DOING THEOLOGY AS IF PEOPLE MATTERED

DOING THEOLOGY AS IF PEOPLE MATTERED

ENCOUNTERS IN CONTEXTUAL THEOLOGY

EDITED BY

DEBORAH ROSS

AND

EDUARDO C. FERNÁNDEZ, SJ

WITH

STEPHEN B. BEVANS, SVD

A Herder & Herder Book
The Crossroad Publishing Company
New York

A Herder & Herder Book
The Crossroad Publishing Company
www.crossroadpublishing.com

The text of this book is set in 12/15 Adobe Garamond Pro.

Composition by Rachel Reiss
Cover design by Sophie Appel
Cover image by John August Swanson

Library of Congress Cataloging-in-Publication Data
available upon request from the Library of Congress.

ISBN 978-0-8245-9996-6 paperback
ISBN 978-0-8245-9995-9 cloth
ISBN 978-0-8245-9997-3 ePub
ISBN 978-0-8245-9998-0 mobi

CONTENTS

ACKNOWLEDGMENTS

As with any worthwhile endeavor, this collection could only become a reality through the support of many friends and colleagues. We are indebted to Steve Bevans, who not only worked with us at the envisioning and consultative stages, but who also saw the project to completion, literally writing the afterword. Our gratitude similarly goes to Robert Schreiter, who wrote an informative foreword. Their pioneering contributions to contextual theologies continue to bear fruit for the Kingdom of God. The Ignatian Center for Jesuit Education at Santa Clara University provided us with a substantial grant that was supplemented by our own Jesuit School of Theology. In addition, in terms of administrative accompaniment, we were well supported by the Dean's Office at our school, particularly Dean Kevin O'Brien. We are equally grateful to our contributors and the rest of the faculty, who gave us feedback, often at monthly faculty colloquia. Among them, the institutional memory of former Dean George Griener proved to be particularly helpful. We owe much, similarly, to fellow faculty members Thomas Cattoi and Kathryn Barush. Thomas helped us procure a publisher, while Kate pointed us toward the artwork that appears on the cover. Fr. Robert McChesney, SJ, who, among his other responsibilities, served as director of intercultural initiatives, was also supportive of the effort to create this book. We are grateful to the Pacific Lutheran Theological Seminary, one of our sister schools here at the Graduate Theological Union in Berkeley, which gave us permission to use Sandra Schneiders's address delivered during the ecumenical celebration of Founders' Day, 2017. The copy editor who helped us bring all of this together for submission is Melody Layton McMahon. Her meticulous eye and endless patience have been genuine gifts.

We applaud the support of Chris Myers and colleagues at Herder and Herder, who shepherded us through the process of bringing this work to publication. We wish to thank our own JST students, alumni/ae, past and present JST faculty and staff, the Berkeley Jesuit community, JST board members, benefactors, and community partners both local and worldwide, including St. Patrick Parish in west Oakland and the San Quentin Prison Ministry. We would also like to acknowledge Santa Clara University's president, Father Michael Engh, SJ, a colleague, brother, and friend whose unwavering support was a welcome blessing in uncertain times. These countless individuals and communities have made and continue to make possible the doing of contextual theology *in situ*. Finally, we thank the person who served as our president from 1998 to 2008, our beloved Father Joseph Patrick Daoust, SJ, a man who not only listened to us but worked tirelessly to keep the vision front and center. In gratitude, we dedicate this collection to him, *con mucho cariño*—with much affection—thanking the good Lord for sending him our way.

FOREWORD

Doing theology has taken on many forms throughout the long history of the Church. In some moments it has been principally a commentary on the scriptures; in other instances, the quest for wisdom and mystical union was its paramount concern. At yet other times it has been a dialogue of a living tradition with other ways of human knowing. And in still other settings, it has been a prophetic call to transformative action.

A particular development in theology in the past half-century has been a more conscious and sustained engagement with the context in which theological reflection is taking place. Although hardly a new idea, this approach was animated by the Second Vatican Council's call to read the "signs of the times" as a moment in which God is speaking to us in a very special and concrete way. "Context" is broadly understood here to include factors shaping the environment in which theology is being done, the inner experience of those engaging in creating a theology, as well as the consequences of such a theology for Christian discipleship and mission. Such attention to context brings multiple voices into the theological conversation in a way that some other kinds of theology have not done as effectively.

The Jesuit School of Theology of Santa Clara University has been consciously attending to a contextually sensitive way of doing theology for more than two decades. Such an approach involves a careful and continual reading of tradition, sensitive to the contexts in which elements of the tradition emerged as well as those new contexts it has encountered in the course of history. It requires, too, a critical attention to the factors shaping the multiple contexts in the World Church where that tradition is being received today.

There is no one method or single formula for doing contextual theology; it might best be described as a path, a *poesis*, and a performance. It is a path upon which a community embarks as a kind of journey or pilgrimage, evoking the image of the pilgrim people of God presented in the Dogmatic Constitution on the Church, *Lumen Gentium*. As such, it is a mystagogy, a being led deeper into the mystery of the Triune God, reminding those who undertake it that they are always *in via* as the Church enters more completely into the embrace of God. Contextual theology is also a *poesis*—a making or doing that involves construction and engagement on the part of its participants. The process is not a mechanical one, but rather requires intuition, critical thought, careful listening, and aesthetic sensibility. And contextual theology is performance, in the sense that doing something engages our reality in a way that transforms it. Contextual theology is not a spectator sport, if you will; rather, it requires full engagement on the part of persons and communities.

This volume by the Jesuit School of Theology faculty is a record of their paths taken, the discoveries they have made along the way, and how engaging in this contextually sensitive theology has transformed them and the students they have accompanied over the past twenty years. Sometimes elements of the path will be front and center in their reflections, as in the case of student pilgrimages and cultural immersions. At other times, the *poesis* of rearticulating the tradition in new and different settings will be most in evidence. And at yet other moments, the outcome of performance of theology is registered in the transformations that occur for them in parishes, prisons, and interfaith settings.

Contextually sensitive theologies are always works in progress as new challenges arise, new insights are gained, and new voices are introduced into the dialogue. *Doing Theology as If People Mattered* stands as an invitation to others to accompany God's people through a way of doing theology that will bring them all closer to the fullness of God's Reign.

Robert J. Schreiter, CPPS

INTRODUCTION

Deborah Ross and Eduardo C. Fernández, SJ

Veritatis Gaudium, or "The Joy of Truth,"[1] contains two powerful images one might not expect to find in such an official Church document. In describing the setting where scholars and pastoral agents are trained, Pope Francis identifies the need for preparing the whole people of God for embarking on a new stage of "Spirit-filled" evangelization, one characterized by a "resolute process of discernment, purification and reform." Ecclesiastical studies, such as those carried out at our own Jesuit School of Theology of Santa Clara University (JST) in Berkeley, California, part of an interfaith consortium, the Graduate Theological Union, are said to play a key role, offering "opportunities and processes for the suitable formation of priests, consecrated men and women, and committed lay people." The innovative pontiff goes beyond the normal functions of these schools of theology to speak of how these formation centers are, at the same time,

> called to be a sort of providential cultural laboratory in which the Church carries out the performative interpretation of the reality brought about by the Christ event and nourished by the gifts of wisdom and knowledge by which

---

1. This Vatican Apostolic Constitution on Ecclesiastical Universities and Faculties, issued on December 8, 2017, updates *Sapientia Christiana*, published almost forty years ago.

the Holy Spirit enriches the People of God in manifold ways—from the *sensus fidei fidelium* to the magisterium of the bishops, and from the charism of the prophets to that of the doctors and theologians. This is essential for a Church that "goes forth"![2]

"Providential cultural laboratory"? Did we read that right? A far cry from the old theology manuals that Karl Rahner and Edward Schillebeeckx sought to surpass with a new theology based on scripture and the history of salvation.[3] This image not only sounds quite worldly in terms of its evocation of culture but dares, at the same time, to invoke Divine Providence. Its incarnational sense can hardly be overlooked.

The second image, this time one taken from creation and the writings of Pope Benedict XVI, is that of tradition as a flowing river: the Church's tradition

> is not a transmission of things or of words, a collection of dead things. Tradition is the living river that links us to the origins, the living river in which the origins are ever present.... This river irrigates various lands, feeds various geographical places, germinating the best of that land, the best of that culture. In this way, the Gospel continues to be incarnated in every corner of the world, in an ever new way. (VG 4d)

As the document states emphatically, still citing Pope Benedict, our theology must be rooted and grounded in Sacred Scripture and in the living tradition (VG 4d).

---

2. Francis, *Veritatis Gaudium* (2017), no. 3, https://w2.vatican.va/content/ francesco/en/apost_constitutions/documents/papa-francesco_costituzi one-ap_20171208_veritatis-gaudium.html.

3. Massimo Faggioli, *Vatican II: The Battle for Meaning* (New York/Mahwah, NJ: Paulist Press, 2012), 50.

The experience of putting together these essays penned by our colleagues has entailed reflecting on what happens in our own little "providential cultural laboratory" on the West Coast of the United States, which draws students from all over the globe, as well as considering how our openhanded God continues to water not only this corner of the vineyard but also other areas throughout the planet. Contained within this volume are stories, many of which surprised us, the collection's editors. As we gradually began to get a sense of where the Spirit was leading us by listening with discerning hearts and utilizing the tools our training provides us, especially in light of the truth and wisdom of the tradition we are entrusted to pass on, we discovered that in sharing the story of contextual theology at JST we are not passing on an idea, or even a set of concepts, but describing a relationship with Someone who has gathered us together in this work and prayer setting to do "God talk." This approach sees theology as the second moment (not the first)—a moment that reflects on a lived reality. But this reality is not limited to our time and space, as the river of tradition reminds us. Echoing Stephen Bevans's oft-quoted statement in these essays that "All theology is contextual," we are reminded that good theology emerges from reflecting on both our religious experience and that of our ancestors in the faith.

This book explores the practice of contextual theology at our school, JST, within the classroom and beyond. Our lay, religious, diocesan, and Jesuit students come not only from the United States but also from Latin America, Africa, Asia, and Europe. JST students study for a variety of degrees, including civil degrees such as the MA, MDiv, and MTS degrees and the STL and STD ecclesiastical degrees. The school is one of two theology centers in the United States for Jesuits studying theology prior to ordination.[4] A

---

4. JST became incorporated with Santa Clara University in 2009. The other theology center for Jesuits is the School of Theology and Ministry at Boston College.

good number of international students also make up the Sabbatical Renewal Program.

As mentioned above, JST is also one of the eight member schools of the Graduate Theological Union (GTU), also located in Berkeley. The GTU, formed in 1962, is an ecumenical and interreligious consortium that dedicates itself to preparing students for ministry, teaching, research, and service. It offers academic programs in theology and religious studies and is the most extensive partnership of graduate schools and seminaries in the United States with the largest theological faculty in one location. In addition, the GTU has a significant number of Latino/Latina doctoral students and prominent alumni/ae scholars.

In the mid-90s, our school made a methodological decision to consciously do contextual theology. Since then, context has provided a point of departure and a hermeneutical key for theological endeavors at JST, including, for example, pedagogy in the classroom, the celebration of liturgy, and international student immersion experiences. Contextual theology has become a way of *doing* theology at JST and beyond. This collection provides a narrative that explains how contextual theology has developed at the school and how it has molded us as an educational faith community. Certain faculty members, notably T. Howland Sanks, in conjunction with other scholars such as Robert Schreiter who pioneered reflections on constructing local theologies, were instrumental in gradually establishing a contextual theology paradigm and envisioning how this would shape us as a theologate.[5]

Since then, newer faculty members have joined our efforts and enhance this theological paradigm, paying particular attention to context, both historical and contemporary, in their teaching and research. Similarly, students—many of whom are international—have

---

5. During a faculty retreat held in January 1999, the then academic dean, George Griener, assisted by a Lilly Endowment grant, invited Robert Schreiter to reflect with us on the vision of the school becoming an international center for the culturally contextualized study of theology and ministry.

been introduced to and informed by this theological method, and, as these essays reveal, themselves experience its fruits as they are constantly learning from one another's contexts and cultures. Years back, the late Virgilio Elizondo, considered to be the father of U.S. Hispanic theology, encouraged us not to hide our lamp under a bushel basket but to share with a wider audience what we were learning and helping to create at the school.

In assembling this volume, we have considered how contextual theology is now part of our institutional memory, a memory that propels us forward as we contribute to the academy that ought to remain at the service of God's people. The ancient term *mystagogy* references moving deeper into the mysteries of faith, and we have moved deeper, in a mystagogical sense, into what the memory and practice of contextual theology means for us as a school.

Steve Bevans's *Models of Contextual Theology* has operated instrumentally as a "classic" text for our faculty, staff, and students. A classic text, a concept developed by theologian David Tracy, has the capacity to prompt changes in ways of being, thinking, and living.[6] The six models that Steve presents in *Models of Contextual Theology* reveal classical ways of describing theology in action. It became clear to us that Steve articulated something really important that has been there all along. His *Models of Contextual Theology* prompted us to engage in the lived practice of contextual theology and acted as a springboard for classroom pedagogy, an interpretive framework for doing theology at the school, a reflective lens, and a way of analyzing and describing experiential learning in the classroom and beyond. Theological contextual method enables us to bring the experience of the past tradition together with the present and engage in mutual critical dialogue. Further, Steve's scholarship has inspired faculty and students at JST to exercise a contextual theological imagination, a way of imagining how to do theology,

---

6. See David Tracy, *The Analogical Imagination: Christian Theology and the Culture of Pluralism* (New York: Crossroad, 1981).

especially given its diverse student body. We were delighted when he agreed to work with us, the editors, and with our faculty in assembling this collection.

The Second Vatican Council sanctioned the exercise of a contextual imagination and the practicing of contextual theology. This historic ecumenical council heralded a theological vision that embraced the graced sacramental reality of all of creation. This same vision affirms the revelatory capacity of all human experience and has opened new horizons within Catholic theology. The opening of new theological vistas after Vatican II led to an innovative way of being Church and of doing theology. For example, contextual scriptural exegesis has transformed our approach to understanding scripture. The Church has since engaged in new expressions of ministry including lay ecclesial ministry, and interfaith dialogue has flourished. As this volume attests, the collective JST contextual imagination has revealed an innate potential for appreciating the pedagogical and ministerial opportunities within the lived experiential realities of the school and wider community. As Steve notes, our contextualizing involves us engaging in a *locus theologicus*—a dialogue involving scripture, tradition, and experience.[7]

Our conversations with Steve during the writing and editing of the collection you hold in your hands helped us to see that this is not just a book about teaching people to do contextual theology. Rather, it is about their discovering *how* to do it, and then helping the people they teach to become contextual theologians. As the authors of this collection share their individual commitment to pay attention to context, we hear much about their own personal learning, pedagogy, the integration of new scholarship in the classroom, and, as Christianity continues to become global, how dialogical learning within an international setting becomes an incredible gift.[8] One-third of

---

7. Stephen B. Bevans, *Models of Contextual Theology*, rev. and exp. ed. (Maryknoll, NY: Orbis, 2002), 4.

8. Because in many ways these essays reflect a type of conversion in the Lonerganian sense of a broadening of one's horizons, we encouraged the

our full-time faculty members were born outside the United States, which is a more recent gift to our learning environment.

We have chosen to name our collection *Doing Theology as If People Mattered: Encounters in Contextual Theology*. Inspired by the 1973 compilation of essays by German-born British economist E. F. Schumacher, *Small Is Beautiful: A Study of Economics as If People Mattered*, we wish to highlight the role of "the little people," the biblical *anawim*, whose lament is not lost on the God who "hears the cry of the poor." As the reader journeys through this book, he or she will encounter populations often ignored or oppressed, such as the Indian *Adivasi*, members of tribal groups outside the standard caste system, who appear in Thomas Cattoi's patristics chapter, alongside the African experience that shaped the work of the Christian ethicist William O'Neill. Julia Prinz's essay likewise describes some of the challenges of Asian women religious seeking to find their theological voice. San Quentin chaplain George Williams's haunting narrative of an imprisoned theology packs a prophetic punch, and Deborah Ross's description of the complexity of ministering in a predominantly African American and Latino/a inner-city parish brings home the point that ultimately the Christian, like Jesus, must be both guest and host. Kevin O'Brien's chapter on Pope Francis as a contextual theologian highlights a similar rich, pastoral tradition at the level of the universal Church, one that demonstrates magisterial leadership through compassionate praxis, not simply in terms of concepts or jurisdiction. This divine concern for those often overlooked, whether in society or even in the Church, flies in the face of the belief that "bigger, stronger, or more famous is better," for as Jesus teaches us, "small is beautiful."

---

contributors to use a narrative style and to build a narrative tension in their writing. A chapter by Susan Rabiner and Alfred Fortunato proved to be very helpful in this regard. See Susan Rabiner and Alfred Fortunato, "Using Narrative Tension," in *Thinking Like Your Editor: How to Write Great Serious Nonfiction and Get It Published* (New York: Norton, 2002), 177–95.

The "aha" moments, or glimpses of insight, found throughout these pages, the fruit of contemplative hindsight and group reflection, are often the result of a dialogic pedagogy, one created in a community of fellow learners and teachers.[9] Subjects such as liturgy, scripture, ecclesiology, ecumenism, and inter-religious dialogue and theology probe new depths when explored in intercultural and interreligious contexts. For example, Gina Hens-Piazza's chapter describing a student immersion in Jerusalem, or Anh Tran's chapter depicting international immersions in Indonesia, Nepal, and India, stress interreligious learning through actual contact with the religious "other," resulting in experiences of friendship and hospitality. Paul Janowiak explores the transformative pedagogy of students' sharing of diverse cultural liturgical experience, and how it encourages a deeper appreciation of the universal Christian tradition. Contextual liturgical and sacramental theology demands appreciation of the interplay among inner faith, personal cultural and social realities, and the outer realms of liturgical worship, and Hung Pham and Kathryn Barush's piece on the *Camino Ignaciano* pilgrimage weaves together the conceptual terms of St. Ignatius with student anecdotes and experiential reflections. In some ways, their engaged method of pilgrimage embodies Steve's translation model as they explore what it means to translate Ignatius's method of following Jesus for a contemporary audience.

Jean François Racine's chapter, which describes New Testament contextual distance education, specifically regarding Paul as a contextual theologian, challenges the notion that contextual theology is a new thing or that it is outside the tradition, a point Cattoi makes equally well in writing about the Fathers and Nicaea as contextual theology. Alison Benders, in her contribution, argues for a greater accountability to the theological enterprise as she explores

---

9. Several of these essays, for example, set the agenda for the monthly JST faculty colloquium, an opportunity to present our written works in progress. Consequent sessions with Steve Bevans similarly yielded valuable insight into our operative theological method.

the problem of testing the outcomes of doing culturally contextualized theology and proposes a set of criteria to evaluate the results of this theological practice.

Another theme that surfaces from this volume's various theological reflections is the famous "so what?" question—or, to put it another way, to what end is our theologizing oriented? Good theology comes out of praxis, and good praxis leads to good theology. As Gustavo Gutiérrez has been telling us for decades, and as mentioned above, theology is but the second moment. "Talk about God (theo-logy) comes after the silence of prayer and commitment."[10] Steve's definition of praxis as "reflected upon action"[11] makes a similar point. Lived contextual theology is often a catalyst for action. Williams's piece describing his prison ministry, for example, pushes us beyond mere speculation toward the radical option for gospel values. His chapter reflects the mysticism of Johann Baptist Metz, one of "open eyes"—in this instance, eyes set on the conversion of sinful social structures that promote mass incarceration. In his concluding remarks, O'Brien does not mince words: bringing pastoral theology to the heart of theological inquiry means asking challenging, often uncomfortable questions.

To help the reader understand how the theological community came to develop and appreciate a contextual theological paradigm, we open this volume with Sandra M. Schneiders's keynote address delivered at the 2017 Founders' Day celebration for the Pacific Lutheran Theological Seminary (PLTS), a GTU partner school of JST. Sandra, in advocating for a biblical spirituality that might orient systematic theology, draws our attention to the method of theopoetics. Theopoetics involves returning to a poetic and spiritual understanding of theology and faith, an understanding that is not averse to, yet less metaphysical than, philosophical systematic

---

10. Gustavo Gutiérrez, *We Drink from Our Own Wells: The Spiritual Journey of a People* (Maryknoll, NY: Orbis, 1984), 136.

11. See Bevans's *Models of Contextual Theology*, Chapter 6, "The Praxis Model."

theology. This is not a new departure for theology, as this way of doing theology draws on the wisdom of the Church Fathers.[12] As Schneiders reminds us, doing theology contextually is made possible by the theopoetical vision of Vatican II's heralding of a new language and consciousness. Theopoetics informs our contextual theological imagination as it allows us to engage rich biblical, polyvalent devices such as image, metaphor, and symbol.

The Founders' Day celebration so strongly impacted our recent faculty hire Christopher Hadley that he opens his own reflection referencing Schneiders's presentation and its subsequent panel discussion, as well as his participation in the worship held in conjunction with this event. Inspired by this experience, as well as the theme of theopoetics, Hadley reflects on both ecumenical dialogue and his JST course on Theological Aesthetics, the Cross, and Race. The course, which explores racism, adopted ecumenical course texts, facilitating students' dialogue and contextual encounter in class and influencing their writing projects. Likewise, Hens-Piazza employs texts in a course engaging biblical and interfaith disciplines entitled Children of Sarah, Hagar, and Mary. The course culminates with students participating in a contextual education immersion experience in Jerusalem, a context providing lived interfaith encounter, the building of common ground, and creation of personal contextual narratives. As with the other authors, we are invited not only into their minds but also into their hearts, as they find themselves being invited through encounter, again and again, to broaden their horizons and contemplate the mysteries unfolding before them.

There is a hidden author here, a brother who deeply marked our way of theologizing but does not have an essay in this collection. Our beloved Alejandro García-Rivera died in December of 2010. His writings continue to bear fruit, as Prinz's essay reminds us. Alex had a love for the "community of the beautiful," and he

---

12. Amos Niven Wilder, *Theopoetic: Theology and the Religious Imagination* (Lima, OH: Academic Renewal Press, 2001), 4.

was a "people's theologian" in every sense of the word, meeting every Thursday with his Bible study group at the parish of St. Leander in the San Francisco Bay Area.[13] Alex kept reminding us of the importance of doing theology *in situ*—right there—or being physically present with a community to contemplate the life-giving Spirit's presence in all. As this theological locus emphasizes, and what quickly became apparent to us as editors, is that doing theology contextually takes us out of the classroom and into places of human and cosmic encounter. From a parish in west Oakland to a state prison in San Quentin, from student immersions in Indonesia, Nepal, or Jerusalem to the *Camino* pilgrimage in Spain, not to mention the myriad communities represented by our students from Asian and African countries, our encounters with the world have taught us that the planet is much bigger, yet much closer, than we had ever imagined.

Good contextual theology, as we have repeatedly been reminded during the compilation of this collection, must be embodied, dialogical, incarnational, relational, and conversant with Pope Benedict's living river of tradition. This awareness allows us to encounter God in unforeseen and stirring ways, not only within ourselves but also with multiple contexts unfolding. Contextual theology, as expressed through worship, teaching, ministerial encounters, and contact with other ancient traditions, continues to be revelatory as we pilgrimage together on this sacred journey.

---

13. Eduardo C. Fernández, "A Litany for Alex: Remembering His Contributions to Pastoral Theology," *Diálogo* 16, no. 2 (Fall 2013): 29–32.

Part I

FOUNDATIONS

Chapter One

RECONCILED DIVERSITY
THEOLOGY AND SPIRITUALITY IN
THE ECUMENICAL JOURNEY
Sandra M. Schneiders, IHM

Introduction[1]

I am very grateful for the invitation to deliver the 2017 Founders' Day Lecture of the Pacific Lutheran Theological Seminary in this year, which is very special from several points of view. This is, I believe, the first major public event of Pacific Lutheran Theological Seminary since its move, just twenty days ago, from its erstwhile hilltop location to its new home in downtown Berkeley—a "new beginning" within a venerable tradition. I'm sure this move is symbolic in many ways, but one, pertinent to our discussion today, is of the transition in the whole Church in our time from the emphasis on the traditional and very legitimate seclusion of the theological academy as a privileged locus and haven of reflection to the necessary emphasis today on the engagement of theology with the world that God so loved. And it is perhaps also symbolic that this event is taking place in one of the member schools of the Graduate Theological Union, the Jesuit School of Theology, to which I am happy to welcome all our Lutheran and other GTU friends and

---

1. Editors' note: Reproduced here is Dr. Schneiders's keynote address, which she delivered on September 20, 2017, at the Jesuit School of Theology in Berkeley.

colleagues, for what we hope will be the first of many shared experiences now that we are geographically so much closer to each other. But most of all, I am personally deeply honored and humbled to be addressing you, carriers of Martin Luther's important legacy, in this extraordinary year when we commemorate, on October 31, the 500th anniversary of one of the most momentous events in the history of Christianity, the posting of Martin Luther's ninety-five theses on the portal of the Church of Wittenberg (or so the myth has it!), the symbolic beginning of the Reformation in which we must all—in our distinctive ways—remain forever engaged.

I cannot resist recounting to you an event I've shared with some of you in the past. Shortly after my arrival on the faculty here at the Jesuit School, after some event in which, I suppose, we had been discussing the nature and interpretation of scripture, one of my Catholic colleagues said to me, I suspected only partly in jest, "Sandra, I think you are a closet Lutheran." I replied, also not entirely in jest, "I deeply resent that. There is nothing closet about it." In fact, I was, at that point, very recently returned from doctoral studies in New Testament in Rome, where my work on the biblical spirituality of John's Gospel had been deeply enriched by study not only of the new generation of Roman Catholic biblical scholars, like Raymond Brown, and others who had come into prominence in the wake of the just-concluded Second Vatican Council, but also by my wide reading of the giants of nineteenth- and early twentieth-century Protestant scholarship, such as Karl Barth and Rudolf Bultmann, and the great Lutheran ecumenist, Oscar Cullmann, from whom Pope Francis has borrowed a term that is at the heart of our reflections this morning, namely, "reconciled diversity," which is the true aim of any ecumenism worthy of the name. Reconciled diversity is not uniformity, however achieved, but something that, I will try to show, probably could not have been envisioned, at least by Catholics, prior to Vatican II. In any case, with the exception of Raymond Brown, perhaps the premier Catholic biblical scholar of the postconciliar period, the most influential biblical scholars in my early academic life were mainly

Protestants, who, of course, certainly outnumbered Catholic biblical scholars until well into the late twentieth century and who
were, without doubt, the real mentors and teachers of the first generation of postconciliar Roman Catholic biblical scholars. And as
my biblical interests became increasingly hermeneutical it was the
Protestant giants of the twentieth-century conversation, the new
hermeneuts like Gerhard Ebeling, Ernst Fuchs, Heinrich Ott, and
their philosophical contemporaries like Hans-Georg Gadamer and
Paul Ricœur, who were my primary mentors and dialogue partners.

Over the years I have continued to appreciate and appropriate
the rich heritage of biblical scholarship that comes to all of us Christians from the Reformation which has been integral to my own
work in biblical spirituality. I also had the privilege of directing the
doctoral dissertation in Christian Spirituality of one of your increasingly influential newer colleagues, Dr. Lisa Dahill, in the process of
which I learned a great deal about Lutheran spirituality. And given
all the topics in regard to Lutheran-Catholic relations that we might
discuss, none is more important than scripture, and no perspective on scripture more important than spirituality. Although the
Wittenberg theses were specifically concerned with the controversy
over indulgences and its implications in regard to authority in the
Church, the fundamental issues of church, ministry, and Eucharist
which we are still discussing, were, in depth, more about the nature
and interpretation of scripture and its role in the Church and in the
spirituality of believers than about practices or discipline.

We certainly do not have time, nor do I have the competence,
to retrace in detail the important progress that has been made in
the fifty years since the close of the Second Vatican Council in Lutheran-Catholic relations. But just to recall the major milestones of
this extraordinary journey, the process began even in the last year
of the council, 1964, before the first official dialogue in 1967 that led
to the 1983 landmark Joint Statement entitled *Justification by Faith*
and then to the *Joint Declaration on the Doctrine of Justification*
of October 31, 1999, and then to the 2010 common statement *The
Hope of Eternal Life*, and finally, in 2015—explicitly in preparation

for the observance of the 500th anniversary of the Reformation this year—to the *Declaration on the Way,*[2] which undertakes the movement beyond doctrinal agreement toward greater visible unity between our two communions. The *Declaration on the Way,* which was the impetus for my reflections in this lecture, specifically articulates thirty-two consensus statements on the topics of justification, church, Eucharist, and ministry, the topics which have long divided Lutherans and Catholics. The document also identifies a few areas, fewer than half as many as the thirty-two statements on which there is working consensus, which still require further discussion. Given the preceding five hundred years of virtual mutual excommunication, we are living in an exciting time when this half-millennial-old rift in the Body of Christ might finally be healed. Even now both communions are seeking increasingly visible signs of reunification, especially in expanded opportunities for eucharistic sharing and mutual recognition of ministries. And what better year in which to anticipate and pray for full reunification with the realistic hope that we will live to see this happen?

Where Are We, and What Is Going On?

There would be many ways to examine the progress that has been made in Lutheran–Roman Catholic dialogue, the most obvious of which would be to examine the theological content of the

---

2. Some of the various documents of the ongoing consultation can be found on the website of the United States Conference of Catholic Bishops. See http://www.usccb.org/beliefs-and-teachings/ecumenical-and-interreligious/ ecumenical/ecumenical-documents-and-news-releases.cfm#CP_JUMP_ 106445. However, the full documentation for the latest and most operative document has been published as *Declaration on the Way: Church, Ministry, and Eucharist by the Committee on Ecumenical and Interreligious Affairs,* United States Conference of Catholic Bishops / Evangelical Lutheran Church in 2015, http://download.elca.org/ELCA%20Resource%20Repository/Declaration_ on_the_Way.pdf.

discussions in which, little by little, both sides have reached the conclusion on one issue after another—thirty-two of them—that the differences between us on that issue are "not Church dividing." I was profoundly struck, and fascinated, by this formulation and it became the center of my reflections as I began to prepare this lecture. How were we able to get to this remarkable point, this striking formulation, that on these long-polarizing topics, our diverse positions were "not Church dividing"? Stated positively, this was a claim that the two sides to the conversation, Lutheran and Catholic, were not claiming some kind of uniformity, not saying there were no differences between us on these issues, nor that the differences were not substantive or important, nor that they were inconsequential historical oddities that had lost their relevance and were no longer worth discussing much less fighting about, nor that one side or the other would abandon its characteristic approach on the subject and simply accept that of the other for the sake of verbal harmony—but that the differences, though real, substantive, and significant and probably permanent, were "not Church dividing." In other words, there is room in the Church's identity, faith, and life for real, substantive, and significant differences on important issues. To me, this is a far more significant position than the positions taken on the subject matter itself of the thirty-two issues, individually or taken together. It marks a new, shared approach to *truth* that was not really imaginable prior to Vatican II. It is an approach rejected by Luther in his posting of the ninety-five theses and by the Roman Church in its condemnation of Luther's positions at the Council of Trent. For Luther, truth and integrity demanded his "Here I stand; I can do no other" and for Trent that same truth and integrity grounded the only possible response, "Let him be anathema." The important change to which the *Declaration on the Way* witnesses—that is, the move from intransigent mutual condemnation based on a certain understanding of the truth rooted in the principle of non-contradiction, to the possibility of holding simultaneously and without compromise more than one valid and life-giving position on a single subject, that is, to "reconciled diversity" on matters of faith and morals, is what I would like to reflect on with you. I think this change is monumental, and we are just beginning to glimpse its theological importance and ecumenical potential as well as to ask, "How have we come to this?" How have we been able to move—in regard to the same topics—from mutual anathema to "not Church dividing"? It has tremendous significance, in my opinion, for the long-desired internal reunification of the Church and the shared mission of the Church to the world, and it is situated at least as much in the area of spirituality, and especially biblical spirituality, as in the area of systematic theology, which is where Catholics and Lutherans have historically situated such discussion. By way of anticipation, I am going to suggest that it is the epistemological move from metaphysically based theology to experience-based theopoetics that opens the way to reconciled diversity.

The history of the twenty-one ecumenical councils of the Church reveals that the Council of Trent, whose documents run to about 130 pages in the standard edition—and which "canonized," so to speak, the split between the Roman Catholic Church and the churches of the Reformation—and the Second Vatican Council, which runs to 300 pages, and which began to heal that split, together almost equal the output of all the other nineteen councils put together. And Vatican II, the council that gave birth to a dream of reunification, produced twice the documentation of Trent, the council of definitive division. This might suggest that hostility is a far easier course than unification. One might say that Trent represented the apotheosis of the development of the Church toward an inward-focused, doctrinally and theologically deductive and monolithic, pyramidally organized, clerical, authoritarian, and static entity positioning itself "outside of" and "in opposition to" the world—defined as everything other than itself—while Vatican II represented a stunning re-evaluation of, and even reversal of, this posture. Vatican II was a turning of the Church toward the world, an opening to theological pluralism rooted in lived experience, the emergence of an egalitarian and communitarian self-understanding of the Church as first and foremost the people of God, in which office and authority were to be at the service of the community and the ecclesial community was to be at the service of the world. Not only were the so-called separated brethren invited to the council—and not only did they accept the invitation—but several documents of the council espoused and promoted the project of reunification of the Church from within and positive relations with non-Christians and even the secular order from without. This is the context in which projects such as the Lutheran–Roman Catholic dialogues were born and have unfolded, moving beyond anything that looked possible in the 1960s.

The Spirit of the Council

Anyone who wants to really understand Vatican II can do no better than to read the masterful treatment by Catholic Church historian John W. O'Malley entitled *What Happened at Vatican II*[3] and especially the introduction and first chapter, which together contextualize the council *historically* and then analyze its *language* in order to lay bare its fundamental *dynamics*. I borrow here especially from the section O'Malley entitles "The Spirit of the Council" to capture the issue I want to develop further, namely, the distinctly postmodern ethos of the council which was in play before most people, even in the academy, were using the term "postmodern."

O'Malley begins by describing Vatican II in contrast to all its predecessors. which were essentially, from the standpoint of genre and vocabulary (that is, language), juridical and legislative assemblies underwritten by the Greek philosophical tradition and, for the more recent councils, that Greek tradition in its medieval scholastic form. These councils were concerned with formulating

3. John W. O'Malley, *What Happened at Vatican II* (Cambridge, MA: Belknap Press of Harvard University Press, 2008), 1–52.

doctrine and passing laws expressive of doctrinal positions, executing judgment on those who deviated in belief or behavior from
those positions, and decreeing appropriate punishment—often in
the form of anathemas—for those judged guilty.

By contrast, Vatican II adopted a completely different style, that
is, a different language or rhetoric, embodied in a different genre
and vocabulary. And this was not a purely decorative, or even
political, development. Vatican II moved from grand conceptual
schemas and a conflictual agenda in defense of the positions based
on these concepts to an espousal of the Church's role as servant
of the mystery of God at work in the world. The Church's task,
according to Vatican II, was to be of pastoral service to all people
and to work together with others for the Church's mission rather
than to fight with them over who was theologically right. O'Malley
calls the rhetorical style, or what theologians would later call the
"spirit of Vatican II," embodied in a new genre and vocabulary, pan-
egyric or epideictic. In other words, Vatican II adopted a rhetoric
of admiration and appreciation for its interlocutors rather than
defensiveness and aggression, of persuasion rather than coercion,
one in which ideals are presented and people, on both sides, are
urged to embrace them, not out of fear but because of their intrinsic attractiveness, their beauty. It is a rhetoric not of threat aimed
at conformity but a rhetoric of appreciation aimed at community,
mutual conversion, and ultimately at holiness. And the conversion
in question was proposed first to the Church itself and then to its
interlocutors. It was—and this is crucial to my argument—a literary or theopoetic genre rather than a philosophical or legal genre.
This is often captured in ordinary language by referring to Vatican
II as a "pastoral" council rather than a doctrinal or legislative or
juridical or disciplinary one.

O'Malley says that Vatican II was really a matter of the adoption
of a new language. The council, in other words, was a "language
event" in the sense in which the New Hermeneuts referred to the
preaching of the gospel not as a proposition of dogma or explanation of theology, but as a language event. Anyone who has ever

really learned a new language knows that it is not a matter of learning vocabulary and mastering grammar. Learning a new language is a matter of cultural conversion, of becoming a new person through language, which incorporates one into a new community. So, says O'Malley, if we want to understand what was going on at Vatican II we have to analyze the *language* of the Council, its new genres and rhetoric of persuasion and reconciliation and its new vocabulary that replaces the language of judgment, alienation, exclusion, intimidation, coercion, punishment, and so on with the language of inclusion and participation and equality, of welcome and cooperation. He organizes this new vocabulary into three categories: "horizontal words" of equality, reciprocity, and humility (words such as collegiality and "people of God"); "change words" (such as *aggiornamento*, progress, development, evolution) coupled with words of empowerment and participation in this change; and "interiority words" (such as charism, conscience, conversion, holiness, commitment, and ministry).

O'Malley argues that style is not a linguistic decoration. Style—including both genre and vocabulary—is the ultimate expression of meaning. He says that style "does not adorn meaning but style *is* meaning." It is the "hermeneutical key par excellence"[4] to the meaning of the council and the key to interpreting it authentically.

Vatican II and the Emerging Intellectual Zeitgeist of the Twenty-First Century: From Metaphysics to Phenomenology; From Theology to Theopoetics

In this context, I want to turn to my primary concern in this presentation, namely, the real nature of this new, emerging style or spirit—not unique to the council but increasingly pervasive in

---

4. See O'Malley, *What Happened at Vatican II*, 49.

contemporary theology as a whole—that offers such hope for the reunification of the Church in our time. (This will involve—for the sake of time—gross, almost criminal oversimplification, but I hope such a tactic is less dangerous among educated people, like my present audience, who will not be led astray by it.)

Vatican II did not invent its linguistic/cognitive novelty—which O'Malley displayed so well—out of whole cloth. The council was, in a sense, channeling the major intellectual developments of the second half of the twentieth century which, at risk of serious oversimplification, we might call the move from metaphysics to phenomenology or from the priority of objectivity to the priority of subjectivity, or from the transcendental controlling ego to the engaged and receptive subject. As the dominance in Western thought of Descartes and Kant, descendants of the classical Greek philosophical tradition by way of medieval Western scholasticism, began to yield to the challenges of Husserl and Heidegger and their disciples and descendants in the twentieth century, the centrality in the understanding of knowledge (what we call epistemology) of the controlling knower began to yield to the centrality of that which gives itself to be known, no matter how unruly, unsystematic, idiosyncratic, and so on it might be. Rather than the mind imposing its categories on that which it seeks to understand, ruling out of court any data which do not fit or could not be handled by those categories, the new philosophies were tending to valorize the individuality and distinctiveness of what offers itself to be known, whether or not that "what" fit or could be handled by the pre-existing categories. As Gadamer captured so well by the challenging title of his famous treatise, *Truth and Method*[5] (which perhaps should have been called "Truth *or* Method"), the dominance of method—scientific, rational, discursive, quantitative, demonstrable, and often socially dominant method—in the search for truth was actually

---

5. Hans-George Gadamer, *Wahrheit und Methode: Grundzüge einer philosophischen Hermeneutik*, tr. Joel Weinsheimer and Donald G. Marshall as *Truth and Method*, 2nd rev. ed. (New York: Crossroad, 1989).

often a subordination of truth *to* method. What rational, provable, and always discursive method could not handle was seen as idiosyncratic, subjective, private, in short, not true knowledge but personal opinion or (suspect always!) merely personal experience. Rather than being seen as the royal road to knowledge, personal experience was seen as virtually the enemy or at least a threat to genuine knowledge. (Parenthetically, that is why spirituality has had such a difficult time being taken seriously in the academy—because spirituality was perceived as a matter of "experience" rather than, like theology, a matter of "knowledge." The battle was between "objectivity" and "subjectivity.")

What existentialism, phenomenology, deconstructionism, hermeneutical theory, and other strands of postmodern thought brought into the picture, introduced into the discourse about God, self, society, religion, morality, and so on, was not the clear and distinct idea, the demonstrable proof, the universal law, but the phenomenon, the singular, the unique—what presents itself to be known as it presents itself—in its integrity, in its challenging, mysterious, original, uncontrollable, complex, uncategorizable originality. The great scientific ideal of stripping from reality its individuality, its uniqueness, its unruly selfhood and reducing truth to the universal, the transcendental, the classifiable, the manageable was being called into question in favor of the unique, the richly textured original, the diverse, and non-classifiable. The individual was achieving a certain ascendancy over the genre. The strict equation of the quantifiable and generic with the intelligible was giving way to a new appreciation of the unique, the original, the individual. Whether in the study of cultures which resist homogenization (in theory as well as in practice) and hierarchical judgment, so-called natural moral laws which were proving to be non-universal, popular religiosity arising from diverse religious and cultural sensibilities, religious (including mystical) experience, sacred texts, psychological phenomena, literature, or art—the ideal of stripping phenomena of what made them phenomenal, what makes them unique and individual, in order to subsume them within classes that could be handled scientifically was giving way to the desire to know, in the biblical sense of "know," the individual in its, her, his, their particularity and wholeness. And the road to such inter-subjective knowledge was not the laboratory (or intellectual) experiment but communication, listening, understanding, dialogue.

What has this to do with the striking originality of Vatican II and its remarkable ecumenical fallout? Rather than, as at Trent and its predecessors, struggling to come up with, even fighting over, abstract dogmatic formulations, transcendent and unchangeable liturgical rubrics, universal moral norms, pristine ecclesiastical structures, divinely sanctioned roles and responsibilities and powers—that is, over universal, transcendental truth which was to be enunciated clearly, proven apodictically, imposed universally, and enforced without exception, this council was concerned with the actual, existential experience of the enormously diverse community called church and its unbelievable individuality, its experientially and historically based *diversity*. The council chose to affirm the phenomena that the mysterious reality "Church" presented rather than try to suppress, to anathematize out of existence, or just ignore as cultural idiosyncrasies anything that did not fit a transcendental definition of church. That meant taking seriously such existential experiences as the real existence of church outside the juridical boundaries of Roman Catholicism; that faith was not restricted to church, Catholic or Protestant or Orthodox, but manifested itself also outside Christianity; that morality was at least as much, if not more, about conscience, which is always individually personal even when instructed and guided by more general norms, than about universal norms; that the true God might be experienced outside the categories of trinitarianism; that true worship of the one true God might be embodied and expressed in cultural behaviors and indigenous languages and symbolic rites that were not invented by the Western Church nor sanctioned by its traditions nor expressed in "universal" languages (such as Latin or French were thought to be!).

The openness, welcome, inclusiveness, tolerance, and so on so characteristic of the attitudes and rhetoric of Vatican Council II were not a clever modern tactic for getting everyone on board before pulling up the gangplank or of selling a patented generic ecclesiastical product presented in new local packaging. These traits were the integral, even if sometimes disjointed and awkward, expression in the experience of the Church assembled in council, of a new understanding of how humans come to know, to express, to share, and to grow. Although unnamed at the time of the council, postmodern sensibility, with its repudiation of a priori dominative structures of thought and control of experience, its embrace of the variety, the unpredictability, the diversity, the originality of persons and behaviors and cultures, was, surprisingly, operative in the vast majority of the participants in the council as witnessed by the votes on the various documents which were, even in the case of the most vigorously debated, lopsidedly in favor of the new articulations with a few of the old guard trying to hold the line against the "wishy-washiness" of the new.[6] The council started with the spontaneity and irrepressibility of John XXIII, who courageously called a very different kind of council than any, certainly, in modern times. And it emerged surprisingly in the majority of the attending bishops, many of whom, in their individual dioceses, had never evinced the kind of originality, openness, and even daring that they discovered in and among themselves when they came together in council. Indeed, when many of these bishops returned to their dioceses after the council they seemed to wonder what had possessed them—knowing in their hearts that it had been the characteristic manifestation of the Originality of God that we call the Holy Spirit, but wondering how they were going to live into their own words. Some of

---

6. Symbolic of the lopsidedness of the preference of the council for the new approach over the old was the vote on the first document that the council passed, and one of the most original in terms of past theory and practice. The extraordinary vote was 2,147 for to 4 opposed on *Sacrosanctum Concilium* (The Constitution on the Sacred Liturgy). None of the council documents was passed by anything like a close vote, even though some of the topics were vigorously debated.

them, unfortunately, didn't. And others, themselves filled with the "spirit of the Council" but aged out by the system, were succeeded by "pharaohs who did not know Joseph"—or John XXIII—who was, himself, succeeded by a much more timid pontiff, Paul VI.[7]

The Effect of Vatican II in the Emerging Theological Climate of the Twenty-First Century

We might describe this phenomenon, which emerged so clearly in the *Declaration on the Way*, as the move in theology away from the ascendancy of metaphysical discourse toward theopoetics understood both as method and product. This has been closely associated with the ascendancy of spirituality in the areas of the Church's life that had been controlled almost exclusively by systematic and moral theology. Rather than spirituality (often called piety) being the behavioral offshoot of theology, spirituality was coming to be seen as the global term for the Church's life, one aspect of which is theology. We should not be surprised, therefore, at the rediscovery and re-emergence—especially among Catholics—of the primacy of scripture, the Church's inspired imaginative literature, over metaphysics, the best-honed tool of intellectual control in the Western armory.[8]

So, let us attend for a few minutes to how this new consciousness, this new sensibility, developed and expressed itself at the council

---

7. For a very readable, but extremely authoritative, discussion of the process of what is called "reception" of the council, that is, its acceptance/rejection/renegotiation/etc. by the Church at large after the close of the council, see Massimo Faggioli, *Vatican II: The Battle for Meaning* (New York/Mahwah, NJ: Paulist Press, 2012).

8. The strongest statement of this new valorization of scripture occurs in chapter 7 of *Dei Verbum* (Dogmatic Constitution on Divine Revelation), where the study of scripture is defined as "the soul of sacred theology" (24), http://www.vatican.va/archive/hist_councils/ii_vatican_council/documents/vat-ii_const_19651118_dei-verbum_en.html.

(even though the word *theopoetics* was never used) and how that has led to the progress that has been made and promises to be made in finding, in the aftermath of the council, true ecumenical unity that does not suppress diversity, does not sacrifice it to uniformity, but celebrates that "reconciled diversity" that Pope Francis exalts as integral to, indeed the very condition of, genuine unity. The term that is beginning to be used, namely theopoetics, to designate this phenomenologically based new epistemology and rhetoric is hard to define.[9] (In fact, my spell-checker will not accept the word, no matter what unladylike rhetoric I use to insist that it is indeed a word, not a misspelling of "theology"!)

The term "theo-poetics" is used in deliberate contrast (not contradiction) to "theo-logy." Theology is talk/discourse about God but specifically, at least in modern times, it has meant philosophically based and philosophically structured talk about God, and the philosophy in question has been classical metaphysical philosophy and its offshoots. Theopoetics is actually older than philosophical theology, but it has been long in abeyance and its contemporary form is somewhat different from its original patristic and then medieval forms. Theopoetics is the language of spirituality which is not anti-philosophical or anti-theological, but is not primarily metaphysical.

The first clue to the nature of theopoetics is its source—both what presents itself to be known and how that "what" is grasped. I have already suggested that the object or subject matter of this new kind (and yet very old) form of thinking about God is "religious experience" as religious and as experience—in other words, spirituality as lived revelatory experience. It is the engagement of people, individually and in community, in liturgy, ministry, moral decision making, personal prayer, civic participation, and so on, which is the site and the content and the interpretation of God's presence and action in the

---

9. A very useful introduction to this subject is L. Callid Keefe-Perry, *Way to Water: A Theopoetics Primer* (Eugene, OR: Cascade Books, 2014), which introduces the reader to both the history of the development of the contemporary field of theopoetics and the major authors and schools of thought in the field.

world. In other words, it is religious experience in all its density and diversity and difficulty and beauty and richness which reveals who God is in and for the individual and the community in this time and place and culture. Theology, or systematic philosophically structured discourse about God, comes "after the fact," and it is theology's task to illuminate experience, not prescribe it or proscribe it or render it abstract and coercive. However, in the nature of the case, as theology became less and less an interpretation of scripture through liturgy, preaching, art, prayer, and so on and more and more a philosophically based and structured articulation of what was believed to be the theological content of the faith stripped of cultural particularities in favor of universal intellectual categories, theopoetics was restricted to spirituality understood as less rigorous, less generalizable, less scientifically provable, and so on.

We have excellent examples of the fruitful relationship between theopoetics and revelation, that is of theology as articulated spirituality, in our history, some of which is being appreciatively rediscovered today. Some of these examples fell into disrepute with the rise of ever more abstract models of theology, but they are being rediscovered in our own time as remarkably rich and interesting. And some which have fallen into desuetude are only being rediscovered today. The classical model of biblical interpretation, for example, somewhat dismissively called in recent times "patristic exegesis" rather than "patristic interpretation," was judged by the norm of nineteenth-century historical-critical exegesis and, since it wasn't intended to be exegesis but to use exegesis in the theopoetic enterprise of fostering spirituality, it was dismissed as woefully unscientific, if not fantastic, and was consigned to the playpen of piety. Today we are beginning to realize that the principles of patristic biblical interpretation, while not productive of certain kinds of important information about biblical sources, nevertheless yield today, as they did in the earliest centuries, rich avenues to engagement with the critical questions of faith and life.

Martin Luther instinctively knew that the hymns he wrote, resonant with biblical imagery, played a role in the people's engagement with the "New Testament as scripture" (that is, not merely as stories or laws, etc., but precisely as the Word of God in their lives) as did theological treatises which ordinary people seldom read and even less often understood. The Western Church in the Middle Ages lived on the beauty of the cathedrals, often called the "catechism of the common people," and the Eastern Church wrote (not painted, but *wrote*) its theology into the icons. St. John of the Cross offers the hugely instructive example of theopoetics in dialogue with theology in his great masterpieces on the mystical life which originated in his mystical poems, the "Dark Night," the "Spiritual Canticle," and the "Living Flame of Love." First, out of his intense personal mystical experience, he wrote the poems. Then, he discursively "unpacked," in his lengthy and scholastically sophisticated prose commentaries on these ecstatic poems, their theological content. Together poems and commentaries constitute a normative canon on the mystical life, but just as, given the choice between preserving the theopoetic texts of scripture or even the best commentaries on scripture, anyone would choose the scriptures themselves, so given the choice of John of the Cross's poetry or his treatises, I think most people experienced in the spiritual life would choose the poems. Hildegard of Bingen in her paintings, her plays, and her poetic writings created a stupendous theopoesis that quite rightly has earned her the title of Doctor of the Church.[10]

---

10. Hildegard of Bingen was named a Doctor of the Universal Church in 2012 by Benedict XVI. Teresa of Ávila and Thérèse of Lisieux, both Doctors of the Church, would be more easily placed in the category of theopoets than theologians in the scholastic sense of the term. The latter was hardly theologically literate, and the former, though avaricious of theological knowledge, was largely unschooled in theology but the intellectual refinement of her treatises cannot be questioned. I addressed this issue recently in an article entitled "The Jesus Mysticism of Teresa of Avila: Its Importance for Theology and Contemporary Spirituality," *Berkeley Journal of Religion and Theology* 2, no. 2 (2016): 43–74 (special issue in honor of Judith A. Berling and Arthur G. Holder).

One of the great innovations of the Second Vatican Council was its rooting of the renewal in the reform of the liturgy understood as the participation of the people of God in the great "drama" of our redemption, rather than the legally regulated re-enactment of a juridically effective event on Calvary. And the return of the Bible understood as scripture, that is, as divinely inspired "literature" rather than a historical record of God's actions and communications, to the Catholic people who had been largely deprived of it for four centuries while they were fed on a catechism version of systematic theology and morality, was one of the greatest gifts of the council.

In other words, theopoetics or the aesthetic engagement with the faith in and through the great works (liturgy, painting, poetry, dance, music, drama, architecture, popular piety, and so on) and through the embodiment of the faith in the works of liturgy and community life and ministry, is increasingly being recognized as the royal road to a living faith, leading to a new appreciation of the spirituality of peoples who never lost touch with the imagination and never really got in touch with systematic theology. Philosophically based systematic unfolding of the faith in theology has an important role to play, but if it has nothing experiential on which to exercise its characteristic rational activity and no field of experience in which to express its reflection, it becomes a sterile scholasticism, a bloodless exercise of academics rather than a red-blooded participation in the faith life of a struggling community. There are times and places in which theology—rational discourse about God—in its most academic embodiment has pride of place but never to the exclusion of or in the absence of theopoetics—the experience of the living God in and through the embodied praxis of believers. One of the great gifts of Vatican II, appearing under the rubric of "the return to the Sources," was its re-orienting of theology not away from its philosophical and rational methods and content but into a retrieval of the role of experience, of spirituality, as the matrix and expression of revelation. In other words, the placing of theology at the service of revelation, which is never a body of doctrine but an experience of God, has rejuvenated and re-enlivened theology itself.

The importance of theo-logy is that it can abstract, universalize, criticize, compare, render intelligible, argue, defend, and plumb the depths of the connections and the wellsprings of meaning that are available to the intellect in its most creative and disciplined activity. But only if it is rooted in the spirituality, the lived experience, that expresses itself in and is expressed by the concreteness of the aesthetic, only if it generates and is generated by a theo-poesis that comes to expression not primarily in rational discourse but in the rich diversity and multiplicity of religious experience, can theology play its true role in the Church and the world.

Conclusion

So, in conclusion, let me now circle back and make my point about the success, both that achieved and that which we can realistically anticipate, of ecumenical dialogue—dialogue between Lutherans and Roman Catholics and indeed in the Church in all its diversity, east and west, north and south, premodern and modern and postmodern—and even interreligious dialogue with Christianity's elder sibling Judaism and those ancient paths to transcendence that predate and postdate the Judeo-Christian experience. I have been trying to suggest that the reason Vatican II has succeeded in launching what no council before it has been able to launch—not the reform of a recalcitrant or wayward institutional Church; a ringing condemnation of paganism, heresy, or laxity; a disciplinary house-cleaning at home and a vigorous proselytism abroad; but genuine, mutually enriching dialogue among all those who seek God and even, potentially, those who do not yet seek God—is that it has re-connected its doctrinal discourse to the deep springs of human religious experience. How this project can continue as postmodernity unfolds is certainly not clear, but I find great hope in the re-integration of sense and sensibility, of reason and feeling, of thought and art, of prose and poetry, indeed of soul and body, in the path Vatican II opened out for us, the path the founders of the Graduate Theological Union set out on and of which we are the inheritors and, I trust, the safe-keepers and cultivators, and promoters, as we celebrate the 500th anniversary of the Reform in which we are all still, by the grace of Jesus Christ, engaged.

Chapter Two

FROM FIRST-CENTURY MEDITERRANEA TO TWENTY-FIRST-CENTURY NORTH AMERICA
A LONG TRADITION OF CONTEXTUAL DISTANCE EDUCATION

Jean-François Racine

To the Jews I made myself as a Jew, to win the Jews; to those under the Law as one under the Law (though I am not), in order to win those under the Law; to those outside the Law as one outside the Law, though I am not outside the Law but under Christ's law, to win those outside the Law. To the weak, I made myself weak, to win the weak. I accommodated myself to people in all kinds of different situations, so that by all possible means I might bring some to salvation.

1 COR 9:20–22, NJB

Introduction:
No Conversion in Sight, Only Core Convictions

The order put before the authors of this collection of essays is to tell about their "conversion" to contextual theology. If by conversion one means a "change of mind" about something, I cannot

23

think of any such conversion.[1] Instead, I can speak of an intellectual journey. Changes in spatial locations prompted the main shifts that occurred during this intellectual journey. All along, two key convictions, acquired in my early twenties, served as bearings to guide me. To these two key convictions I should add a growing awareness of the environmental impact of our lifestyles, including professional lifestyles and educational formulas.

The first key conviction is that effective teaching focuses on the learner as much as on the topic. I gained this conviction while training to obtain my certification in education and teacher's license during the mid-1980s. It came through formal coursework, personal reading about teaching effectiveness, and reflection about whom I considered to have been the most effective teachers in my education.

The second conviction is that biblical interpretation should focus on the text and its various contexts: (1) the historical, geographical, social, and theological contexts in which biblical texts came into existence and were transmitted; (2) the literary contexts of the portions of texts under scrutiny, that is, how these portions connect with the surrounding passages and play a role in the discourse; and (3) the historical, geographical, social, and theological contexts of the various interpreters.[2]

While my initial training in theology and biblical studies prepared me to address contextual aspects (1) and (2), the third aspect, that is, the context of the interpreters, was rarely, if ever, mentioned. Is this surprising? Not so much, according to an operational model of scientific investigation that was formulated in Western modernity. This model assumes a clear distinction between the object under examination and the subject who examines. It therefore assumes the possibility of a disinterested study of the object. As a

---

1. As expressed by the Greek word *metanoia*.

2. Margaret Nutting Ralph considers attention to various contexts to be the hallmark of biblical interpreters trained in the Roman Catholic tradition. See Margaret Nutting Ralph, *A Walk through the New Testament: An Introduction for Catholics* (New York/Mahwah, NJ: Paulist Press, 2009), 3.

result, biblical scholars often give the impression of uttering normative interpretations that remain valid through times and cultures.

Four decades ago, Michel de Certeau remarked that historians
have succeeded at giving the impression of connecting their audience with an unmediated past and at making the audience forget
their presence.[3] Similarly, biblical scholars often succeed at giving
the impression of directly connecting their audience to the word of
God and at making their presence unnoticed.

I became convinced of the importance of the interpreter's context when, as a doctoral student, I attended for a few years both
the annual meetings of the Canadian Society of Biblical Studies
(CSBS) and the annual meetings of the Association Catholique des
Études Bibliques au Canada (ACÉBAC). These scholarly meetings
were held a few days apart from each other in different locations.
Not only were they held in different languages (English and French)
and attended by different people, but they also addressed different questions using different methods and approaches. While the
English-speaking CSBS meetings focused on the historical and social contexts of the formation of biblical texts, the French-speaking
ACÉBAC meetings were mostly preoccupied with the question
of making these texts relevant for contemporary audiences.[4] As a
French-speaking student attending an English-speaking university
in Ontario, I had the rare opportunity to move across these two academic worlds and to see how incompatible they could sometimes be.
For instance, I would be asked the "so what" question, that is, to
address the contemporary relevance of my research at the ACÉBAC

---

3. Michel de Certeau, *L'écriture de l'histoire*, Bibliothèque des histoires (Paris:
Gallimard, 1975), 77–95.

4. This preoccupation on the part of the members of ACÉBAC surfaced
in section IV of the 1993 Pontifical Biblical Commission document
L'interprétation de la Bible dans l'Église (*The Interpretation of the Bible in the
Church*) that used the term *actualisation* (actualization) to describe the pro-
cess of having the scriptures speak to the situations of their audiences. See
Commission Biblique Pontificale, *L'interprétation de la Bible dans l'Église*
(Paris: Cerf, 1994), 103–7.

meeting, after explaining how a first-century C.E. audience would have understood a passage of the Gospel according to Matthew. On another occasion, when risking a question at the CSBS meeting about the impact of a text on a contemporary audience, I would be reminded that biblical scholars focus on the origins of biblical texts and on how their initial audiences would have understood them.

In the meantime, I had been hired by a public university as an adjunct faculty to teach a survey course on the New Testament aimed at elementary school teachers in training. The goal of the course was to enable them to teach children about the biblical aspects of the Catholic religious education program.[5] As a result, the "so what" question became part of my daily life and has remained so. As a biblical interpreter attentive to the context, I have therefore become aware that my task is not accomplished until I have, on the one hand, addressed various types of context and, on the other, signaled my presence as an interpreter trained in certain ways and commissioned by institutions to accomplish specific tasks. I have tried to live up to these core convictions, something that is not always easy or obvious.

Going North:
Saguenay and Lac-St-Jean Regions

In July 1996, I was standing in the office of the chair of the religious studies and ethics department at Université du Québec à Chicoutimi. I had been hired a few days before as an adjunct faculty,

---

5. Until the early 2000s, Catholic or Protestant religious education was offered by default in all schools of the province of Québec, public or private. Parents could petition for an exemption that replaced religious education with moral education. The Catholic and Protestant committees of the provincial board of education designed these programs. Public and private universities had to provide dedicated courses to enable those who trained for teaching at the elementary (grades 1–6) and secondary (grades 7–11) levels to teach these topics.

following a phone interview, to teach a course on Paul in an off-campus center. The theology program director joined the meeting and told me that the title of the course I would teach was "Le défi théologique de Paul," which in English sounds like "Paul's Theological Challenge." He briefly explained that his idea about giving the course this title was that Paul faced the task of making relevant a message that initially came into existence in Aramaic Palestine and used cultural categories specific to that society. The message had to be translated and adapted for a Hellenistic audience whose culture was very different. Next, he added that I similarly needed to design a course that would make Paul's letters intelligible and relevant to the students.

I did not realize at that moment how much this perspective on Paul as someone who navigates across cultures would have lasting effects on my teaching. When I asked for more information about the audience, I was told that they were about to complete their bachelor of theology degree, which they had been pursuing together as part-time students for the last nine years, taking one course per semester. I was also told that they would need to accept me as an outsider and was asked if I had family from the Lac-St-Jean region, a circumstance that would save me from being seen as a complete stranger. Fortunately, I could say that my maternal grandfather was from St-Gédéon and that my maternal grandmother was raised in Métabetchouan after the family had moved there from Woonsocket, Rhode Island. Finally, I was told that the students would let me know how they wanted to organize their semester.

This first semester of teaching for Université du Québec à Chicoutimi went well, as did the following ones. I taught courses at the same off-campus center and also on the main campus for three years. I spent much time on the road every week; some courses required a six-hour, round-trip drive...in fair weather. I became used to driving for long hours at night in snowy conditions. I also adapted my way of teaching to the culture of the place. For instance, students continually asked questions in class. As a result, a three-hour class period would mostly be a three-hour Q&A session. To make sure that we would cover a section, I would at some point tell students that we needed to move on so that we could explore the next section, which was even more interesting than the present one.

After three years as an adjunct, I was offered a full-time position as a visiting professor at the university. I therefore moved to Chicoutimi, where I lived for four years. I came to know and understand better the profile of students both on the main campus and in off-campus centers. The student population was ethnically fairly homogeneous. Most students were French Canadians born in the region. There was also a significant number of students from the First Nations—mostly Innu-Montagnais—or connected to the First Nations through one parent. About half of the students trained for ministry, lay or ordained. The other half was made up of people who had an interest in religions or in religious writings. Hence, in addition to equipping those preparing for ministry, courses included a significant component about the reception of biblical texts in Western visual arts and francophone literature.

I also came to understand better what is involved in living outside of major cities. Practically, it means that the governments' financial resources, which are allocated generously to develop major cities, are allocated sparingly in the development of outer regions. It means, for instance, that physicians are rare and tend to leave as soon as they can work in major cities. It means high unemployment. It means that major employers, such as the aluminum plants and paper mills, are all-powerful and therefore that environmental regulations are applied leniently. It means that younger people leave the region and that one realizes when walking in the streets of some towns that the 25- to 35-year-old age group is underrepresented in the population.

The department of religious studies and ethics at the university offered three undergraduate programs and two graduate programs in theology. The graduate programs were offered only on the main campus, while the three undergraduate programs were offered in six off-campus centers, one of which was accessible only by airplane.

Six full-time faculty and about twelve adjuncts staffed these pro-grams. All were committed to the mission of the university to offer quality higher education to people scattered over a vast territory who could not afford taking courses in major cities because their situations made it impossible to drive for hours to the main cam-pus. Most of the faculty came from the region and had gone to major centers, often overseas, for their training. They had neverthe-less returned, had their feet rooted in the clay of the region, as they said, and were thus there to stay, despite the odds of a demographi-cally declining region. In off-campus centers, the size of cohorts oscillated between eight and twenty-five students. With smaller cohorts, distance education began to look appealing. The faculty of our department undertook inconclusive experiments with video conferencing. At the turn of the twenty-first century, video con-ferences still necessitated the installation of costly equipment. In addition, six phone lines were needed to convey voice and image in both directions. The phone networks of most off-campus centers could not support such demand, and class periods frequently relied on one or two phone lines. Yet a promising alternative, the internet, was around the corner.

Going West: California

In 2002, I moved to California to take my present position. What a contrast with the Saguenay and Lac-St-Jean region! California did not suffer from depopulation. Indeed, it was rather the opposite. There were people everywhere; there were cars everywhere. Oceans of cars! Saguenay and Lac-St-Jean were ethnically homogeneous; California was superlatively diverse, ethnically speaking.

From an academic standpoint, the ethnically and denomina-tionally diverse student body was not without reminders of the student body of the doctoral program at the Toronto School of Theology. As I now held the position of instructor, I quickly re-alized that ethnic diversity also meant that students had been schooled in various educational systems, all of which were, of course, different from the one in which I had been schooled. In retrospect, I can say that my students and I experienced culture shock. I had to quickly adapt my teaching style to the new situation. For those students schooled in systems where lectures are the *modus vivendi*, I did lectures. Since U.S. students like having the impression that they cover much ground in a course, I broke course sections into smaller units to give the impression of a Hollywood film montage in which the camera angle changes constantly. Yet in spite of the ethnic, denominational, and educational diversity, most students were training for some type of ministry. In addition, students tended to stand more at the center of the ideological spectrum than my students from the North: no more clashes in class between agnostics and ultra-conservative Catholics.

While I was reorganizing my two core classes to suit the needs of the students and of the programs, I began to experiment with new courses. For instance, I created a course about a contextual reading of Matthew, the purpose of which was to read this Gospel from one's particular location. Since the eight students enrolled in the course were all white males, among whom six were U.S. Jesuits, everyone basically read from the same place and tended to come up with the same perspectives on Matthew. I scheduled a similar course the following year on the Gospel according to Luke, telling myself that I would probably have more diversity in the classroom. I was not completely mistaken: besides seven U.S. Jesuits, one female student with an interest in art history enrolled in the course. At some point during that semester, I decided that this type of course did not promise a bright future. The time had come to try something else.

This "something else" was a course about exegesis for preaching. The first time I offered it, I had the good fortune of teaching it with a doctoral student in homiletics who shared my interests for Moodle, the course management system that the consortium had just adopted. We decided to see what Moodle could do and to push it to its limits. That course proved to be a good idea: male and female students from various denominations enrolled in it. They brought to the course different sensitivities about preaching. In addition, preaching is intrinsically contextual: It typically reads the lives of people in the light of scriptures. It is tailored for a specific audience at a specific time. For this reason, all homilies—even great ones—come with an expiration date. During that semester, we heard outstanding preaching. We also heard about the pastoral needs and sensitivities of various communities across the Bay Area and beyond. We heard about the challenges of addressing these needs effectively. This course was offered two more times, always team-taught with a colleague of the Episcopalian school in our consortium. These remain among the most rewarding courses I have ever taught; they allowed me to evenly address all the various contexts of biblical interpretation.

In some courses in biblical studies I remain the expert on the topic from beginning to end and may even be considered by students and colleagues as some sort of gatekeeper. I cease being the expert early on in the process, however, when teaching a course of exegesis for preaching.[6] At some point in the interpretive process, I indeed have to recognize that if I know well enough the historical and literary contexts of these readings, I often know very little about the preaching standards in other denominations and about the ethos of the audiences for whom the homilies are created. I therefore come to the point where I have to trust that situations and audiences are well presented. I have experienced the same situation when supervising some theses and dissertations. Since I

---

6. I owe the image of biblical faculty as gatekeeper to Dale B. Martin, *Pedagogy of the Bible: An Analysis and Proposal* (Louisville, KY: Westminster John Knox, 2008), 14–17. Martin's book is based on visits he made to ten Protestant seminaries to see how biblical studies were taught. For his work, he interviewed faculty who taught biblical studies, asking how they perceived themselves. He also interviewed faculty from other disciplines and students to see how they perceived biblical faculty and the role of the curriculum in biblical studies. In all seminaries, he found a wide discrepancy between the self-perception of the biblical faculty and how other members of the faculty and students perceived them.

arrived at the Graduate Theological Union, all the students whom I have supervised have come from other continents. I have never lived in Uganda, Vietnam, South Korea, China, India, Indonesia, or Poland. I therefore do not know and do not fully understand these students' situations. I am simply grateful that they make the effort of describing their world to me. Each time, I feel like the clumsy visitor who does not know the social codes and needs to be guided by the hand. I have therefore come to accept that if I want students to do theology and preaching from their own context, I eventually reach a point, beyond the initial guidance, where I have to "let it go" and trust the student, who has now become my guide.

Paul as a Role Model

Before moving to the last step in this journey, I wish to return to Paul. More specifically, I wish to return to the perspective that considers him to be a cultural navigator. Whereas this perspective was initially imposed on me from outside, it has become an interpretive lens to help me read my teaching career, has provided the impetus to launch new ventures, and has given me comfort when such ventures meet with failure or mixed success due to my own limitations.

Let me therefore reflect on this perspective. I make no claim of objectivity for this reading, but I consider it to be well supported by evidence in the letters themselves and by contemporary scholarship on Paul.

After a little more than twenty years in theological education, I have yet to meet a student who dislikes Jesus or critiques him. The same does not hold true with Paul. Attitudes toward Paul are mixed. Some consider him the paradigmatic convert, the paradigmatic missionary, and the paradigmatic theologian. Others consider him the archetype of the misogynist theologians who populate the history of Christianity and/or as a far too cerebral thinker who, early on, turned Jesus's highly accessible message about the kingdom of God into a labyrinthine discourse on sin, death, and justification.[7] In fact, a reading of the Pauline corpus may leave one with the impression that Paul's discourse is not always clear and comprehensive, that its formulation may cause misunderstandings that prompt him to reformulate it in new writings, which themselves may fuel new misunderstandings. In addition, the letters indicate that Paul's relationships with communities were frequently conflicted. Far from solving conflicts, the sarcastic tone of some letters is apt to amplify conflicts.[8] In other words, Paul's letters relate not only his success stories, but also his less successful ones.

Let me nevertheless put such considerations aside and focus on different features. The first aspect to take seriously is Paul's affirmation that he was a Pharisee (Phil 3:5), a member of a progressive religious group that had adopted a belief in the resurrection of the dead, that attempted to make the Torah accessible to all Jews, and was interested in having Gentiles become part of Israel.[9] Paul's interest in Gentiles may therefore originate partly from his belonging to the Pharisees. Next, Paul is a diaspora Jew from Tarsus. Hence he is fluent in Greek, used to dealing with Gentiles and

---

7. Some websites offer collections of negative opinions about Paul. See, for instance, http://3oce.com/paulstatements.htm and http://www.atheists-for-jesus .com/paul.php. I have not been able to locate a similar website about Jesus. In fact, one may have the impression that the last person to have uttered a negative opinion of Jesus was Celsus during the second half of the second century.

8. For instance, when addressing Galatian Christians as "You stupid people in Galatia!" (Gal 3:1) or telling the Corinthian Christians that not many of them are wise or influential by human standards (1 Cor 1:26).

9. Matthew 23:15 alludes to the Pharisees' efforts to gain proselytes. On Pharisees and their ideological proximity to the Jesus movement, see, for example, E.P. Sanders, *Paul and Palestinian Judaism: A Comparison of Patterns of Religion* (Philadelphia: Fortress, 1977), 33–83. A recent collection of essays edited by Jacob Neusner and Bruce D. Chilton nevertheless reminds us how little we know about the Pharisees, despite the fact that they are mentioned in numerous documents. See Jacob Neusner and Bruce D. Chilton, eds., *In Quest of the Historical Pharisees* (Waco, TX: Baylor University Press, 2007).

negotiating his Jewish identity within a Hellenistic environment.[10] In contrast to Palestinian Jews such as Peter and James, he is in a better position to navigate among Gentiles and to convey the Gospel to them.[11] Paul is in fact so committed to spreading the Gospel among the Gentiles that the letter to the Romans announces his tentative travel plan to Spain, the extreme western end of the Mediterranean, for this very purpose (Rom 15:28).

Paul's zeal in spreading the Gospel among the Gentiles results in the founding of, or relations with, churches in Asia Minor (Ephesus, Colossae, Galatia), Macedonia (Thessalonica and Philippi), Achaia (Corinth), and Italy (Rome). This constitutes a vast territory difficult to cover, assuming that travelers could not travel much distance each day using the means of transportation available to them. In addition, circumstances often prevented Paul and his co-workers from staying for very long with these churches. It is therefore not surprising that he and his co-workers made use of the very short list of media available at that time, that is, the letter, carried and expounded by a co-worker.

The letters of the Pauline corpus served various purposes. For instance, they can be letters of recommendation, as in the case of the letter to Philemon on behalf of Onesimus. They may attempt to mend relationships, as in the case of 2 Corinthians. They may serve to inform about recent events, to keep in touch, and to express Paul's longing for seeing members of a church, as in the case of Philemon 1. Yet in many instances these letters serve to complement the initial instruction about the Gospel and its implications, to solve misunderstandings on some questions—for example, the resurrection of the dead in 1 Corinthians 15, an idea some Corinthians rejected—and to address situations that are proper to certain groups. For instance, 1 Thessalonians 4 addresses

---

10. On this, see, for example, Calvin J. Roetzel, *Paul: The Man and the Myth* (Columbia: University of South Carolina Press, 1998), 11–14.

11. This is precisely the point of Ronald Charles, *Paul and the Politics of Diaspora* (Minneapolis: Fortress, 2014).

a question from these people about the fate of those who have died prior to Christ's return. In the same vein, 1 Corinthians 8 provides some deontological guidelines when one is being served meat from an animal that has been sacrificed to a pagan god. In such cases, Paul appears to be a contextual theologian: the letters originate from specific needs and questions. They are tailored specifically to address these questions in relation to the needs of the audiences. Still, in some cases, the letters serve to enforce a perspective and practice alien to a church, as can be seen with Paul's imposition of the format of the Passover meal to the Corinthians (1 Cor 11:17–34), who likely envisioned the common meal as following the practices of a Greek banquet.

Anyone familiar with standard letters from the Hellenistic world nevertheless notices that Paul's letters are usually much longer than the typical one-page Hellenistic letter from the same period and often convey long instructional sequences about his understanding of the Gospel and its ethical implications. Furthermore, several copies of Paul's letters were made and circulated from one church to another.[12] For this reason, I suggest looking at Paul's letters as the earliest instance of a wide-scale theological distance education program using the most appropriate medium of that time: the letter. As with any distance education program, it provided education to people in their own location and minimized the need for costly and hazardous travel. Interestingly, this model set a standard that is still in use today when one thinks of encyclical letters.

Going to Cyberspace

In 2009, I was given the opportunity to revisit the interests I had developed for distance education in my previous position by

---

12. See Colossians 4:16–17 and the absence of mention of Ephesus in several ancient manuscripts of Ephesians.

teaching a fully online survey course on the New Testament for the MA in Ministry offered by Creighton University.

Over the years, I had added online components to all the courses that I offer at the Graduate Theological Union, first by posting the course calendar, readings, and digital slides on the consortium's course management system, and second by creating electronic sign-up sheets. Concurrently, I experimented with various formats of discussion forums to address the challenge of often having more than twenty-five students enrolled in a course. I noticed that in such larger groups I heard the perspectives of only a fraction of the group during in-class discussions. Mandatory online discussion forums allowed me to read perspectives from all the students enrolled in the class. In addition, for introverted students who needed time to formulate their perspective, an online discussion forum that lasted between forty-eight and seventy-two hours provided enough time for reflection and allowed me to enter into dialogue with every student at least once during the semester. In some courses, I frequently moved away from the standard questions that monitor the acquisition of basic concepts to ask about their reception and use in a student's own context. Finally, I went paperless for several courses by having the students place their written assignments into digital dropboxes and returning electronically the graded assignments with comments. When the offer came to teach an online course at Creighton University, I was therefore ready for this next move, which was facilitated through short audio (and now video) podcasts that provided an orientation to the course material and to salient points of the topic under discussion.

Seeing Paul as a contextual theologian and "cultural navigator" has been a source of inspiration in the context of online distance education. As I offered this first fully online course, I knew that all the students enrolled in the course were engaged in some kind of ministry. I also knew that they were based in Nebraska, Iowa, Missouri, Utah, and Louisiana, and I designed the course to include their own geographical and ministerial context in the learning process. As with any survey course on the New Testament, we spoke a great deal about the first-century historical, geographical, and social contexts. We also used a few literary methods to read the text itself, but in addition I had individual students describe their context, as well as issues, questions, and challenges about biblical interpretation they encountered in ministry by writing a case study that their classmates would address as "consultants." The next step was to discuss these situations as a group. We all realized that challenges could be very different from place to place and that an approach that was successful in a particular setting was not going to apply in another one, even if all students were based in the United States. Personally, I realized that if students had had to move to Omaha to take the course, something of their daily context would have been lost as a result of that move.

I initially became interested in distance education as a means of fulfilling the mission of the institution for which I previously worked. This made much sense in the context of a small population scattered over a vast territory served by few human resources. Instead of having this population converge on major centers to benefit from higher education, programs were made available to these people wherever they were. For me, distance education also cohered with a tradition of contextual theology and distance education exemplified in the earliest Christian writings that have been preserved, Paul's letters.

Even though my work situation has changed and I now live at the other end of our continent, I am still interested in distance education for the same reasons I was originally: I consider that theological education should be available to people where they are and that it should address them in their particular situation instead of rooting them out from that situation in order to educate them.

In California, distance is not the primary hindrance to access to theological education. The main obstacles are road congestion and its corollary, an underdeveloped system of public transit. To these aspects, one can add the cost of higher education and how busy the life of working adults is, especially if they are raising children. If one is nevertheless determined to commute to centers of theological education, one ends up adding to traffic congestion, which makes one's commute even longer. Another aspect of traffic congestion is the amount of air pollution that it generates by having thousands of motor vehicles creeping along roads and burning fossil fuels to no advantage.

The environmental impact of our professional lifestyles and pedagogical formulas is overlooked or dismissed as being irrelevant in our educational models. It nevertheless has an accumulative negative effect on our environment. Yet no such concern is allowed to stand in the way of the achievement of educational goals as they are usually defined in U.S. education. Paul traveled a great deal in the Eastern Mediterranean. Still, how does the carbon footprint he left in a lifetime compare with the one I leave in the course of a year? Did the three shipwrecks in which he was involved (2 Cor 11:25) have much negative and lasting impact on the environment?

Let us consider that Paul's lifestyle and travels likely caused less damage to the environment than the lifestyle and travels of the average North American.[13] His adoption of a model of distance education was likely prompted by the difficulty of visiting, in person, all the churches with which he had a relationship—within a reasonable amount of time and without putting his life at risk.[14] Circumstances have changed: airplanes and automobiles make it possible to cover much distance within a short time and indeed help to create and maintain webs of human relationships that are mutually enriching. However, we now live in a context of ecological

---

13. Not that human beings who lived in these times and places had no capacity to generate "trash." In fact, a visit to an archaeological dig gives a good idea of the human capacity to produce an amazing amount of trash, often in the form of pieces of broken pottery, which was the common mode of packaging at that time.

14. 2 Corinthians 11:27 mentions the dangers inherent to travel in Paul's society. One of these dangers was the presence of brigands on the roads. The parable of the "good Samaritan" (Lk 10:30–37) also features road brigands (Lk 10:30).

crisis.[15] This present context demands a readjustment of lifestyles to reduce the damage we have been causing to our common home.[16] Yet this readjustment should not result in the disappearance of the rich web of human relationships made possible by modern means of transportation, or even in its impoverishment. Paul's letters constitute an early example of the use of means of communication to maintain and foster relationships, to instruct and to minister at a distance. How can our modern means of communication better serve these goals in our educational systems? Should the achievement of educational goals necessarily imply being physically present in a classroom?

Conclusion

By relating my own intellectual journey, I have come to perceive contextual theology as an effect of three elements rather than something I have pursued intently. These three elements are the geographical moves that I made over the years, a conviction that teaching should focus on the learner as much as on the topic, and the inspiration provided by Paul as an innovative contextual

---

15. The phrase "ecological crisis" is precisely used by Pope Francis in the third chapter of his encyclical letter *Laudato si'* (On Care for Our Common Home) (2015), http://w2.vatican.va/content/francesco/en/encyclicals/docu ments/papa-francesco_20150524_enciclica-laudato-si.html.

16. Francis, *Laudato si'*, chap. 6. Two years after it has come out, one may ask whether this encyclical letter has had much impact among U.S. Catholics, since it is mostly absent from church-related conversations and discussions. I asked a group of students in class during the Fall 2016 semester when was the last time they heard a homily that discussed environmental issues; all thirty students said that they actually had never heard such issues mentioned in homilies. A recent article attempts to explain the lack of impact of *Laudato si'* among U.S. Catholics. See John D. Wilsey, "Does American Exceptionalism Clash with Pope Francis's Call to Care for Creation?" *America*, November 14, 2016, http://www.americamagazine.org/ issue/whose-land.

thinker. In this regard, the "context" element of contextual theology focuses primarily on a geographical location, but also on a situation that can be experienced across times and social settings such as foreign domination, warfare, or economic downturns.

My move to distance learning was initially prompted by the challenges that a particular geographical situation posed to the accomplishment of an institutional mission. A few years later, in a new geographical setting, it is also prompted by taking seriously the context of the ecological crisis in which we live and the need to change our lifestyles accordingly, while still providing quality theological education to all those who want it.

Chapter Three

WHY READ THE CHURCH FATHERS?
TEACHING NICAEA AS CONTEXTUAL THEOLOGY

Thomas Cattoi

As a teacher and scholar who has had the privilege of working at the Jesuit School of Theology since 2006, I have met and worked with students from a variety of countries of the Global South: Jesuits and diocesan priests from India and Latin America, religious sisters from Asia, Protestant ministers from Korea, and many others. To an Italian who studied in the United Kingdom and completed his doctorate in the United States, the points raised by these students reflected an experience of life and an intellectual horizon that was often very distant from mine. At the same time, the material I was teaching often appeared to be very distant from my students' theological concerns and did not always help me address their questions. What is the relevance of fourth-century trinitarian debates for a Vietnamese sister who is going to return to her country and work with battered women? Why study the spirituality of the desert fathers if your job after graduation will be running a parish in Lagos, an African metropolis of over thirty million people?

Attitudes toward patristic theology in contemporary academe vary, but they tend to fall into two mutually opposing camps. Some view the Church Fathers as hopelessly outdated representatives of a culture that no longer exists, and therefore as mere archaeological curios that can entertain scholars insulated from the demands of reality. Why study the Arian controversy and the story of the Council of Nicaea when, after graduating, you will return to India and minister to local tribals? Surely, a vigorous contextual theology has no use for classical trinitarian theology, articulated within a frame of reference that is utterly foreign to anyone living in the twenty-first century. Others, however, wonder why anyone would even want to develop new contextual theologies when really everything that could possibly be known about God—our experience of God—can be found in the pages of the Church Fathers. Just read the Cappadocians, and everything will be revealed to you. Who needs context anyway?

Caught between these two extremes, I found myself wondering whether there wasn't a better way. After all, people like Gregory of Nyssa and his Cappadocian peers were not operating in a vacuum—they were trying to articulate a theology for their educated contemporaries, bringing the Gospel into conversation with a sophisticated culture rooted in the Neoplatonic philosophical paradigm. Then it dawned on me that the theology of the Church Fathers was actually a form of contextual theology—indeed, one that built on the encounter between the Christian message and Greek philosophical culture that is already unfolding in the Gospel of John and the Pauline letters. If this insight were retrieved, it would then be possible to teach this material from a different perspective, presenting these authors as pioneers of an intellectual search for dialogue with the surrounding culture. What seemed to me crucial, then, was to recover a sense of the contextual—and indeed experiential—root of classical trinitarian and Christological doctrine so that students could recognize that the challenges faced by the Church Fathers were not too dissimilar from their own as they try to become contextual theologians.

My reflection on this topic has been greatly helped by the work of the Canadian Jesuit Bernard Lonergan (1904–1984), whose work on theological epistemology ensures that one can recover a sense of the experiential and historical roots of classical doctrines. Another important resource was the conceptual "map" of contextual theology drawn by Stephen Bevans in *Models of Contextual Theology*.[1] In the course of this essay, I will rely on the writings of Lonergan and Bevans to uncover the experiential and contextual character of the teaching of *homoousia* in the writings of Athanasius of Alexandria (296–373). After this historical survey, I will offer some suggestions toward a possible contextual reformulation of classical Christology, prompted by my work with a number of graduate students at the Jesuit School of Theology.[2]

Bernard Lonergan famously defines theology as a set of "related and recurrent operations cumulatively advancing towards an ideal goal,"[3] while more broadly thinking of the discipline as mediating between religious experience and culture. Lonergan deplores the tendency of contemporary theology to be so specialized and fragmented, and suggests that we reflect on the way in which different functional specialties are related to each other so as to develop an overarching understanding of theology as a single discipline with a number of distinct, yet integrated, subfields. The interdependence of the various specialties reflects the different stages of the subject's engagement with her own religious experience, her attempt to offer a cogent account of the latter, and the community's eventual assessment and appropriation of this experience.[4] Unfortunately, we only have direct access to our own religious experience; when

---

1. The main reference works cited in this essay are Bernard Lonergan, SJ, *Method in Theology* (Toronto: University of Toronto Press, 1971), and Stephen B. Bevans, SVD, *Models of Contextual Theology*, rev. and exp. ed. (Maryknoll, NY: Orbis, 2002).

2. The literature on the Arian controversy and Athanasius's defense of *homoousia* is, of course, extensive and constantly growing. Useful reference works are Khaled Anatolios, *Athanasius: The Coherence of His Thought* (London: Routledge, 1998); Lewis Ayres, *Nicaea and Its Legacy: An Approach to Fourth-Century Trinitarian Theology* (Oxford: Oxford University Press, 2004); John Behr, *The Nicene Faith*, Parts 1 and 2 (Crestwood, NY: St. Vladimir's Seminary Press, 2004).

3. Lonergan, *Method in Theology*, 125.

4. Lonergan, *Method in Theology*, 126.

it comes to someone else's experience, we need to rely on other sources—most often texts, where individual practitioners give an account of their own encounter with ultimate reality or the divine. Lonergan views *research*, which includes the study of texts, but also inscriptions, symbols, and art, as the first step toward the development of a coherent theology. What follows is *interpretation*, where one applies the tools of contemporary hermeneutics to whatever research has made available. *History* will then attempt to contextualize this interpretation in a particular chronological context, offering an evaluation of this experience "with regard to the sum of cultural, institutional and doctrinal movements in their concrete setting."[5] As different individuals having the same or analogous religious experiences may develop different interpretations of those experiences, there will then be a need for a comprehensive viewpoint that mediates or adjudicates between conflicting positions. Lonergan uses the term *dialectic* to indicate the moment when distinct assessments of a religious experience are compared with each other and a meta-judgment emerges seeking to integrate different insights or discarding one in favor of another.[6]

Lonergan views these four functional specialties (research, interpretation, history, and dialectic) as reflecting the different stages of the epistemic trajectory, whereby the individual processes the content of an experience. The specialty of research seeks as much as possible to capture the moment when the individual undergoes the initial experience that starts the whole speculative process. The ensuing interpretation mirrors the individual's effort at understanding the experience, whereas historical contextualization reflects the individual's ultimate judgment on the experience. The dialectical moment, then, marks the stage when the individual chose to share her experience with her community or the world at large; in the history of Christianity, the first ecumenical councils could be regarded as paradigmatic of

---

5. Lonergan, *Method in Theology*, 128.

6. Lonergan, *Method in Theology*, 129–30.

this dialectical moment, when different "judgments" on Christological or trinitarian questions came to the fore and required a definitive assessment on the part of the ecclesial community.[7]

The four other specialties (foundations, doctrines, systematics, and communication) explore the gradual emergence of a theological horizon that grounds the speculative articulation of a particular doctrine in conversation with a specific cultural milieu. Lonergan defines the fifth specialty—*foundations*—as "the horizon within which the meaning of doctrines can be apprehended."[8] Foundations differ from what is traditionally known as fundamental theology—a set of doctrines or *loci* on particular *praeambula fidei*—inasmuch as entering into one such horizon requires an intellectual conversion that is existential as well as communal, in the sense that its terms are set by the community known as church. Implicit in these foundations are speculative principles that will serve as guideposts in the development of the following functional specialties, of which *doctrines* will be the first. Doctrines are a judgment on a religious experience that comprises a factual as well as an axiomatic component—a doctrine seeks to establish what is to be affirmed about a certain experience, along with its soteriological import. Since doctrinal definitions inevitably give rise to more questions, and are often accused of fallacy or inconsistency, *systematic theology* attempts to "work out appropriate systems of conceptualizations" that support the system within which the doctrines are articulated. Most importantly for the purposes of our broader argument, the functional specialties of doctrine and systematic theology will have to rely on the resources of the surrounding culture, so as to properly convey the meaning of the original religious experience. Lonergan rounds off the list of specialties with *communication*, which,

---

7. Lonergan's great work of theological epistemology, where the operations of the subject are discussed at great length, is *Insight: A Study of Human Understanding* (London: Longmans, Green, 1957), whose publication preceded the Second Vatican Council by a few years.

8. Lonergan, *Method in Theology*, 131.

he claims, "concerns theology in its external relations" and also includes pastoral theology. Communication will have to develop differently in different contexts so as to ensure that doctrines and their systematic frameworks are adequately received by an audience that may not necessarily be equipped with the philosophical or historical knowledge necessary to fully appreciate the import of the formal doctrinal definitions.[9]

This brief survey of the functional specialties should make it clear that Lonergan's theological epistemology navigates the balance between the classical emphasis on the "givenness" and metaphysical character of the deposit of faith and the modern emphasis on the heuristic role of the subject's cognitive faculties. The main implication of this synthesis is that doctrinal statements do not lose value because they emerge from culturally contextual speculative articulations of specific experiences; on the contrary, they *derive* their value from the fact that they develop out of this encounter between a metaphysical reality and a historically specific context. Historical knowledge is always the result of cumulative insights, each of which reflects the perspective of a particular scholar or school of thought. In the same way as there can be no such thing as a "neutral" historical account, there will never be a "neutral" theological perspective, since all doctrinal judgments will reflect a foundational horizon emerging from a specific dialectical moment.[10]

If we consider the emergence of classical Christology, we will see that Lonergan's functional specialties offer us a map to chart the trajectory from the plurality of Christologies that are present in the New Testament to the doctrinal clarity of the definition of Nicaea. In Lonerganian terms, each of these Christologies can be regarded as a "judgment" on a religious experience: the authors of the different New Testament texts deploy their distinctive hermeneutic

---

9. Lonergan, *Method in Theology*, 131–33.

10. Lonergan explores the relationship between historical experience and historical knowledge in *Method in Theology*, chap. 8, 175–85, where the notion of an "objective" history is problematized.

lenses to articulate the salvific import of their encounter with Christ in ways that can be understood by their particular audience. The authors of the Synoptic Gospels may be more grounded in the scriptural tradition of the Old Testament, while the author of John adopts a more speculative perspective and engages in a qualified retrieval of philosophical notions from the heritage of Neoplatonic philosophy. Each of these Christologies mirrors a particular social, cultural, and theological outlook that results in different conceptual articulations of what is ultimately the same experience of salvation through the person of Christ. The question then is how the many Christologies of scripture were superseded by the one Christology of the Council of Nicaea, which eventually provided the basis for the development of trinitarian theology. This move from plurality to uniformity, or perhaps from conceptual fluidity to normativity, is what Lonergan characterizes as the "moment of dialectic," wherein different judgments compete in a conceptual struggle for the emergence of a unified foundational horizon. In the case of classical Christology, the foundational horizon was provided by different elements of Neoplatonic thought, and it is through a critical appropriation of its conceptual and terminological armory that the Christology of Nicaea came to life.

In his seminal work *Christianity and Classical Culture*, Orthodox theologian Jaroslav Pelikan identifies the fourth century as the pivotal moment in the development of a Christian speculative philosophy.[11] While earlier centuries had already witnessed remarkable instances of apologetic reflection—Justin Martyr's *Apologies* are one of the earliest examples[12]—the cessation of religious persecution after the Constantinian edict and the gradual reshaping of the Christian Church into a public institution marked

---

11. Jaroslav Pelikan, *Christianity and Classical Culture: The Metamorphosis of Natural Theology in the Christian Encounter with Hellenism* (New Haven, CT: Yale University Press, 1993).

12. Justin Martyr, *The First and Second Apologies*, trans. and ed. Leslie William Barnard (New York/Mahwah, NJ: Paulist Press, 1966).

a move toward greater and more explicit theological "normativity," where particular doctrinal positions would be taken as benchmarks for orthodoxy as well as badges of loyalty to the institution of the Church. The Christology of Nicaea, its defense by Athanasius of Alexandria, and its later re-elaboration by the Cappadocians can thus be regarded as a classic example of theology mediating between experience and culture in the Lonerganian sense, but also as a paradigmatic model of theological inculturation, drawing on a plethora of speculative sources to develop a meaningful Christology for the educated audience of the time.

The teaching of *homoousia* affirmed at Nicaea and so eloquently defended in Athanasius's *Contra Gentes* and *De Incarnatione* represented a marked deviation from the slew of subordinationist theologies that had largely controlled Christological discourse in the first centuries of the Church.[13] Athanasius's contribution to Christology rests on a distinct cosmological vision, which then becomes the basis for his theological anthropology and ultimately his understanding of the incarnation. The harmonious character of the natural order cannot possibly be mistaken for a deviation from an undifferentiated noetic reality;[14] rather, it is a manifestation of God's providence, as well as a way in which humanity can come to know and eventually encounter God himself. In *Contra Gentes* 35, Athanasius stresses that God wanted to remedy our ignorance of his nature and his plan, and, as a result, he "ordered creation through his Word so that, while he is invisible by nature, he might nevertheless be known to people from his works." The universe is God's *praxis*,

---

13. See Athanasius, *Contra Gentes* (PG25b: 3–94); *De Incarnatione* (PG25b: 95–197).

14. In the Origenist tradition, the creation of the material universe was an afterthought that was not part of God's original plan, but was made necessary by the turning away of some disembodied rational beings (*logikoi*) from a primeval experience of intellectual communion with the divine. See Jean Daniélou, *Origen*, trans. Walter Mitchell (Eugene, OR: Wipf and Stock, 2016), part III, chap. 1, 209–19.

and while the mystery of God may also be accessed through inner contemplation, only a few are able to do so, whereas many more will be able to discern God's imprint in the world's order (*taxis*) and harmony. While Origen argued that ontological homogeneity was on a higher plane than contingency and plurality,[15] Athanasius claims that the unity within distinction that is present in creation offers a far greater witness to God's omnipotence and wisdom: only a divine power could bring together opposite elements such as fire and water into a coherent whole. In *Contra Gentes* 40, this divine power is identified with "the Father of Christ..., who like a supreme artisan (*demiourgos*), by his own wisdom and Word, our Lord and Savior Christ, steers and orders all things for our salvation."

Athanasius's argument is that the cosmos is fundamentally rational; it is not a divine afterthought but is part and parcel of God's plan from the beginning of time. Since the universe unfolds according to reason, it is clear that "the one who governs and ordered it must be none other than the Logos of God" (CG 40). As Khaled Anatolios points out in his study of Athanasius's theology, the Alexandrian father resorts to the conceptual and terminological legacy of Stoicism to discuss the presence of God in the universe, but moves beyond it to affirm God's independence over creation.[16] While the Stoics postulated an immanent and ultimately impersonal *logos spermatikos*, Athanasius argues that the Word of the Father is endowed with individual subjectivity and intentionally orders the created order: the *logos* of the philosophers "is soulless and can neither reason nor think but acts merely by an extrinsic art according to the skill of the one who applied it," whereas the Christian Word "is the living and acting God, the Word of the good God of the universe," who, most importantly, "is other than the things that are made and all creation" (CG 40). The Word is the one proper (*idios*) of the Father, and he "has ordered

---

15. Daniélou, *Origen*, part III, chap. 1, 209–19.

16. Anatolios, *Athanasius*, 49–51.

the arrangement of all things, combining together contrary things and composing from them a single harmony" (CG 40).

How does Athanasius move beyond the Stoic framework while retaining its trademark terminology? On the one hand, it appears that the Logos of *Contra Gentes* is partly inspired by the *demiurge* in the *Timaeus*, who brought about the natural order on the basis of pre-existent matter.[17] This *demiurge*, while not fully personal in the sense of the Johannine Logos, is, however, distinct from the Stoic *logos* to the extent that it is set apart from creation itself. On the other hand, Athanasius retrieves the Platonic notion of participation (*metochē*), which enables the eternal Word of God to transcend the opposition between immanence and transcendence, as well as that between being and becoming. This approach enables him to move beyond a Neoplatonic notion of the divine as utterly removed from the created order to one where God is actually the ground of all contingent beings. In *Contra Gentes* 42, we are told that "it is the omnipotent, all-holy, and perfect Word of the Father himself who dwells in all things and extends his power everywhere, enlightening all things visible and invisible, containing and tying all things to himself." All things obey the Word, and it is the Word that sets the boundaries between opposites such as hot and cold, or heaven and earth, without blurring their distinction. This creative blend of Stoicism and Platonism turns the Word into a new *demiurge* who mediates between creation and the Father, making sure that the created order has access to the Godhead: "everything was created through and for him," who is "the power of the Father and his wisdom and Word" (CG 46). This speculative framework is then deployed to interpret the prologue of John's Gospel, ensuring that Johannine Christology is buttressed and articulated in a way that can be understood by the educated audience of the time.

In Lonerganian terms, this dialectical moment between the different early Christologies creates a foundational horizon where the

---

17. See Plato, *Timaeus*, trans. H. D. P. Lee (Baltimore: Penguin Books, 1965).

Logos Christology of the Gospel of John becomes the basis, as well as the organizing principle, for all future Christological reflection. As a result, the Christian soteriological vision is able to clothe itself in the garments of Neoplatonic thought, while simultaneously subverting many of its assumptions about the futility of the cosmos or the inferiority of matter. The doctrine of *homoousia* that emerged at Nicaea can then be seen as an ecclesial judgment on the mystery of the incarnation based on this fundamental insight into the intrinsic worth of the natural order.

In *De Incarnatione*, which further develops the argument of *Contra Gentes*, Athanasius introduces the incarnation as the renewal and reaffirmation of God's relationship with the world. The Greeks, we are told, ridicule Christians for their "absurd" (*atopon*) set of beliefs about the world, even if some of them—for example, the Stoics—do believe in the existence of a divine Logos. If then they confess—Athanasius rhetorically asks—that the Word of God is the governor over all things, and that it descends from the Father, and that "by the works of his providence (*pronoia*) he is known" and through him the Father is also known, why should it be against reason to believe that the Word could also become incarnate in a body? Indeed, "if it is suitable for him to come into the world and be known in the whole of it, it would also be suitable that he should appear in a human body," and that this body should be enlightened and moved by him (*De Incarnatione* 41). Athanasius uses the term providence (*pronoia*) to indicate God's immanent activity in the cosmos, and this comes to comprise whatever God does to prevent creation's slide into nothingness because of sin. If God is able to be present in the whole cosmos as in a body, it is not at all unsuitable that he should assume our human condition.

Athanasius does not offer a paradigm mapping the relationship between the divinity of the Word and the humanity of Christ— that is something that will only emerge at Chalcedon and will be the object of further refinements at the Second and Third Councils of Constantinople. What matters to him at this stage is simply to outline how it is not unreasonable to assert that the incarnate

Christ that we encounter in the Gospel is none other than the Word that sustains the universe, and that this Word, being the eternal wisdom of the Father, is invested with all the powers and attributes of divinity. Athanasius's defense of Nicaea's termino-logical choices—especially the adoption of the contested term *ousia*—flows from his commitment to the ultimate rationality and congruence of his soteriological vision with his understanding of the cosmos and of God's activity within it. The term *homoousia* is not introduced arbitrarily but rather is chosen because it encap-sulates the relationship between the Father and the Logos and emphasizes not only the unique status of the latter, but also the way in which the Word's activity in creation is the manifestation and the channel of the Father's providential love. Athanasius's *Contra Arianos* and *De Incarnatione*, as well as the no less influential *De Decretis*, fulfill the very task that Lonergan envisages for systematic theology: they chart and evaluate the speculative implications of a particular doctrinal position. The retrieval of the Aristotelian dis-course on causality, which is used to present the eternal Word as the first cause of the universe, offers yet another way to articulate the ontological link between the created order and the creator, as well as their ultimate distinction. The consubstantiality between Father and Son, apart from being the starting point for all sub-sequent Christological reflection, also becomes the starting point for trinitarian speculation—especially with regard to the divinity of the Holy Spirit—and eventually for the theology of deification that would build on the Nicene paradigm and the later paradigm of the hypostatic union.

The normative speculative horizon whose foundations were laid in the fourth and fifth centuries of the Christian era would remain largely unchallenged until the late eighteenth century, when Schlei-ermacher's *On the Christian Faith* questioned the received wisdom of the Church and wondered why certain traditional doctrines had to be preserved when it was clear that they seemed totally unrelated to the religious experience of the believers of the time. The slow emergence of contextual theology as one of contemporary theology's most important directions of research is rooted in the rediscovery of the fact that while divine revelation surpasses human culture and all historically determined expression, theology—speculative reflection on the human encounter with revelation—necessarily reflects the cultural context of its place and time of origin. As Stephen Bevans points out in his *Models of Contextual Theology*, explicit attention to context may be a departure from the traditional way of doing theology; at the same time, contextualization is also something very traditional, since the study of the history of theology—as we saw in the case of the Nicene dogma—inevitably reveals that all theology is grounded in a particular context.[18] Lonergan's reflection on the distinct moments of the theological endeavor shows beyond all doubt that even classical Christological doctrines such as the teaching of *homoousia* grow out of a specific religious experience and constitute a meta-judgment on this experience grounded in a specific foundational horizon. To be faithful to the spirit of Nicaea, then, means that contemporary theology should transmit the teaching of the early councils, but also be open to new culturally based Christological formulations.[19]

Is there really a need for such new doctrines? Bevans observes that in the First World, the classical theology inherited from the patristic era is often sidelined and replaced with "existentialist, personalist, and linguistic philosophies," while in some cases theology abandons philosophy completely and seeks to develop its reflection on the Christian faith on the basis of narrative, biographical, or sociological approaches. In the Global South, on the other hand, many traditional theological positions appear to be in tension with deeply held beliefs characterizing certain non-Western cultures; the absence in many Asian cultures of clear analogues to Western notions of personhood and substance is a case in point, as is the Buddhist rejection of the principle of non-contradiction central to

---

18. Bevans, *Models of Contextual Theology*, 3–4.
19. Bevans, *Models of Contextual Theology*, 8–9.

Aristotelian thought.[20] While the realization of the culturally conditioned nature of many of our deeply held speculative beliefs may initially be unsettling, we should remember that "the doctrine of the incarnation proclaims that God is revealed not primarily in ideas but rather in concrete reality,"[21] and the encounter of humanity with God continues to take place in the world through concrete realities such as culture, human experience, and history.

Bevans proposes a variety of contextual models of theology ranging from the translation model, which distinguishes a "core" Christian message from its linguistic articulation, and sets out to translate the meaning of doctrines into different cultural contexts, to the anthropological model, which views scripture and tradition as themselves culturally conditioned and therefore "incomplete," and argues that the Gospel is already present in all cultures and traditions as long as we are able to discern it and "pull the gospel out of it."[22] Other approaches, such as the praxis model or the synthetic model, also emphasize the centrality of the context but acknowledge that the latter should not be idealized, because it can be distorted by structural sin and may have to be challenged and transformed.[23] The synthetic model nuances the praxis model by claiming that the resources of other cultural contexts may help us to dismantle sinful social structures—for example, the experience of societies that have left slavery behind can be of help to Christians who live and work in places where analogous forms of exploitation are still commonplace.[24] The coun-

---

20. Bevans, *Models of Contextual Theology*, 9–10.

21. Bevans, *Models of Contextual Theology*, 12.

22. Bevans, *Models of Contextual Theology*, 61.

23. Bevans, *Models of Contextual Theology*, 72–73, 88–89. Liberationist approaches, for instance, will emphasize orthopraxis as opposed to orthodoxy, and argue that Christian revelation encounters a sinful world, and that authentic Christians must work to supplant these sinful structures.

24. In *Models of Contextual Theology*, 93, Bevans uses the metaphor of cross-pollination to describe how new and "sturdier" theological strategies might be developed to suit a particular environment.

tercultural model goes even further in asserting the radical ambiguity and insufficiency of human context, viewing the Gospel as a narrative that challenges and questions contemporary practices.[25] Often, local culture is seen as marred by sin, so that it is resistant to the message of Christ and needs "weeding" and "fertilizing" before the seeds can be planted. Finally, the transcendental model focuses on the religious experience of the individual or the community, emphasizing how revelation takes place in individual or communal encounters with the divine that may even offer correctives to scripture or tradition.[26]

All six of Bevans's models resonate with the Lonerganian notion that theology mediates between religious experience and culture, while differing in terms of the importance they ascribe to either end of this spectrum or the way in which they conceptualize their interrelationship. At the same time, most of the approaches outlined in *Models of Contextual Theology* do not view doctrines as central to the contextualizing endeavor. Some models, such as the praxis or the countercultural model, seem to imply that a reduction of the Christian message to doctrinal statements is actually a betrayal of the spirit of Christianity—a Christianity viewed primarily as a struggle for social justice—while the transcendental model seems to propose an open-ended dialogue with a supernatural horizon that resists all doctrinal closure. The translation model, however, emphasizes the centrality of an essential context that can be separated from a contextually bound mode of expression. The first step in contextualizing a specific doctrine, therefore, is to try to strip it of its culturally contextual husk and find what could be named as the "naked Gospel." As Bevans notes, "experience, social location, and social change" are acknowledged to be important, but they are never as important as the supra-cultural Gospel message. If there are cultural values that are in conflict with the original Christian message, it is clear that it is the latter

---

25. Bevans, *Models of Contextual Theology*, 118–19.
26. Bevans, *Models of Contextual Theology*, 101–2, 143.

that has to be preserved. In the opening speech of the Second Vatican Council, Pope John XXIII appeared to approve this approach when he stated that "the substance of the ancient doctrine of the deposit of faith is one thing, and the way in which this is presented is another."[27]

In the wake of this speculative reflection, however, one may still wonder how a new Christological vision could build on the insight of Nicaea and incorporate the elements of non-Western cultures—cultures that are only now freeing themselves from the shackles of political and, most importantly, intellectual colonialism. On the road toward more inculturated Christologies, there are no easy recipes for success; indeed, the imposition of a preconceived schema developed in Euro-American universities could very well mean the return to a form of theological subordination. As such, it is important to proceed by trial and error, sampling the resources of these cultures and seeking to attain a synthesis with the evangelical message that is attentive to classical tradition but is also forever open to revision.

I will now offer a brief example of this method. In working with students from sub-Saharan Africa but also from the Indian subcontinent, especially members of tribal groups outside the standard caste system, one is bound to learn of the crucial role played by ancestor worship in most of their cultures.[28] Beliefs about the

---

27. "Pope John's Opening Speech to the Council," in *The Documents of Vatican II,* ed. Walter M. Abbott (New York: Herder and Herder, 1966), 715.

28. See Anthony Ephirim-Donkor, *African Spirituality: On Becoming Ancestors* (Lanham, MD: University Press of America, 2011); John Lakra, *Tribal Spirituality: A Way of Life* (Gumla: John Lakra, 2006); K. Thanzuava, *Theology of Community: Tribal Theology in the Making* (Bangalore: Asian Trading Corporation, 2004). See also Francis Minj, SJ, "Jesus Christ Paramādivāsi: A Liberative-Inculturated Christology from an *Ādivāsi* Context of India" (STD diss., Jesuit School of Theology, 2009); Wandahilin Kharlukhi, "East-West Cultural Synthesis: Toward a Cosmic-Pneumatic Christology for Indigenous Khasi Christianity of Northeast India" (PhD diss., Graduate Theological Union, 2015).

ancestors' dwelling places vary substantially from tradition to tradition—some *Adivasi* cultures in India believe that ancestors are benevolent figures who continue to dwell in the places where they used to reside during their earthly life, whereas other cultures in Africa claim that ancestors have to be appeased, and only return at certain appointed times to ensure that customs and traditions are being upheld. Ancestors are distinct from the more strictly divine figures that are in charge of different natural phenomena or aspects of the cosmos, but the boundary between the different worlds is often blurred. In these particular contexts, it is helpful to present the figure of Christ as the ultimate ancestor; he is the head of our race and intercedes for us with the highest God and has come once and for all to bestow eternal life on all those who put their trust in him. The language of ancesterhood comes to play the role of the substantialist language of *ousia* taken from Neoplatonism—and yet, as with this philosophical tradition, this conceptual framework has to be purified and transformed in order to express what the Church teaches about the salvific mission of Christ.

First of all, the notion of ancestorhood entails an element of subordinationism; Christ as the ultimate ancestor and mediator, on the contrary, must be understood as equal in dignity to the creator of the universe, whose plan he manifests and carries out in the course of time. As such, the difference between Christ and other ancestors is not merely one of degree, but one of kind; Christ is one with the fundamental divine ground that sustains the universe. Second, the notion of creation has to be freed of all pantheistic overtones; while Christ as ultimate ancestor indwells the whole of creation, he is not identical to it, but he is ontologically distinct from the natural order, which is destined to an eventual eschatological transfiguration. Finally, fear of the ancestor's anger has to be replaced with an appreciation of the notion of God's merciful justice: Christ chooses to share our fate as human beings, and his judgment at the end of time will be informed by his understanding of the human condition. The ultimate ancestor will thus be someone who experienced what it is like to be human, but also transcends this reality and as a result grounds our humanity in the heart of the divine mystery.

This approach may be devoid of the conceptual and terminological precision that characterized the Nicene doctrine of *homoousia*, opting for a more narrative approach grounded in ethnography and the reception of oral folk traditions. It will, however, lay the foundations for a new Christological vision—one that, in line with Bevans's translation model, will convey the soteriological and cosmological import of the classical doctrinal tradition but will use the resources of a very distinct cultural context. The foundational theological horizon that emerged in the first centuries of the Christian era will be preserved, but a new theology of the incarnation will be developed after the model of Nicaea's creative appropriation of the surrounding culture.

Lonergan's exploration of the cognitive operations of the individuals, as well as the resulting notion of functional specialties, can help us recover a sense of the experiential roots of early Christian theology and the contextual character of the classical doctrinal definitions that emerged out of the first councils. After exploring the culturally conditioned nature of a notion such as *homoousia*, one should finally be able to break the spell of the Church Fathers' historical uniqueness, setting contemporary theology free to appreciate classical doctrines as historically significant expressions of the Christian worldview. Such doctrines will be cherished and preserved for posterity but will also serve as models for new contextual articulations of the Christian faith that reflect the multicultural face of the Church of today.

Chapter Four

THE THEOPOETIC CONSTITUTION OF THE CHURCH
CHRISTIAN ECUMENISM AS A THEOLOGICAL CONTEXT
Christopher M. Hadley, SJ

The Context and the Question

On September 20, 2017, the Pacific Lutheran Theological Seminary (PLTS) in Berkeley, California, held its Founders' Day Celebration on the campus of the Jesuit School of Theology, an event that marked the 500th anniversary of the Reformation in a quite special way. In her keynote address (included in this volume), Sandra Schneiders advocated for the centrality of an intellectually rigorous biblical spirituality as systematic theology's primary reference point. She considers this biblical, liturgical, existential spirituality to be a kind of theopoetics. The subject matter of this theopoetics, as Schneiders sees it, is:

> spirituality as lived revelatory experience. It is the engagement of people, individually and in community, in liturgy, ministry, moral decision making, personal prayer, civic participation, and so on, which is the site and the content and the interpretation of God's presence and action in the world. In other words, it is religious experience in all its

density and diversity and difficulty and beauty and richness which reveals who God is in and for the individual
and the community in this time and place and culture.[1]

The source matter for theopoetic action becomes the source matter
for a theopoetic theology. Schneiders pointed to the Second Vatican
Council's emerging self-understanding as "Church" as a theopoetic
phenomenon that could also be characterized as a "language event."
A language event, in hermeneutical theory, is not simply a successful
maneuvering of grammar and semantics, but rather an existential
conversion experience mediated by the very mode of communication.[2] The council was an event of the Catholic Church humbly
striving for a more adequate response in thought and speech to the
concrete realities it faced and to the mysteries that have sustained it
through the centuries. Vatican II's way of ecclesial self-understanding
was perhaps not truly "new" at the time, because it flowed from and
resonated with the ecclesial self-understanding of the fathers and
mothers of the early church. But in another way, it was new, because
it was made possible by the depth and freedom of Protestant biblical
scholarship. That is to say: a renewed ecclesial spirituality focused
on God's witness to God's self in scripture, in Eucharist, and in the
hearts of gathered believers was made possible for Vatican II and for
all the Catholic scholarship and life that flowed into it and out from
it by the abiding fidelity of the reformed churches to the word of
God. This historical unfolding of grace, even under the initial conditions of such painful strife, is why some Catholics and Lutherans
went on to say on October 31, 2017 (over a month after the Founders'
Day event), that together they "are very thankful for the spiritual
and theological gifts received through the Reformation."[3]

---

1. Sandra M. Schneiders, IHM, "Reconciled Diversity," pp. 17–18 in this volume.

2. Schneiders, "Reconciled Diversity," pp. 10–11, citing John O'Malley.

3. Joint Statement by the Lutheran World Federation and the Pontifical Council
    for Promoting Christian Unity on the Conclusion of the Year of the Com-
    mon Commemoration of the Reformation (October 31, 2017), http://press

The group that gathered in September from all over the Graduate Theological Union of Berkeley for the PLTS Founders' Day celebration was made up mostly of Lutherans and Catholics. We ended the day together with a Lutheran Liturgy of the Word and renewal of our common baptismal covenant in our Jesuit chapel. We stood together to sing beautiful Lutheran hymns and sat to listen to biblical preaching on Jonah's judgmental impatience with the pagan Ninevites and on Jesus's parable of wages for day laborers—stories of God's supreme generosity to all of us, *together*, receiving the same forgiveness, the same grace, the same love. During the luncheon that followed, the people I spoke with all expressed a desire to become more thoroughly what we were supposed to be, which was the Graduate Theological *Union* in Berkeley. This desire was percolating in the academic panel discussions that day, in our communal acts of theological and biblical interpretation. But I daresay it was solidified in the communal prayer, in the common hearing of scripture.

This chapter seeks a theopoetic understanding of the GTU as a context for teaching theology and thinking theologically. My understanding of what I do at JST and in the GTU is informed by an experience of common worship and by my participation at the eleventh Leuven Encounters in Systematic Theology conference in Belgium in response to the 500th anniversary of the Reformation.[4] Behind the questions related to my present context at the GTU are questions of how the Bible might become "the church's book" in this context and how the GTU might be seen as a living instantiation of "the book's church."[5] The Founders' Day event has

---

.vatican.va/content/salastampa/en/bollettino/pubblico/2017/10/31/171031a .html.

4. Leuven Encounters in Systematic Theology (LEST) XI: "*Ecclesia semper reformanda:* Renewal and Reform beyond Polemics," at the Katholieke Universiteit Leuven (KU Leuven), October 11–14, 2017.

5. This question is considered in more detail in my unpublished paper for LEST XI: "The New Testament as the Church's Book: Which Church?" given October 12, 2017.

served as an interpretive key to my teaching of a course entitled Theological Aesthetics, the Cross, and Race. Reading Hans Urs von Balthasar and James Cone with a multidenominational group of graduate students on the campus of PLTS in 2017 accentuated for me the Protestant influences on Balthasar and the catholicity of James Cone's theological vision. As these two interdenominationally situated authors mutually interpreted each other in our reading of them, and as we did the same with them and each other as members of a classroom community, I had a profound sense that we were participating in and transmitting one common Christian tradition. The teaching and the learning in our classroom took on the characteristics of language events, of a creative theopoetics within a commonly shared paschal imagination. In doing this together, we were certainly one learning community. We were also one *Christian* community. Were we participating together, even if only in a fragmented way, in a locally instantiated reality of one church? That is my question as a Catholic theologian.

This chapter is, therefore—at least in part—about a renewed Catholic understanding of communion. That is to say, the question of whether a sacramental understanding of the scriptural word of God could provide any insight into the practice of shared scriptural prayer in common among separated churches forms a theological worldview from which to ask whether other kinds of language events—teaching and learning in an ecumenical graduate institute—might also be church-constituting. The present work offers no hard conclusions, but I hope some ways forward might be glimpsed from here.

Some Terms:
Sacramentality, Theopoetics, and Communion

My theological starting point falls within a Roman Catholic and (somewhat) Eastern Orthodox perspective, even if my professional context and my hopes are ecumenical in an explicitly interdenominational sense. The notion of sacramentality as applied to the scriptural word comes to me from my reading of Sandra Schneiders's *The Revelatory Text*. The notion of church as communion comes to me from Metropolitan John Zizioulas's eucharistic ecclesiology, which is Eastern Orthodox in its origin and approach but also resonates with a Vatican II conciliar self-understanding that exists in the Catholic Church. The link between Schneiders's sacramentality of the Word and Zizioulas's eucharistic ecclesiology is solidified for me in John Baldovin's exploration of the analogous sacramentalities of Word and Eucharist. Baldovin begins this exploration with the understanding of "Christ as the primary sacrament," which he clearly shares with both Schneiders and Zizioulas. The Church derives its sacramentality from Christ alone. Baldovin follows Gordon Lathrop and Louis-Marie Chauvet, who say that the gathered church is "the primary place where the Scripture becomes Scripture and the canon is constructed."[6] But the gathered church's act of interpreting the scripture is the dynamism within which, as Lathrop says, "Ancient texts are made to speak a new grace."[7] This is a theopoetic language event, in Schneiders's terms, one that reconstitutes the gathered community. My use of the more ontological word "communion" is obviously a departure from Schneiders's "horizontal" and theopoetic language of "people of God."[8] It is, in fact, a look *back* from her phenomenology to Zizioulas's ontology, back from theopoetics to a more traditional theological language. But I draw attention to an analogy between the two methodologies and their resulting conceptualizations of "people of God" and "communion" in order to strengthen and broaden a Catholic sacramental worldview to be more inclusive, and thus more adequate to the mysteries of which it treats.

---

6. John Baldovin, SJ, "The Sacramentality of the Word: An Ecumenical Approach" (unpublished paper, School of Theology, Sewanee, June 21, 2017), 6.

7. Baldovin, "Sacramentality of the Word," 6; citing Gordon Lathrop, *Holy Things: A Liturgical Theology* (Minneapolis: Fortress, 1993), 19.

8. See Schneiders, "Reconciled Diversity," pp. 11, 20.

People of God and Scripture,
Communion and Eucharist

Schneiders's "people of God" metaphor connotes a unity constituted by persons, but also one constituted in a creative encounter with the self-revealing God: "As in the tent of meeting Israel, through Moses, encountered God and gradually learned what it meant to be God's people, so in the prolonged engagement with the biblical text the Church as community learns what it means to be people of God, and individual Christians what it means to be disciples of Christ today."[9] The scriptures become the "Text of Meeting" in a communal act of interpretation within the context of the liturgical gathering. This mutuality between the gathered church and the text concerns both a deeper understanding of God through the text and a deeper self-understanding of the assembly as church in the light of God. In this mutuality of interpretation between the gathered people and the revelatory text, the people seek an understanding of both the meaning of the revelatory text and what they are becoming by being confronted *by* this very meaning.[10]

But is the scriptural word of God functioning sacramentally in nourishing the desire for unity experienced in common scriptural worship? One of the issues in ecumenical dialogue is the very meaning of "sacrament." The meaning with which I operate includes, in Baldovin's words, a foundational sense of God being "actually at work in and through our created world" through "finite" symbols that are "really capable of communicating the infinite."[11] This sense of sacramentality is widely shared among many Christian traditions, but many churches do *not* share the conciliar Roman Catholic Church's self-understanding as a sacrament of Christ for the world.

---

9. Sandra M. Schneiders, *The Revelatory Text: Interpreting the New Testament as Sacred Scripture,* 2nd ed. (Collegeville, MN: Liturgical Press, 1999), xix.

10. Schneiders, *Revelatory Text,* 18–19.

11. Baldovin, "Sacramentality of the Word," 2.

Since my goal lies presently within the self-understanding of the Catholic Church, a deeper inquiry into the possibility of an ecumenically shared meaning of "sacrament" can be conveniently, if unfortunately, bracketed.

Schneiders construes the sacramentality of the scriptures in and for the gathered assembly not in terms of a metaphysical, ontological structure but a phenomenological, theopoetical process. In becoming the revelatory text for the gathered people, the scriptures as proclaimed and preached facilitate the people's growing union with God *as* the people of God.[12] A new grace is spoken via the text to a gathered people, and Christ becomes present to them by the working of the Holy Spirit. This is analogous, at least in a basic way, to the view that the Eucharist makes the people into what it is, the Body of Christ, by the working of the Holy Spirit. The gathered people are constituted as a local, particular church in that event.

The Catholic sacramental schema obviously implicates the notion of "communion," about which there is even less ecumenical agreement.[13] Given the renewed privilege accorded to the liturgy as the primary locus of scriptural interpretation, the question of what constitutes a communion is bound up with the question of who actually does the interpretation of scripture in the church. The latter question, of interpretation, is addressed at times by both Zizioulas and Schneiders, although my focus will be on Schneiders's position. While ordained leadership is essential to a truly ecclesial and communal act of interpretation, it is the community as a whole that makes the interpretation actual. In Zizioulas's Eastern Orthodox Eucharistic ecclesiology, *"the Church constitutes the Eucharist while being constituted by it.* Church and Eucharist are interdependent;

---

12. Schneiders, *Revelatory Text*, xviii–xix.

13. This is true even within Catholicism. Note particularly the Ratzinger-Kasper debate over the universal and local dimensions of church catholicity. For a summary and commentary, see Kilian McDonnell, OSB, "The Ratzinger/Kasper Debate: The Universal Church and Local Churches," *Theological Studies* 63 (2002): 227–50.

they coincide, and are even in some sense identical."[14] In this view, the church gathered for Eucharist is not only most visibly itself, but also most ontologically itself. The church is a being-in-act of eating because eating together is the fundamental human way of being. But the celebration of Eucharist is also the event of the gathering of the people, the *synaxis* itself, from their dispersion near and far. Laypeople, ministers, and clergy are all absolutely necessary for the church to be the church and the Eucharist to be the Eucharist in Zizioulas's thought. The Body of Christ becomes actual not only on the altar when the gifts are offered by the gathered community but also, in another way, in the gathered community itself. The mutuality of gifts and people in the constituting of Eucharist and church is a living dynamic, an event that cannot be reduced to either one of its oppositional poles. The church needs the sacrament to be church, but the sacrament only properly comes into being in the context of the gathered church.

Based on this proposed analogy between becoming a renewed people in the act of interpreting scripture as a mode of being on the one hand and gathering in the Eucharistic assembly to receive communion on the other, "communion" cannot be reduced to something willed into being by willing participants. Communion is an ontological reality, a reference point for an understanding of the Church's being. But there is an eschatological dimension at work, too, one of becoming something new in the process of becoming more fully what the church is called to be as the Body of Christ. The analogy between Zizioulas's and Schneiders's ways of construing the way of being-human-in-act that I am proposing is a metaphysical construction, but it is also open to the dimensions of phenomenality that Schneiders perceives. While Zizioulas's view of the human is the being-in-act of eating, Schneiders follows Gadamer and Heidegger in presupposing the act of understanding

---

14. John Zizioulas, *The One and the Many: Studies on God, Man, the Church, and the World Today*, ed. Gregory Edwards (Alhambra, CA: Sebastian Press, 2010), 68.

as the "characteristically human way of being, our fundamental mode of being-in-the-world."[15] It is in this latter dynamism of understanding self and other that the text becomes truly revelatory. So, to adapt and very loosely apply the structure of the above-mentioned phrase from Zizioulas: "The Revelatory Text makes the Church and the Church-as-gathered-in-the-act-of-interpreting makes the Bible a Revelatory Text." God is the primary agent when the text becomes revelatory *as* the church's book *in* the gathered church. Through the text, God (dynamically, progressively) gives form to the gathering *as* the church.

Of course, there is no identification between church and revelatory text in Schneiders's consideration, but the parallel between her and Zizioulas on the interdependence and mutually constitutive natures of church and scripture together and church and Eucharist together is significant. Neither author is claiming that the existence or the "validity" of scripture or Eucharist is absolutely dependent on the existence of a validly existing church, without also being a factor in the very existence of that church. I would hazard that both authors would agree with Paul that the very validity of a gathered "church" depends on how attentive they are to God's grace working through their openness to the scriptures and in their "discernment of the body" (both one's own and the gathered "body") in the very practice of liturgical eating (1 Cor 11:17–34). Both positions preserve the authority of faith in the interpretation of scripture and in handing on of tradition, which is construed as an ongoing, integral response of the individual Christian and of the Christian community to the revelatory event of salvation in Christ.[16] The church also becomes what it is in these acts and cannot *be* the church

---

15. Schneiders, *Revelatory Text*, 17.

16. See especially chaps. 5 and 6, "The Status of Scripture in the Church" and "Scripture in Theology," in Roger Haight, *Dynamics of Theology*, 2nd ed. (Maryknoll, NY: Orbis, 2001). The authority of scripture in the church ultimately depends on the authority of faith as a communal response to the event of God's salvation in Christ (104).

without doing them, regardless of whose job it is to be the presider, chief interpreter, and representative gift-offerer. The church both constitutes and is constituted by the acts of interpreting scripture and offering and receiving gifts in Eucharist.

Are we Catholics becoming a new church with our "separated brothers and sisters" when we gather to interpret the revelatory texts with them? A church *not* of our own making, but one constituted by the revelatory power receiving together the narrative of Jesus's "priestly" prayer in John 17, that we all may be one? Pope John Paul II in his *Ut unum sint* speaks of "the fundamental importance of doctrine" (18–20), but also at even more length of "the *primacy* of prayer" (21–27).[17] The pope highlights in this document the inspiration, fostered by prayer in common, for members of separated churches to grow in love and to engage in common actions for the common good. But my question is whether by virtue of their very common intention to gather and read the text, and in hearing it together for the purpose of changing their lives together, they are being constituted as *the* church in that time and place. The need for theological dialogue and the healing of memories notwithstanding, perhaps the very act of gathering is more *efficacious* than we have been able to acknowledge.

Teaching in the GTU during the 500th Anniversary Year of the Reformation

Participating in an act of gathering on the Founders' Day in September 2017, followed closely by participating in an act of gathering at the Catholic University of Leuven to reflect on the Reformation "beyond polemics" a month later, had an effect on my teaching in the GTU in the 2017 academic year. These two ecumenical gatherings

---

17. John Paul II, *Ut unum sint* (On Commitment to Ecumenism) (1995), http:// w2.vatican.va/content/john-paul-ii/en/encyclicals/documents/hf_jp-ii_ enc_25051995_ut-unum-sint.html.

had both academic and liturgical moments, but in both cases the liturgical moments were the culminations—and not the opening reference points—of the gatherings. But my experience as a teacher and scholar in the wake of these two experiences has been richer and truer to its purpose to the extent that I now refer any gathering to interpret texts theologically to the primary, *theopoetic* act of gathering in common prayer. Hans Urs von Balthasar, Andrew Prevot, and James Cone, the authors of the main sources for my course, Theological Aesthetics, the Cross, and Race, make this reference to the revelatory text in prayer and liturgy in their own theological work.[18] They come from different ecclesial contexts and traditions, but bringing them together in an ecumenically diverse classroom in the GTU constitutes yet a new context. This 500th year of the Reformation is itself a new context, with its own effect on the theology we did.

My choice to teach a course on theological aesthetics, the cross, and race at JST is part of my own commitment to our commonly adopted contextual theme of racism as a theological problem in society. To do research and teach on the topic of race as an American Catholic, one simply cannot rely exclusively on Catholic sources. The Catholic Church has been comparatively silent on racism compared to other denominations, particularly on the virulently anti-Black form that it takes in the U.S. context.[19] I witnessed a dimension of this silence of the Catholic Church firsthand in the

---

18. Our primary texts were Hans Urs von Balthasar's *Glory of the Lord: A Theological Aesthetics,* vol. 1, *Seeing the Form,* pref. and ed. by John E. Riches, trans. Erasmo Leiva-Merikakis (San Francisco, CA: Ignatius Press, 1983); *Glory of the Lord,* vol. 7, *The New Covenant,* ed. John Riches, trans. Brian McNeil, CRV (San Francisco: Ignatius Press, 1989); Andrew Prevot, *Thinking Prayer: Theology and Spirituality amid the Crisis of Modernity* (Notre Dame, IN: University of Notre Dame Press, 2015); and James H. Cone, *The Cross and the Lynching Tree* (Maryknoll, NY: Orbis, 2011).

19. This tragic and frustrating fact has been amply documented by Bryan Massingale in *Racial Justice and the Catholic Church* (Maryknoll, NY: Orbis, 2010) and by Jon Nilson in *Hearing Past the Pain: Why White Catholic Theologians Need Black Theology* (New York/Mahwah, NJ: Paulist Press, 2007).

parish church I attended after the deadly White supremacist rallies of August 11–12, 2017, in Charlottesville, which resulted in the killing of Heather Heyer, and after I heard countless laments from friends all over the country who similarly experienced silence in their parish churches that Sunday. I witnessed yet another dimension of this silence in the virtual absence of any Catholic institutions from a rally in Berkeley later that month under the leadership of many Protestant clergy of color who felt that they were marching for the very lives of their people in the face of White supremacy.[20]

Although the voices of Bryan Massingale, M. Shawn Copeland, and now Andrew Prevot are thankfully being heard more and more on theology and race, to take a full account of Black theology in the United States, one simply must turn first to Black theologians who are not Roman Catholic. Hence my obvious choice of the Baptist theologian James Cone as one of my main sources. Cone is an enduringly potent pioneer of Black liberation theology in the United States and a practitioner of theological aesthetics and theopoetics. His theological aesthetics focuses on the cruciform beauty of God, and his theopoetics on Black American church hymnody. Reading Balthasar and Cone side by side, thinkers at once so different but also both so attentive to the aesthetic and experiential dimensions of divine revelation, gave form and content to our course: while the trinitarian and christological form of theological aesthetics as a method came to us through Balthasar, its contextual urgency and content came to us through Cone.[21] The Catholic Balthasar and Baptist Cone as

---

20. This was the "Rally Against Hate" in Berkeley on August 27, 2017, a peaceful counter-demonstration against a planned "Say No to Marxism" rally that never materialized. Although the original rally was ostensibly a rally for "free speech" at the University of California, the racist overtones in its planning were well known and never really denied. The reaction against it was largely, and positively, a march for racial justice in the Bay Area and the United States as a whole.

21. Andrew Prevot also brings Balthasar and Cone together in a theopoetical and theological-aesthetical response to the problems of postmodernity and violence in *Thinking Prayer*.

read together by two Catholics, a Wesleyan, a UCC member, and a Lutheran, pointed us along the pathway of a common Christian tradition to be lived out in a racist, White supremacist American context filled with the potential for reconciliation and beauty. As we plumbed Balthasar's scriptural references and listened to the hymns referenced by Cone and gazed on the shocking images of lynched Black bodies beside the crucified Jesus, a truly ecumenical American Christianity began to take shape for us.

But in 2017, the year of the 500th anniversary of the Reformation, punctuated by two explicitly ecumenical Liturgies of the Word at JST in September and KU Leuven in October, I could not help but long for a fuller realization of this American Christianity in an expression of life in a real, common American church. Could our little group, itself a subset of the GTU, not be a concrete expression of something larger? Such an idea is a very Catholic one: a local, particular church that expresses the fullness of the universal church. I admit that it is my idea, one that was only occasionally discussed in class in any explicit way. We mostly discussed how no one church's theology is yet adequate to the theological problems we face in the United States. But the notion of one American Christianity does seem to implicate the notion of one American church. It is a notion that James Cone himself seems to hope for, an eschatological reality he glimpses from afar: "Unless the cross and the lynching tree are seen together, there can be no genuine understanding of Christian identity in America and no healing of the racial divide in churches and seminaries as well as in the society as a whole."[22]

Andrew Prevot has seen the universal potential of the "contra-whiteness" focus of Cone's project not in terms of any systematic wholeness but rather as a "host" of theological hospitality to all people, a new universal lens through which to see the world

---

22. James H. Cone, "Strange Fruit: The Cross and the Lynching Tree," *Journal of Theology for Southern Africa* 148 (March 2014): 9.

theologically.[23] But there *is* a systematic-theological potential in
Cone, one that must constantly be referred (à la Schneiders) to
the theopoetic realities of Black religious experience. Balthasar, as
interpreted by Prevot through the lens of Cone, helped us as a
class see more deeply how Blackness is a universal theological category that forms a crucial dimension of catholicity for American
Christianity today.[24] This is because Blackness, in response to the
crippling dehumanization of White supremacy, is itself a beautiful
icon of Christ, a crucial dimension of the form of revelation for
our time and place. From the standpoint of its contingency, Blackness also reveals to the world its sin, the sin of rejecting the one
whom God sent. For Cone, Black Christians are therefore called
to "serve" White Christians—with obvious risks—by revealing to
them the true history of sin, in the United States, in Africa, and
anywhere dark-skinned people are rejected.[25] White people are
correspondingly called to receive this great gift. This cruciform
revelation of sin also reveals the beauty of the reconciling God
who is Christ crucified in solidarity with us and in forgiveness of
us, uniting us all—sacramentally—as one Body. The hymns of
the Black church become the hymns of the *human* church, of the
reconciled church. For Cone, "black ecumenism" seeks not only
Christian unity but human integration.[26] In the end, there are
no better terms on which to insist on Christian unity. Theological aesthetics focuses on the perception of God's beauty as God
chooses to reveal it to us. To quote the oft-quoted St. Irenaeus, but
now in the complete form of his thought: "For the glory of God
is a living [human being]; and [this] life...consists in beholding
God. For if the manifestation of God which is made by means of
the creation, affords life to all living in the earth, much more does

---

23. Prevot, *Thinking Prayer*; 319–20, 322–24.
24. Prevot, *Thinking Prayer*, 324.
25. Prevot, *Thinking Prayer*, 322.
26. Prevot, *Thinking Prayer*, 319–20.

that revelation of the Father which comes through the Word, give life to those who see God."[27]

None of the students who signed up in the 2017 fall semester for Theological Aesthetics, the Cross, and Race were African American. But other than me, all the members of our class were U.S. people of color or international students. The Samoan Roman Catholic student had interests in the deep theological issues of the marginalization of Oceania and the devastation of island ecologies. The Japanese American UCC student used Black liberation theology and postcolonial theory to explore newer and more adequate biblical-hermeneutical narratives for the Asian American experience. The Korean student from a Wesleyan holiness tradition wrote a scholarly theological meditation on the spiritual senses in the Balthasarian-Ignatian tradition in preparation for his dissertation chapter on Wesleyan theological aesthetics, with a moving epilogue on the spiritual senses in Cone's Black theology. The Mexican American Lutheran student studied Luther's notion of beauty in dialogue with Balthasar in his own search for a more truly ecumenical Lutheran theological aesthetics. The ecumenical richness in our common search for the theological foundations of human wholeness could only have happened at a place like the GTU, in a course inspired by the common contextual focus on race at JST, with the urgency for Christian unity inspired by the 500th anniversary of the Protestant Reformation. The act of gathering liturgically is theopoetic. Is the theological being-in-act of the church at study analogous to its being-in-act of encountering the revelatory text in prayer? Could, and should, the act of gathering in study not also be theopoetic? What we will hand on to the world as a group, a *Christian* group, gives me hope.

---

27. Irenaeus, *Against Heresies* IV.20.7, in *Ante-Nicene Fathers*, vol. 1, *The Apostolic Fathers, Justin Martyr, Irenaeus*, ed. Philip Schaff (1885), and Alexander Roberts and James Donaldson (Grand Rapids: Christian Classics Ethereal Library, 1996), http://www.ccel.org/ccel/schaff/anf01.html), 1220.

Chapter Five

SACRAMENTAL AND LITURGICAL THEOLOGY FROM THE INSIDE OUT

HOW DIVERSE SOCIO-CULTURAL REALITIES CHANGE THE QUESTIONS AND SHAPE THE PEDAGOGY OF A SHARED TRADITION

Paul A. Janowiak, SJ

To walk together—free and obedient—moving toward the margins of society where no one else reaches, "under the gaze of Jesus and looking to the horizon which is the ever greater glory of God, who ceaselessly surprises us."[1]

POPE FRANCIS

The Jesuit Pope Francis, speaking to his own brothers in an allocution to the 36th General Congregation of the Society of Jesus

---

1. Francis, "Address to the 36th General Congregation of the Society of Jesus," in *Jesuit Life & Mission Today: The Decrees and Accompanying Documents of the 36th General Congregation of the Society of Jesus* (Boston: Institute of Jesuit Sources, 2017), 45. Pope Francis is quoting his own homily for the "Liturgical Memorial for the Most Holy Name of Jesus," Church of the Gesù, January 3, 2014.

in October 2016, paints an imaginative picture for me as a Jesuit teaching in a graduate school of theology and ministry that understands contextual theology as the organizing fulcrum that centers our work. This imagination asks both students and teachers to be firmly grounded—theologically and spiritually—in the divine gaze of love that calls us into this work. At the same time, it orients the fruits of that grounded encounter toward our own ministerial and theological gaze "to the horizon which is the ever greater glory of God, who ceaselessly surprises us."

The pedagogical approach and the questions that arise from the process of grounded horizons demonstrate to me that contextual theology begins from the inside—where that profound gaze of Christ in trinitarian communion is the wellspring of a living faith—but it cannot rest there, nor does it turn back on itself.[2] The road to greater theological and ministerial depth must look beyond the confines of our own theological imaginations to the horizon of surprises that a diverse and global world is always offering up to us. This is a creative tension, calling us to stay grounded in the living Tradition, but to gaze at these veritable truths from a variety of complementary foci, each rich with revelatory possibility and also a challenge to the ways diverse believers understand the same Divine encounter.

This is especially true in my field of liturgical and sacramental theology, which includes a sustained praxis and reflection on the enacted rites that express the sacramental reality we call the Church. I like to think that we all come as professors with a rich foundation in a shared tradition (studied and practiced largely from the

---

2. Peter's enthusiasm in being invited to the mountain and seeing the transfigured Lord prompts him to suggest that they remain and "make three dwellings..." (Lk 9:33) and focus on this theophany. Jesus, instead, gently but resolutely leads Peter, James, and John out of the overshadowing cloud and leads them down the mountain, for "he had set his face toward Jerusalem" (Lk 9:51). The wellspring transfigures, but it also necessarily sends out a mission from the inside out.

Western and Global North), but one that, through the very encounter with the diversity of students we engage, reveals and illumines aspects of that deposit of faith that we could never have imagined. Sacramental faith and worship offer a fertile field for this grounded horizon approach from the inside out. *Lex orandi, lex credendi* is the dictum of this liturgical field; praying (an embodied action together, in union with Christ) shapes believing (the shared truth), which in turn orients the *lex vivendi*, how we live our lives in conformity to this faith and witness. That interchange is never exhausted, and the wider the circle of participants in this dance becomes, the more resonant the grounded horizon becomes.

Learning to reverence the gaze of Christ while looking outward toward an expanded locus of revelation involves, as I have said, a creative tension that is inherently dynamic: it asks us to love and treasure what we have been given, only to surrender our theological and ministerial imaginations to what is often, for each of us, a new reality and a new creation. That grounded horizon becomes a necessary participant in this mutual exchange of gifts. Employing specifically liturgical terms, worship and sacramental faith in the Christian tradition involve an eventful encounter with the Holy One and the assembled Body of Christ. Engaging this ritual dynamism in the classroom, therefore, cannot be a thing we study from afar and passively observe. Carried out in this contextual vein, professors and students soon discover that one can never uncover the gift that each culture and social reality offer to the theological and ministerial whole, nor even appreciate its richness, until it has first been called forth, named, heard, and received. Such a pedagogy is relational, participative, and dialogical.[3] In the classroom, both professor

---

3. This threefold dynamism, rooted in the Trinity's own way of being in communion, is the rhythm and harmony of the liturgy itself. It serves as a helpful perspective for teaching, which is an exchange of gifts and rooted in a shared faith and tradition. See Paul Janowiak, SJ, *Standing Together in the Community of God: Liturgical Spirituality and the Presence of Christ* (Collegeville, MN: Liturgical Press, 2011), esp. 12–18.

and students share in the mutuality of this exchange. It cannot be otherwise if we are to take a sacramental imagination seriously, because the locus of ongoing revelation is not "out there," disembodied and statically encoded. It is in our midst, and together our common horizon of shared faith in *this* world, engaged at *this* time, with *these* particular people, each bringing a history very different from others in the classroom, all coalesce to reveal a fresh Word of God and a Sacramental Table that has many sides and offerings.

The Contextual Setting for Worship, Its Teaching, and Its Study: A Living Community of Faith as the Totus Christus

From that perspective, the field of communal worship and sacramental practice is the particular focus of this essay. From a professor's experience, it will address how the lived experience of teaching students from a variety of cultural contexts can help all of us to re-imagine and deepen our appreciation for the universality of this shared, sacred Tradition. The common faith is housed in a living church, a global household of faith, in which Christian liturgy and sacramental theology play such a communal and identity-making role in the life of a Christian. This Church's sacramental economy is not encased in frozen, principled dogmas or fixed ritual scripts, but is first and foremost expressive of an eventful, embodied encounter with the living God. So our way of studying must engage the inside and the outside, both of the individual and the communal whole, what the Tradition since Augustine calls the *totus Christus* ("the whole Christ, Head and members"), in order to plumb the depths of this field of study and pastoral practice.[4]

---

4. In a letter he wrote in 1958 before he entered the conclave in which he was elected pope, Pope John XXIII prophetically articulated the Church's raison d'être: "We are not on earth as museum-keepers, but to cultivate a flourishing garden of life and to prepare for a glorious future." The words

For me, these dimensions and questions and possibilities only became alive in my theological imagination when I was faced with real students with real questions and diverse ecclesial contexts. My contention, therefore, is that our teaching "habitus" changes when we expect that relational, dialogical, and participative dynamism to be the operative mode. Such expectation demands that we have something to hear from the other, that we listen first to the experience of faith and practice that brings us to this study, in order to draw the theological richness of a common tradition illuminated by the nuances of our social location.

This does not mean that there are no grounding theological principles to our work—in fact, it is quite the opposite! As Vatican II's first document, *Sacrosanctum Concilium,* The Constitution on the Sacred Liturgy, insists at the outset, the liturgy's theological claim and *modus operandi* is that it is "the outstanding means whereby the faithful may *express in their lives* and *manifest to others* the mystery of Christ and the real nature of the true Church."[5] The gaze of Christ and the Magis horizon that is constitutive of a pilgrim people on the way to the kingdom share together in Francis's own mode and way of proceeding: animated from the inside (Christ's gaze and our experiences of faith), directed always to the marginal horizons (the liturgy's conversation partner about the mighty deeds of God throughout all generations). We do not invent these rites or beliefs in every age. Rather, this tradition of faith and practice has been handed down to us, from communities

---

appeared originally in *Giovanni XXIII—Lettere 1958–1963,* ed. Loris Capovilla (Rome: Edizioni di Storia e Letteratura, 1968), 481, and are quoted in English in Peter Hebblethwaite, *John XXIII: Shepherd of the Modern World* (New York: Doubleday, 1985), 269.

5. *Sacrosanctum Concilium* (hereafter SC), 2 (emphasis mine). Notice how the "inside" and the "outside" coalesce and mutually inform one another, both in the activity of liturgy and in the enduring faith foundation it expresses; http://www.vatican.va/archive/hist_councils/ii_vatican_council/docu ments/vat-ii_const_19631204_sacrosanctum-concilium_en.html.

of believers who had seen in this tradition and its practice an enduring truth about who they were, while providing for us a graced horizon for deepening the encounter with the Lord they served in mission. There is one way and truth and life, that liturgical legacy proclaims, but it gathers depth and solidarity along that way through the diverse paths by which we have tried to be faithful to that summons.

In this manner, all the documents of Vatican II expansively describe our own contemporary summons to participate in the generations of faith handed down to us and received in every age. All that we receive has been lived and prayed and proclaimed before us, beginning with the Father's own gift offering of his own Son, and who, in the Spirit, shares the gift and promise through the church which is his Body. Christian prayer and sacramental practice, our communal "doing this in memory of Him," has always had cultural and diverse ways of speaking to this common experience of Love loving us, incarnate love poured out and shared, drawing those who gather in liturgical assembly to see their own identity in Spirit-filled communion with one another who gather in this triune Name. Noting those founding experiences that make us who we are, *Sacrosanctum Concilium* states:

> From that time onwards the Church has never failed to come together to celebrate the paschal mystery: reading those things "which were in all the Scriptures concerning him" (Lk 24:27), celebrating the eucharist in which "the victory and triumph of his death and resurrection are again made present," and at the same time giving thanks "to God for his unspeakable gift" (2 Cor 9:15) in Christ Jesus, "in praise of his glory" (Eph 1:12) through the power of the Holy Spirit.
>
> To accomplish so great a work, Christ is always present in his Church, especially in her liturgical celebrations.... (SC 6–7)

That enduring presence of Christ in the church "pitches his tent"[6] in the lives and experiences of faith and of church that all students carry within them when they cross the threshold into the classroom. I have found that asking them to begin from the *inside* in order to understand the *outside* is the most daring and honest thing we can do in order to study theology, to express a living faith that engages this Tradition, and then to communicate this graced experience to others in class and in their ministry. Believers can hear this, because they, too, have heard the same calling of Love and desire the same holy communion we "professionals of divine reality" can be tempted to believe belong to us alone. So I always ask some free-write questions at the outset, beginning with "How does your longing and deep desire for God, your life of faith that struggles to give shape to that desire, express itself in your prayer, both alone and in community?" Then, widening the parameters of that theological tent, I may ask, "How is the Creator God and Father active as Source of all existence, through and with Christ as Incarnate Word that speaks forth and names that offer of grace, and in the Spirit as the hallowing ground of all life?"[7] Once the trinitarian dynamism is set in dialogue with our own lives, then something wonderful happens. I believe that. It has changed the way I understand the role of the professor, the sacramental and theological tradition I am charged to share, and the richness that

---

6. In referring to Jn 1:14, the theologian Herbert McCabe, OP, prefers this translation to the more common "dwells among us," which he considers "an impoverishment of St. John's words." This integrates God's "dwelling in the ark" among the people of Israel with "the new Creation" of the baptized and redeemed. McCabe, *The New Creation* (New York: Continuum, 1964, 2010), 11.

7. As Eucharistic Prayer III in the 1985 revised edition expressed so poetically, "All life, all holiness comes from you through your Son, Jesus Christ our Lord, by the working of the Holy Spirit. From age to age you gather a people to yourself...." We are in relational, dialogical, and participative communion with the Trinity's own life.

can occur when people know the faith, reasonably and expansively, and wrestle with it together "from the inside out."

This pedagogical approach requires skilled shepherding, for it is not a communal free-for-all, but a creative and tensive wrestling. Risking to toss the net of this Tradition into the deep waters of people's diverse experiences, their unique sense of communal identity, and the embodied ways each student's cultural and social location strives to give utterance to that treasure of this universal household of faith yields surprises and gifts, but also questions and challenges. The creative tension has to be honored and also trusted. Together, this dialogue will tell us all something new. We need to remember: "Christ is always present in his Church, especially in its liturgical celebrations," the Constitution tells us. We *will* meet him there, like the disciples on the road to Emmaus (Lk 24:13ff.). The vision starts with "our hearts burning within us," to use the Emmaus imagery to which *Sacrosanctum Concilium* (6) refers, yet it precisely animates and moves its vision to the road ahead, the eschatological horizon and God's greater glory (the *Magis*). We do not know for sure where that road leads. We do know that Christ is present. The horizon is the signpost that signals, "See, I am making all things new" (Rv 21:5).

In short, the guiding assumption for a contextual theology of worship and sacramental life is that symbolic exchange in communal prayer and spirituality is dynamic and must take seriously real people and their histories of faith and worship. As French sacramental theologian L.-M. Chauvet says, Christ's Body needs a body in this world; bodiliness in all its diverse manifestations is constitutive of liturgical practice. Noting how Christian faith cannot be separated from the sacraments and their enactment, Chauvet says this "fact" (a theological faith)

> means that faith cannot be lived in any other way, including what is most spiritual in it, than *in the mediation of the body*, the body of a society, of a desire, of a tradition, of a history, of an institution, and so on. What is most spiritual always takes place in the most corporeal.... Are not the

sacraments the most powerful expression of a faith that
exists only "at the mercy of the body"?[8]

The whole self and the unity of the community share this media-
tion. Our bodies are not divorced from our minds or our hearts.
The integration of all these is necessary for any good theology, but
especially for a liturgical/sacramental tradition that takes the performative rite and its participants as crucial to its expression.

Three Pedagogical Questions and Examples of a Contextual Liturgical and Sacramental Theology

To illustrate how an "inside out" pedagogy engages these realities
in a contextual paradigm, I would like to offer three possible examples in the liturgical and sacramental context that are of particular
note and will shape the structure of the rest of this chapter. They
center around the relational, dialogical, and participative "matter
and form" of liturgy, worship, and sacramental rites in our diverse
and global context as a universal church today. They do not address all issues or answer all questions, nor do they necessarily have
easy solutions or answers, but they have been pertinent examples
of a new vision for me when I have listened and engaged with my
students as an exercise in mutual gift giving and not as a handing
down of facts that must be absorbed.

These examples roughly follow these areas of concern: (1) the
acknowledged experience of one's cultural and social reality in
shaping images, symbols, and their communal meaning, and the
consequent transparency of the traditional categories of "matter and form"; (2) the understanding of community identity, its

---

8. Louis-Marie Chauvet, *Sacraments: The Word of God at the Mercy of the Body*
    (Collegeville, MN: Liturgical Press, 2001), xii. The title itself eloquently
    expresses that dynamic and necessary correlation.

primacy (or not), and the type and role of leadership that flows from or expresses liturgical practice as *theologia prima* ("primary theology"); and, finally, (3) the role of food and drink and other primary vehicles of sacred communication and how the imagined possibilities broaden or change when they emerge from a specific cultural and social location; this is especially true when that lens in the one prism is neither Eurocentric nor celebrated within a dominant cultural and economic reality. The first example will be more detailed and informs the two that follow, which flow from the symbolic exchange between categories of "matter" and "form" in the ecclesial Tradition[9] and their expression in diverse cultural and social contexts.

Cultural and Social Reality Shape the "Matter and Form" of Images, Symbols, and Communal Meaning

This short excursion, admittedly, is not in any way an exhaustive study of culture or sociological factors informing religious practice and its study. They center out of a concrete pedagogical and social location that emerge from the everyday practice of teaching and study. However, from this active engagement with students and my own wrestling with the primary symbols and images employed

---

9. Following the insight of the twentieth-century theologian Yves Congar, OP, I use the term "Tradition"—with a capital "T"—in dialogue with the multiple faces of a tradition that engages the larger category. Congar scholar Paul Philibert, OP, describes Congar's use of the term "Tradition" as "the continuous authoritative voice that arises in the Scriptures, that is celebrated in the Church's liturgy, that is refracted through the wisdom of the Fathers of the Church and the theologians of the High Middle Ages, leading to such contemporary church teaching as Pius XII's *Mediator Dei* and the documents of the Council." *At the Heart of Christian Worship: Liturgical Essays of Yves Congar*, trans. and ed. Paul Philibert (Collegeville, MN: Liturgical Press, 2010), ix. That "Tradition" has only continued to expand and deepen after the council and its reception, as well as in the theology that has emerged in recent sacramental theology and postcolonial studies in ecclesiology, scripture, and other areas of fundamental theology.

in worship and sacramental practice, certain surprises and fresh insights arise and augment traditional understandings. For example,
it is a humbling and wise admission for any student or teacher to be
aware that we always bring a hermeneutical lens that is profoundly
shaped by how we were raised and where, by our mutual regard or
rejection of that engaged Tradition out of which we have learned
and practiced the faith, and by how the wider community around
us honors this contextual practice of faith as a shared value. Such
realms of the sacred and our place within it may be so ingrained
in us that they are largely inaccessible to immediate awareness. Yet
they are expressed very practically and concretely even before we
begin our classroom study: for example, where we naturally situate
ourselves (where we "belong") in the worship space and our embodied relation to the sacred and focal symbols and to one another
(for example, in the back, the front, or hidden in the middle); or
by what choice of words we use to describe primary symbols (for
example, Holy Mass, service, divine liturgy; chalice or cup, sacred
Host or eucharistic bread, etc.); and by how our personal sense of
worthiness or unworthiness to draw close to the Mystery embodies
itself in the type of affective presence we bring to these rites or in
how we think about them (actively participating in the assembly,
drawn into one's own world in acts of personal devotion and awesome submission, or simply a resolute fulfillment of an obligation
to be present). Our participation itself may be understood as a constitutive act of our faith identity or merely an adjunct to it, which
one is free to accept or not (the necessity of baptism, reconciliation,
weekly Eucharist, marriage in the church, "full, conscious, and active participation" [SC 14], etc.).

The depth of experiential meaning gets more interesting when
we see these practical realities and actions as expressive of a social
construct that reflects the wider cultural understanding that embraces it. For example, if sitting in the front means privilege and
class rather than an eagerness to form a community of shared discipleship, different understandings may give the same action a very
different meaning. Some of my students have never seen or shared

roles of reading the scriptures, ministering at the eucharistic table, or leading the mystagogical catechesis and faith formation of new Christians after Easter, simply because they come from a cultural and social reality where such ministries are "traditionally" reserved for clergy and religious. At the same time, they would never have even thought that they were not actively engaged in the worship life of the parish or community simply because (from a Euro perspective) they are largely passive spectators and consumers at the liturgy or sacramental rites.[10]

Familial practice also carries much more weight than many young adults would care to admit. When we begin to talk about it from the inside out, the deep-lying motivations that shape liturgical and sacramental practice come to the fore. Reflections like this emerge rather spontaneously: "This is the way we have always done it in my family or village or ethnic setting." "Men lead and women serve; or, better yet, clergy lead and other men stand aside. Women are up front praying for us all." "Lay persons who want to be up front as ministers of the Word or servers at the table possess, or wish they possess, a special kind of holiness that many others do not have." "Eating with our hands is not considered sanitary or reverent. We receive on the tongue. The cup is the preserve of the priest and ministers because he is a closer icon to Christ. Besides, sacramental wine must be imported and is too costly for all to receive." "To be Catholic in my culture is to stand over and against practices of African traditional religions that we were taught are sinful." No culture is immune from the role of familial influence. For example, "My parents and siblings stopped going to Mass, so my choice to practice seems an indictment of their loss of faith. This sets me apart from them, both by choice and not by choice."

---

10. Chauvet distinguishes the latter dispensation model as "market exchange," in contrast to a more contemporary sacramental principle of "symbolic exchange" with its "logic of *gratuitousness* or 'gift,'" where the participants themselves are expected *to receive the gift and respond* with their own gratuity. See *Sacraments*, 117–18.

Clearly, the liturgy's proper "matter" and "form" take on a different shape when considered from these perspectives. It is engaged Tradition within a contextual tradition.

Enter the formal study of theology in this dialogue: within the classroom and in private study, these "inside" cultural and social realities that have shaped these students can be addressed specifically by the challenging insights of a renewed ecclesial understanding of often static categories of sacramental and liturgical theology. This contemporary theology emerged forcefully after Vatican II, a faithful expression of Congar's Tradition, and it appropriated the insights of both a collegial model of church in the early centuries[11] and added more relational models of metaphysical truth claims and communication theories characteristic of our current age. The result of this interchange imagines a living ecclesial and historical Tradition attempting to be a partner in dialogue with cultures and not an arbiter of an unnuanced culture-free institution that dispenses these graces and interprets definitively their meaning.[12] Sacramental and liturgical theology in the spirit of Vatican II

---

11. The Pauline notions of the Body of Christ in passages such as 1 Corinthians 10:16–17, 12:27, Romans 12:5, or the Lukan community in Acts 2, and second-century accounts of Justin the Martyr to the Roman authorities in *1 Apology 67* are classic and imaginative models of this understanding of collegial and participative worship that still followed an *Ordo* and was guided by a leadership that gathered that community into communion. An excellent study, written in 1966, soon after the closing of the council, is Congar's *The Ecclesia* or *Christian Community as a Whole Celebrates the Liturgy*, originally published in French as *La Liturgie après Vatican II: Bilans, études, prospective*, Unam Sanctam 66 (Paris: Editions du Cerf, 1967), 241–82. Reprinted in Philibert, *At the Heart of Christian Worship*, 15–67.

12. See esp. SC 37–40. Theologies of liturgical inculturation, the sacramental imagination, and biblical theology in dialogue with literary and cultural studies are also cogent examples of this renewed perspective that emerged in the second half of the twentieth century and that may address these questions in a way that many students may not have considered. This trajectory is the greatest gift of what contemporary theology calls the "return to the sources" (*ressourcement*), the gift especially of French Dominicans in the early to mid-twentieth century.

imagines and invites believers through a doorway, a threshold into God's revelatory activity in our midst, nourishing a living faith that leads to praise and thanksgiving.

Here is where good contextual theology and its pedagogy reshape the questions we have been honest enough to voice that emerge from the "inside." In that theological milieu, legitimate and identity-sustaining cultural norms can be embraced, but historically compromised practices can be challenged as well, all of which is more than simply legitimating or rejecting current practice, as if we even *could* construct symbolic meaning without them. How is this done? We specifically put these received identities in dialogue with the rich nuances of the historical, theological, and spiritual legacy that has been handed down. We examine in the Tradition the variety of understandings of worship that developed from the earliest times to the present, how a new sect maintained its own identity over against a prevailing and often dismissive dominant religious or cultural ethos. This is, in turn, in conversation with a contemporary (largely Western) world discovering new sources of texts and biblical interpretation and struggling to go back to these sources after the upheaval of two world wars in the past century.[13] We examine how, throughout human history, wars and the need for assimilation with prevailing structures of an organized body,[14] along with doctrinal and ecclesial responses to heresies and reformations and new spiritualities, were always altering and augmenting how the Christian

---

13. Although Christian theology and *ressourcement* was largely a Northern and Western project, its process and dialogical rhythm has continued to influence much wider global Christian theology, particularly in Africa, Latin America, and Asian contexts. Each has its own legitimate concerns, but the *praxis* is mutual and broadens the whole theological endeavor.

14. Examples of assimilation with the dominant culture, for better or worse, may be basilicas, bishops as princes, structured orders and hierarchy, and regal adornment and ritual. Examples of contestation with the prevailing culture may be the role of martyrs and their cult, liturgy as sacred mysteries (*disciplina arcana*), mendicant orders of poor preachers and servants of the poor, medieval women's mystical practices, and the Protestant Reformation itself.

people understood themselves when they entered the holy place to pray. The same holds true today. The tent of faith, however, has stretched its poles of inclusion.

The questions and subsequent reflection on the theological Tradition's engagement that history and culture engender are a response to what Augustine calls a "Beauty, ever ancient, ever new,"[15] which God continually reveals in the Church in every age. We begin to ask, is the liturgical rite an awesome mystery to be observed from afar, or can it be an equally awesome event of cohesive ingathering that draws the whole Body of Christ intimately close? This is a new conceptual and practical horizon for many students. And what makes this all the more rich and complex for us as a class is that our shared faith history did not follow the same timelines of addressing these issues. Asian Christianity has a very different trajectory and face from a Latin American or European countenance. African communities' creative tension between Catholic identity and traditional domestic faith practices creates a contemporary dilemma that many of us from the outside had not imagined, locked in our own contextual perspectives. Out of this diverse way of "looking" at the same practice of the faith, we are summoned to return to what God promised "in the beginning" and is doing now, how the Divine communicates that desire in the flesh, and how, in everything, God holds the Body of Christ in mercy through the hallowing of the abiding Spirit.[16] That, after all, is what "faith seeking understanding" is all about. It is vibrant "worship in spirit and truth" (Jn 4:24).

---

15. Augustine, *Confessions, Book X.* This melodic description of a living Tradition comes from his famous ecstatic prayer, which demonstrates precisely the need for a theology from the inside out: "Late have I loved you, O Beauty ever ancient, ever new, late have I loved you! You were within me, but I was outside, and it was there that I searched for you." *The Office of Readings: According to the Roman Rite,* Second Reading for the Feast of St. Augustine <August 28> (Boston: St. Paul Editions, 1083), 1538.

16. My colleague at the Jesuit School of Theology, Anh Tran, SJ, prefers to see our identity as *Imago Dei* in a much wider context of divine communion. He speaks of *Imago Trinitate.*

Given all that, the specifically sacramental and liturgical questions proliferate and emerge: What *does* baptism, for example, mean? Does one leave who one is and become something else? Or is it acceptance into a predominant religious ethos one did not choose? Or is this new reality something beyond all this? Is the celebration of reconciliation an individual piety or immersed within an aching social need for a whole community? The contours of reconciliation then widen to allow a sacramental space to lament and claim their own victimization by, and their responsibility for, violent acts of a privileged class against the dispossessed, stories of genocide, or ancient family enmities that have made estrangement a matter of pride or loyalty. Ecclesial structures and ministry also raise questions. For example, how do largely First World suspicions of exclusive or abusive Church structures, along with a cultural approval to criticize them publicly, affect how a community values a life of religious or priestly service? What does the Church "sanction" regarding covenant commitments? Does a Christian understanding and celebration of marriage address the actual structures of coupled life or polygamous families? The theological treasures continue to yield a greater appropriation of what it means "to manifest the mystery of Christ and the real nature of the true Church," to echo the liturgy constitution's dogmatic claim (SC 2).

It is a pedagogical spiral that intensifies. From my experience, this forces us continually to go back to the trinitarian communion, to the biblical narrative of God reaching in and saving a people and giving that redemptive grace a name and a face in Jesus Christ, to the stories of our theological controversies about real presence and merited grace and even the stubborn and uncomfortable "sense of the faithful" (*sensus fidelium*) that Vatican II reminds us is a constituent part of any dogmatic truth. The patriarch Jacob's wrestling with the angel to find out the Divine's identity in relation to his own is the Tradition's legacy and gift to us (Gn 32:24). And in the end, we have to ask what role the liturgy has played throughout these evolving generations that have handed down this Tradition: does our fidelity to communal public worship still proclaim the

Good News and feed the hungers and desires of people for a transcendent God who communicates within history and peoples, and who we believe and proclaim empties Self to draw so near?

Sacramental theology always insisted on proper "matter and form." Now we are seeing that *the matter is multivalent and the forms diverse.* And yet, through it all, the matter *matters* and the form *forms.* As the great Anglican theologian Dom Gregory Dix wrote in the middle of the last century in his historical and theological treatise on Christian worship, Jesus "had told his friends to do this henceforward with the new meaning 'for the anamnesis' of him, and they have done it ever since. Was ever another command so obeyed?" For better or worse, in every context and intention, throughout history, we begin to learn from every part of the globe and in every cultural and political nuance, Dix's contextual theological claim that "we have found nothing better to do than this." He ends this famous passage with a dictum that I hope all of us who study and practice today might acknowledge, to the glory and praise of God. Dix says, "The sheer stupendous quantity of the love of God which this ever-repeated action has drawn from the obscure Christian multitude through the centuries is itself an overwhelming thought."[17] Each member is a limb in the Body of Christ. Our cultural and social realities throughout our history shape this graced meaning and, I think, keep us struggling together to plumb the depths of meaning embedded there. Three shorter points can augment and give specificity to an active engagement that generates a mutual sharing of gifts.

The Understanding of Community Identity, Its Primacy (or Not), and the Type and Role of Leadership That Flows from Liturgical Practice as Theologia Prima

An essential sacramental principle is that there is a distinct but inseparable relationship between Christ and the church, between

---

17. Gregory Dix, *The Shape of the Liturgy* (London: Dacre Press, 1945), 743–45.

the eucharistic body and the ecclesial body, and the saving activity of the historical and risen Lord as Head of the body. This symbolic mutuality and the reverence shown the Other in their distinctness express an intimate covenantal bond and give resonance to the image of the Body of Christ.[18] In such a sacramental context, a worshiper's cultural and familial understanding of the primacy of the community in establishing one's baptized identity takes shape in different ways. Do prior individual identities come together to make the whole? Or is the whole community the primary referent that gives identity to each member?

Many North American students come out of a social identity that privileges the individual over the community. One brings unique gifts that then go to make up the rich diversity of a community. This is well and good. But when individual needs, wants, and expectations always have primacy over the good of the whole, the liturgy's claim to be "one Body, one Spirit in Christ" presents strong challenges to the unity of a community gathered in Christ's name. In contrast, those students who come from cultural and social backgrounds where family, tribe, or national identity is the primary referent and one comes to know oneself only through that identifying, communal bond, then the same claims of the *totus Christus* (the whole Christ, Head and members) have a qualitatively different shape. Both perspectives wrestle with their understandings of what Vatican II's document on the liturgy maintains is the communal nature of the liturgy. Liturgical services are not private functions; rather, they are celebrations belonging to the church, which is "the sacrament of unity," namely, the holy people united and ordered under their bishops (SC 26). This prior communal identity gives meaning to the personal and requires a certain "handing over" and a surrender to the soul of

---

18. Romans 12:4–5. Chauvet calls this the "threefold body of Christ." This builds on patristic understandings that were also important to Congar, Henri de Lubac, and others. See, for example, Chauvet, *Sacraments*, 139–40, and Congar, *Ecclesia*, 30–40.

the ecclesial body. For some, this seems a violation of personal integrity and freedom. For those from communal cultures, this is life-giving and liberating. How can these two very different contexts mutually enrich one another?

Starting from the inside out can yield a rich synthesis. We wrestle together with the ecclesial Tradition, which claims that liturgical and sacramental practice is *theologia prima* (primary theology). Communal praying shapes believing, which in turn shapes our living. The act of gathering to pray, and the liturgical assembly's understanding of their identity as the Body of Christ at prayer, make theological claims about God's dynamic relationship with the people of God and Christ's presence in the midst of that Spirit-filled gathering (Mt 18:20). That means that what we believe about God, the Trinity, the church, sacred scripture, and ethical living emerge out of that communal eventfulness we call the liturgy. Moses's invocation to the Lord in the tent of meeting is still the sacramental claim: "...Consider too that this nation is your people." To which the Lord responds, "My presence will go with you, and I will give you rest" (Gn 33:13b–14). Jesus in John's Gospel prays in thanksgiving for this intimate union of "those you gave me from the world" and how that unity is an expression of the very communion between himself and his Father (Jn 17:6, 21–24). Paul sees the prior gift of the Body of Christ as "one body with Christ" in which "many members" are the sacramental expression of this gift. It continues to deepen as a source of a "love that is genuine" for one another and expresses itself in our love for the world (Rom 12:4, 9–11). That promise of presence is real and faithful and walks through us in every age. As the sacramental Tradition says, *"lex orandi, lex credendi, lex vivendi."* This is liturgy as *theologia prima.* But our social and cultural contexts approach these differently.

For those from a more secular and individualized sense of the self, priority must be given to honoring the gifts of each member as a necessary component of "full, conscious, and active participation" that the reform intends (SC 14). For those who were raised in a culture where the community bestows on you your identity, the priority of the deep bond of union with Christ and one another may be affirmed and embodied in a much more fluid manner. Full and conscious participation is a "given" because the assembly is praying. The assembly has one voice and one body, and one's gifts are called out and affirmed in their service to the whole.

These seemingly disparate priorities do have different starting points, but when they meet, the complex richness of being a member of the Body of Christ deepens. Each perspective yields a different lens from which to view the Body of Christ as the relationship between Christ and the church, of the eucharistic body and the ecclesial body, and the presence of the glorious and risen Lord as the head of this sacramental body. Each is "distinct" but never "separate." This mutual sharing of gifts yields a nuanced appreciation on all sides of the liturgical assembly's "matter" and "form" in worship, "who we are" and "what we do" as baptized members in this body. Such interchanges, in my experience, give greater meaning to the council's claim, noted above, that the liturgy is the privileged vehicle of communal and personal identity, out of which "the faithful may express in their lives and manifest to others the mystery of Christ and the real nature of the true Church" (SC 2). For both myself as a teacher and, I think, for the students as a whole, we are richer for this exchange. But this yields even more.

The creative tension between the primacy of a communal bond that honors the individual and unique gifts of each member impels us to consider leadership in the ecclesial community and her worship. What kind of authority does the ordained person have in contrast to those who are not? And this is a point of tension. Some are suspicious of any top-down roles, while others are not, considering the prior authority of any leader as a God-given expression of what it means to be, as the American theologian Robert Hovda called, presiders at prayer who are "strong, loving, and wise."[19]

---

19. Robert Hovda, *Strong, Loving, and Wise: Presiding at Liturgy* (Collegeville, MN: Liturgical Press, 1976).

Does leadership of the community match the expectations of gender roles affirmed by different cultures, or does Christian leadership turn such expectations upside down? Does the authority of the community play a role in expectations of shared leadership and the diversity of gifts within the Body of Christ? Who decides—the individual leader or the community, which is seen as calling them to a leadership that is primarily a service to the whole?

I wish I could say that we have resolved this definitively. As a North American with decided understandings about the absolute need to revisit traditional understandings of liturgical presidency at worship, I have fixed ideas on the subject. Students with similar perspectives have also to listen to different cultural nuances regarding how one views the power issues at play in any ecclesial gathering. The fact that we are asking questions like this shows that the identity of the presider as a gatherer of the community into communion is important. The unity of the Body of Christ is a shared value on all sides. Yet how that is concretely expressed differs greatly.

What complicates the discussion even more is that *all* cultures are in flux regarding these matters in our contemporary world, and the church herself must continue to see how the Tradition reflects that shifting understanding of leadership. It invites us to revisit what it means to be shaped into Christ, his "way and truth and life." Every perspective contributes to the evolution of liturgical leadership, but the Spirit's hallowing never rests definitely in one place and time. That realization is a *kenosis*, a self-emptying in the manner of Christ the head.

In that light, historical study of the identity of the early Christian communities and the vicissitudes of shifting political and social factors that shaped those forms over the centuries reveal that our contemporary context is not immune from such calls to deeper discernment of what it means to be the church and to pray as one body in every age. Fixed assumptions on all sides are on shaky foundations. This is a call to faith, to the *sensus plenior*, to a deeper appropriation of what it means to be a global church in a diverse world. Good theology and ministry in a contextual framework call that out of us. One thing is sure: the more voices we hear, especially those who have been silenced or placed at the margins, keeps God as the wellspring of our communal procession into the kingdom. This leads to the final example, which is but another of many concerns a contextual theology can yield regarding liturgical and sacramental theology.

The Role of Food and Drink and Other Primary Vehicles of Sacred Communication

The eucharistic meal is a focal expression of Christian identity. It involves food and drink and a shared table, along with the public reading of the scriptures, the table of the Word, as a necessary ritual component of that meal. How we do this action together and what kinds of food and drink we use are also influenced greatly by our specific cultural and social locations. Further, they invite us once again to re-imagine what it means to "Do this in memory of me," as the eucharistic narrative proclaims.

One issue in particular that has a complex character regarding food and drink and its use in different socio-cultural contexts involves whether the entire assembly is provided the opportunity to commune with both the bread and the wine. Here is where liturgical leadership and local customs provide very different outcomes. The 2010 edition of the "General Instruction of the Roman Missal" (GIRM), in keeping with the Instruction, *Eucharisticum mysterium*, promulgated by the Vatican in 1967, notes the following:

> Holy Communion has a fuller form as a sign when it is distributed under both kinds. For in this form the sign of the Eucharistic banquet is more clearly evident and clear expression is given to the divine will by which the new and eternal Covenant is ratified in the Blood of the Lord, as also the relationship between the Eucharistic banquet and the eschatological banquet in the Father's Kingdom. (281)

This is never to deny that one receives the "whole Christ" under one form, yet the eucharistic action conveys its transparency as a significant action when both are received. The instruction leaves the decision to local bishops and conferences to implement according to local custom. The reasons for withholding the cup in many dioceses and individual communities vary greatly. They also express the understanding of liturgical leadership expressed above. So, for instance, the "Norms for the Distribution and Reception of Holy Communion under Both Kinds in the United States of America" (2002), although permitting the practice, leaves room for denying it under the grounds that

> the need to avoid obscuring the role of the Priest and the Deacon as the ordinary ministers of Holy Communion by an excessive use of extraordinary ministers might in some circumstances constitute a reason for limiting the distribution... or for using intinction.... (24)

This American context raises issues of leadership, power, and control ("to avoid obscuring the role"). The eucharistic meal is thus being used as an expression of making clear the distinction between those who preside and those who celebrate as central to faithful communion. The norms even make a proviso for the permission, even when most others are denied, for "Priests who are not able to celebrate or concelebrate" and for "members of communities at the Conventual Mass or the 'community' Mass" (23). Clearly, the texts and the practice privilege ordained or religious, while they consider an "excessive" use of lay ministers an obfuscation and a suitable reason for denial. The sacramental priority of the "fullness of the sign" for all, therefore, must always cede to the need to distinguish and set apart a clerical and religious culture so as not to confuse the faithful. Depending on how a student feels about ecclesial and priestly identity (and whether one is allowed to be admitted to such an order), these issues raise interesting questions regarding the meaning of food and drink at the eucharistic meal.

As an American professor, and as I hinted above about leadership, I have rather firm opinions in this regard. My students, depending on their vocation and theological perspective, have a variety of opinions as well.

However, our discussion broadens when students from other cultural contexts, even those whose families now live in the United States, share from the "inside" of their own experiences. For example, the economic issue of importing only grape wine can be a hindrance in a region where wine made from grapes is not accessible. The result has been that only the barest minimum of the sharing of the cup (with priest, deacons, religious, and perhaps expanding it to retreatants) has shaped the way the whole Church communes and understands their "fully conscious and active participation…which is their right and duty by reason of their baptism" (14). They would never expect that to change, given the cost of wine and the long tradition of denying it to the larger assembly. Here, as in all cases, is where the "rule of prayer shaping the rule of belief" (*lex orandi, lex credendi*) clearly has liturgical and ecclesial consequences. It even reinforces the clericalism that the economic and agricultural limitations have imposed from the outside.

North American students are surprised and challenged by these perspectives. We can then ask, "What is more important sacramentally, the precise fruit of the vine or the covenantal sharing of the cup? What 'matter' and 'form' are most essential for the sacramental communion of the Body of Christ within the gathered Body of Christ?" This is where contextual theology opens up the discussion beyond the mere canonical requirements. When the Vatican reform calls for unity in the whole church yet "has no wish to impose a rigid uniformity" (37) and imagines parts of the world where "an even more radical adaptation of the liturgy is needed" (40), might questions of the availability and use of local food be faithful partners in that discussion? We look first at the Tradition and how the tradition has interpreted this. As the General Instruction says succinctly at three points:

319. Following the example of Christ, the Church has always used bread and wine with water to celebrate the Lord's Supper.

320. The bread for celebrating the Eucharist must be made only from wheat, must be recently baked, and, according to the ancient tradition of the Latin Church, must be unleavened.

322. The wine for the Eucharistic celebration must be from the fruit of the grapevine (cf. Lk 22:18), natural, and unadulterated, that is, without admixture of extraneous substances.

Can a local church that does not grow or have easy access to wheat or grapes still be faithful to the Lord's example through the use of maize or other kinds of flour or meal and through the use of local wines made from palm or rice, which are clearly abundant and would not require such an economic burden by their use? Even more, would the use of such local materials have a greater symbolic significance and resonance as ordinary food and drink now transformed? "The fruit of the vine" in the scripture is not simply about grapes, but the gladness and joy that come from sharing the Passover cup that Jesus then used in a new way and with a new meaning. It is the ritual act of choosing the lifeblood of Christ to "flow through my veins," as the ancient *Anima Christi* prayer says.

Revisiting the historical Tradition teaches us about diverse Christian ways of praying, remembering, and celebrating, which were not created *ex nihilo*, but grew out of their cultural and religious heritage. These practices illumine for us how each generation's own praying out of, and then handing on to later generations, foundational Jewish ways of praying were slowly reinterpreted and inculturated in the early church with the addition of even more diverse practices and continued through the centuries that followed. Is that not also true today?

Surprisingly, for those from cultures and social locations where such eucharistic gifts are not widely available, the idea of imagining something different and still being united in faith and practice with the global Church provides an eye-opening moment of deeper theological reflection. Given that local bishops and dioceses may have raised this issue in the past and were roundly refused, or in those places where local leadership finds its truest identity in being unequivocally identified with Rome and its ways, most students had not seriously entertained the issue. Yet theology and ministry in contextual conversation with the concrete experiences of life in their own cultural contexts raise questions and, in these faithful and generous young Christians, truly invite them to theology's ultimate purpose, which is "faith seeking understanding."

For North Americans who are also significant partners in this dialogue, the more pertinent issues of ecclesial leadership and a more collegial manner of ministry in service to the whole can also be deepened by witnessing the very different contexts of students who share that faith but whose issues and reasons for actual practice may be very different. I can say without hesitation that my own thinking about the sharing of the covenant cup as a true expression of eucharistic communion has broadened considerably. The same is true about the one loaf, broken and given to the many. This is not a question of sowing seeds of infidelity; it is about listening to the Spirit speaking in different voices in every time and season.

Many more examples could be given regarding focal elements as primary vehicles of sacred communication. The role of physical bodies in other cultural contexts and how they express themselves and show reverence and communicate one to another is particularly pertinent. Bowing or touching one's folded hands to the forehead may be as intimate as a handshake or an embrace at the exchange of peace. Dance may not be simply a window dressing ornament for special occasions and under the aegis of local permissions, but *integral* to the very way a community expresses herself in prayer. How embodied assemblies sing and chant, the instruments they use, all sacred in their proper cultural contexts, help the global church to sing with one heart and mind and voice, a common prayer often distinctly unique to each place but inseparable from the sacramental unity we share.

Unless we hear one another and allow the inside experience of others to communicate the meaning of the outside expression of that in corporate public prayer, we will not be faithful to the Tradition that has been handed down generation after generation, as the Vatican Constitution has insisted (SC 7). Part of my role as a professor is to bring the breadth and depth of the Tradition into conversation with the living faith and practice I see in those who come to study. In turn, this faith and practice deepens my own and, in turn, widens my study. Through this mutual sharing of gifts, we can honor and remain not only *distinct* in our understanding of the sacramental Tradition, but also *inseparable* in affirming our global unity in being faithful to the Lord's command, "Do this in memory of me." I once thought I basically understood the scope and trajectory of liturgical and sacramental theology. Through the richness of the diverse context of our school and its students, faculty, and staff, I realize that what is truly ancient and venerable is also surprisingly renewed "age after age" by a fresh Word and a wider table.

Chapter Six

EVALUATING THE EFFECTIVENESS OF CULTURALLY CONTEXTUALIZED THEOLOGY

Alison M. Benders

Nearly twenty years ago, the faculty at the Jesuit School of Theology committed itself to a new approach for studying theology as a way to make connections between the classroom and the world. Culturally contextualized theology is the cumbersome mouthful that describes both a decision and a pilgrimage that continues at JST until today. It recognizes that there is no single, universally normative "Theology-with-a-capital-T," but that all theology is local or contextual in that it emerges and lives in a particular local church community.[1] All traditions and cultures have a voice in what the Christian revelation means and how it is lived; truly Christianity is a world religion. JST's turn to culturally contextual theology is noteworthy as an explicit recognition that all theology is tied to culture.

After years of doing culturally contextualized theology, it seems time to reflect on what JST has been doing and to evaluate its contributions to the contemporary theological project. As a latecomer to JST's distinctive approach to inculturated evangelization, arriving here in 2014 to serve as associate dean, my driving questions

---

1. See Robert J. Schreiter, *Constructing Local Theologies*, 30th annual ed. (Maryknoll, NY: Orbis, 2015); and *New Catholicity: Theology between the Global and the Local* (Maryknoll, NY: Orbis, 2005).

have been: *What are we doing when we do culturally contextualized theology? How well are we doing it?* These are basically evaluative questions. I've struggled to grasp the phenomenon that has transformed this theology school, which my colleagues have nurtured into greater maturity and clarity in the preceding decades.

This essay, then, endeavors to contextualize JST's concrete achievement within more comprehensive theological and intellectual trends to prompt questions about how to evaluate what we are doing. Evaluation is vital to the full appropriation and acceptance of contextual theology in the academy. As such, I will first locate the practice of doing theology by beginning with culture within a broader shift in the Catholic Church prompted by Vatican II. The next section briefly describes my own foray into culturally contextualized theology and summarizes our approach at JST. The third section discusses the problem of testing the outcomes of doing culturally contextualized theology and proposes a set of criteria to evaluate the results of this theological practice. Overall, I offer a general invitation to reflect more intentionally on the way that theological study in this era of globalization and inculturation can effectively disclose the meaning of the Gospel in ever-new ways.

Why JST Embraced Culturally Contextualized Theology

While faculty and students at JST sometimes speak as if culturally contextualized theology were revolutionary, that is not wholly accurate. What was revolutionary was the school's explicit decision to embrace Vatican II's challenge to read the "signs of the times." Theology should always elucidate God's ongoing revelation as meaning for human living.[2] Culturally contextualized theology means, more

---

2. Theologizing is a single undivided project, with disciplinary moments where one or another kind of expertise is needed: scripture is the (divinely inspired) record of the revelation, which is interpreted through a variety of

specifically, the school's passionate commitment to recover theology as an activity, rather than taking theology to mean defined and normative content. The practice of presenting the *kerygma* in images and terms appropriate to the listeners is as old as Christianity itself. Theology, more properly *theologizing*, reaches beyond the academy "into the whole of human affairs...to translate the word of God and so project it into new mentalities and new situations," according to Jesuit theologian Bernard Lonergan.[3] What is perhaps new in theologizing today is the very explicit discussion of methods and approaches that are needed because we are truly a global, catholic church comprising a plurality of local churches.

From the Council of Trent until Vatican II, Catholic theology had regrettably become isolated, rigidly dogmatic, rejecting modernity; it conceived of truth, especially doctrinal truth, as a permanent achievement to be proclaimed and defended by the Church.[4] Nowhere was this more evident than in seminary education. In 1965, as a breath of fresh air, the Second Vatican Council promulgated *Gaudium et Spes,* which, along with other conciliar

---

critical methods; systematic theology reflects on the meaning of the divine revelation and expresses it discursively; liturgy expresses the revelation in worship and ritual; moral reflection expresses its meaning for community life; pastoral reflection applies theological outcomes for the care of the community; and spirituality nurtures people's relationship to God and others. These disciplinary moments interpenetrate in the experience of individuals and communities as they experience and express for themselves who God is and what God has done according to the Christian *kerygma*.

3. Bernard J. F. Lonergan, "Theology in Its New Context," in *The Lonergan Reader*, ed. Mark D. Morelli and Elizabeth A. Morelli (Toronto: University of Toronto Press, 1997), 408–19, 414.

4. Stephen B. Bevans recounts the types and approaches of theology in *An Introduction to Theology in Global Perspective* (Maryknoll, NY: Orbis, 2009). After the Council of Trent, theology "was developing into a rather arid exposition of church doctrines" (271), in the eighteenth-century theological manuals became the basic seminary texts (278), and into the mid-twentieth century "there was still official opposition to any theology that did not conform to the neo-scholastic model" (293).

documents, revolutionized the Church.[5] The Pastoral Constitution on the Church in the Modern World invited Catholics, theologians included, to read the "signs of the times" and to understand the Church itself as radically engaged in humanity's multidimensional struggle for meaning in the world. In a significant way, the Church's perspectival shift embodied in *Gaudium et Spes* liberated it from its neo-scholastic enclosure to embrace and engage the world's peoples. Lonergan compares the qualities of pre–Vatican II dogmatic theology to theology in its contemporary context along several dimensions. (1) Dogmatic theology was deductive, drawing logical conclusions from the premises of scripture; *now* theology must encounter its current context in the same way that an empirical science interprets the data of experience. (2) Dogmatic theology grounded itself in a classical worldview, where meaning and values were presumed to be universal and fixed; *now* theology, grounded in historical consciousness, recognizes evolution and development in human culture and meaning, which necessarily depends on "detailed studies of the resources, the problems, the tendencies and the accidents of time." (3) Dogmatic theology utilized Aristotelian analyses and concepts appropriated since the Middle Ages; *now* empirically based theology incorporates biblical images and language, which are then "worked out by historicist, personalist, phenomenological, and existential reflection."[6] In the half-century

---

5. For a succinct discussion of Vatican II as the "impetus for a theology of context," see Simon C. Kim, *An Immigration of Theology: Theology of Context as the Theological Method of Virgilio Elizondo and Gustavo Gutiérrez* (Eugene, OR: Wipf and Stock, 2012), 12–21. More comprehensively, see Joseph Komonchak, "Modernity and the Construction of Roman Catholicism," *Cristianesimo nella storia* 18 (1997): 353–85, and Richard R. Gaillardetz, *The Church in the Making: Lumen Gentium, Christus Dominus, Orientalium Ecclesiarum* (New York/Mahwah, NJ: Paulist Press, 2006), for sources for Kim's explication.

6. Lonergan, "Theology in Its New Context," 411–13. See also Sandra Schneiders's essay (the first chapter in this collection) on this shift in Western thought as it plays out in the project of theology.

since Vatican II, Catholic theology has enjoyed a creative richness of original theological approaches and significant local theologies.

Roger Haight's observation, pertaining to liberation theology as an instance of the contemporary theological project, summarizes the give-and-take that must occur in any modern theological reflection:

> Liberation theology is certainly a modern theology, one that translates and reinterprets Christian symbols in dialogue with our contemporary world and culture. But it is at the same time counter-cultural: it calls into question society and culture as it actually is; it mediates God's word and will to unbelief and sin. And this prophetic word is addressed not only to the world but also and especially to the Church wherever it exists in an easy relation with society and culture.[7]

Vatican II motivated the Jesuit seminary of California, Alma College, to move from its remote location in the Santa Cruz Mountains into Berkeley, a university town nationally renowned in the 1960s for its political activism, particularly relating to free speech, the anti-war movement, and the Civil Rights Movement. Moreover, Alma College joined the Graduate Theological Union in 1968 as part of that extraordinary ecumenical, theological consortium of nine seminaries and took the name Jesuit School of Theology in Berkeley. In 1995, nearly thirty years later, the decrees of General Congregation 34 of the Society of Jesus inspired the faculty to renovate JST's theological method even more radically, recognizing culture as an indispensable vector of human life and meaning. GC 34, Decree 4, 25, states:

---

7. Roger Haight, *An Alternative Vision: An Interpretation of Liberation Theology* (Eugene, OR: Wipf and Stock, 2014), 2–3 (italics added). Liberation theology is among the most emblematic products of contextual method. See, for example, Gustavo Gutiérrez, *A Theology of Liberation: History, Politics, and Salvation* (Maryknoll, NY: Orbis, 1988).

It is part of our Jesuit tradition to be involved in the transformation of every human culture, as human beings begin to reshape their pattern of social relations, their cultural inheritance, their intellectual projects, their critical perspectives on religion, truth and morality, their whole scientific understanding of themselves and the world in which they live. We commit ourselves to accompany people, in different contexts, as they and their culture make difficult transitions. We commit ourselves to develop the dimension of inculturated evangelization within our mission of the service of faith and the promotion of justice.[8]

The faculty of the Jesuit School of Theology in Berkeley incorporated the Society's commitment to inculturated evangelization into every degree at the school. This commitment is now established for each degree as Learning Goal II (critical fidelity to Roman Catholic tradition, which establishes an expectation for basic theological literacy) and Learning Goal III (the interplay of faith and culture).[9] JST hired a sociologist on to the faculty to develop the community's skills in analyzing cultural context. It intentionally expanded the faculty's cultural observation skills through immersions to Guatemala and Mexico. The available foci for theses and dissertations were expanded by encouraging students' topics to include issues that emerged from their own situations and communities. Courses on art and religion as well as popular piety were added. While the faculty's choices reflected how they responded to the signs of the times, the school's explicit, intentional, and comprehensive embrace of cultural context was radical and formative.

---

8. See Boston College, *A Portal to Jesuit Studies*, "Decree 4: 'Our Mission and Culture,'" General Congregation 34 (1995), 25, http://jesuitportal.bc.edu/research/documents/1995_decree4gc34/.

9. See the JST Program Handbooks at https://www.scu.edu/jst/academics/degrees-and-programs/.

Thus, in the past two decades, JST has developed its own distinctive approach to culturally contextualized theology. Culturally contextualized theology at JST is more than adapting traditional doctrinal content to a local community. When students have a solid foundation in traditional sources for theology, culturally contextualized theology then becomes a dialogue reflecting JST's distinctive appropriation of the enduring theological task, which is to share the good news of Christ in and through every culture.

How JST Does Culturally Contextualized Theology

The shift in approach at JST has given rise to new theological conversations at the school. These are methodological in some instances, for example, the historical-critical interpretation of scripture; they also ponder cultural identity and experiences, or they consider a variety of social ethics projects and identity-based theologies. Such conversations have explicitly yielded inquiries into process and application. Stephen Bevans's *Models of Contextual Theology* is among the most frequently referenced resources, but other leading voices are also a part of this conversation.[10]

Since joining the faculty five years ago, I have admired the immediacy and relevance of the theological conversations at JST, especially the way that faculty and students are galvanized around pastoral possibilities. While I was not wholly inured to Catholic systematic theology's lingering neo-scholastic tendency to privilege

---

10. Stephen B. Bevans, *Models of Contextual Theology* (Maryknoll, NY: Orbis, 2002). We also turn to other resources on contextual theology, such as Schreiter, *Constructing Local Theologies*; David Tracy, *Blessed Rage for Order: The New Pluralism in Theology* (Chicago: University of Chicago Press, 1996); Angie Pears, *Doing Contextual Theology* (New York: Routledge, 2009); Paul Duane Matheny, *Contextual Theology: The Drama of Our Times* (Eugene, OR: Wipf and Stock, 2011), and Kim, *Immigration of Theology.*

inherited tradition and to suspect doctrinal dilution that might result from excessive inculturation, JST's approach has been freeing
for me. The discussions invited me to focus on outcomes that matter, not on analyzing theological positions for their own sake. Thus,
after familiarizing myself with the paradigm of culturally contextualized theology through sustained conversations with colleagues,
observation, and study, I created a new course in Spring 2017: Race,
Theology, and Justice, which I taught jointly with Professor Margaret Russell of Santa Clara University Law School.

Our overfull classroom opened the first day's discussion with
personal stories responding to the question: Where have you experienced "the color line" in your daily life? In their personal
narratives, students revealed their own racial heritage: six students
from sub-Saharan African nations, one African American, seven
or eight claiming Latino/a ethnicity either as immigrants to the
United States or from Spanish-speaking nations of Central or
South America, and a few Asian or Asian American students. The
remainder were U.S. students of Western European heritage. Over
the course of the semester, I witnessed the students' ever-deepening
awareness that U.S. culture, from its very birth, has built itself on
the oppression, exclusion, and dehumanization of people of African descent and other people of color. I listened as they grappled
with ways to preach, teach, or communicate about racism as an
individual and a social sin that denies full human dignity to all our
brothers and sisters in this nation. I was awestruck as they shared
their evaluations of socially active organizations, which aroused in
many of them the desire to make racism an intersectional issue in
their future ministries.

As formulated, Race, Theology, and Justice conformed to the
JST way. The approach generally functions by (1) diving deeply
into the culture from which a particular issue emerges; (2) exploring traditional theological symbols through established practices
of theological literacy; and (3) mining the culture for symbols
and values that connect with the Christian tradition to offer a
way forward. In class, our three-pronged analysis began with a

robust cultural engagement with racism in the United States and elsewhere. Next, the discussion framed the issue theologically, using a range of relevant authorities on sin and social sin as well as exploring restorative justice. Finally, students expressed their understanding in new ways or by offering new symbols that disclosed the disvalue of racism more adequately; they explored how Christian symbols from theological anthropology, sacramental and ecclesial theologies, and scripture might provide ways to resist racism and its pernicious impact concretely.

Despite students' profound theological reflections, at the end of the class I wondered what they had learned. I considered whether I might have advanced their general doctrinal literacy if we had done a survey course on sin, social sin, and grace by tracing the historical developments and articulations of these doctrines, beginning with scripture and ending with a smattering of feminist, liberation, and identity-based theologies. I wondered whether they had actually learned any *theology*, that is, any of the Church's traditional teachings on sin, redemption, or social ethics.

I realize now that each disciplinary area (that is, scripture, systematics, ethics, and pastoral theologies) has developed its own performance standards for explicating and critiquing dominant traditions and for fostering authentic exchanges between culture and tradition. Our curriculum also relies on practitioners such as prison or hospital chaplains, parish pastors, and formation leaders, and teachers who concretize students' learning in ministry settings. In doing culturally contextualized theology, faculty and students regularly locate their approaches within one or more of the models for contextual theology that Bevans has described.[11] Very often

---

11. See generally Bevans, *Models of Contextual Theology*. In his chapter "Models of Contextual Theologizing in World Christianity," in *World Christianity: Perspectives and Insights*, ed. Jonathan Y. Tan and Anh Q. Tran (Maryknoll, NY: Orbis, 2016), 146–60, Bevans identifies three other additional models: the neglected themes approach, the global perspective approach, and an intercontextual approach emerging from comparative theology.

students also report that they use the pastoral cycle of *See-Judge-Act* as their theological method in theses and dissertations. Overall, the approach presumes strong theological literacy in the foundational areas of scripture, systematics and history, moral theology and ethics, and liturgical and pastoral theology. Building on these, culturally contextualized theology as apparently practiced at JST follows a predictable three-step flow:

- Culture: Students bring questions that emerge from the sufferings, longings, and hopes of their home faith communities. The exploratory questions are: *What is happening in this culture, in terms of who God is and what God is doing among the people? In what ways does this culture bear witness to God's revelation—or fail in that witness?*
- Christian symbols: Within their own expertise, faculty guide and accompany students as they explore traditional Christian symbols and what the tradition may mean for their questions. The exploratory questions are: *What scriptural images, doctrinal themes, or liturgical/pastoral practices disclose God best here? What in the culture already reveals the Christian* kerygma?
- Mutual correlation: This is the movement to articulate what traditional sources of theology mean for their concerns and how the community might respond in light of the Gospel message. The exploratory questions are: *How do established theological positions intersect with this culture? Are there alternate understandings or expressions of the Christian symbols, perhaps using the culture's own resources, which can offer grace here?*

From the experience of a particular culture, faculty and students re-examine expressions of the Catholic faith to find an appropriate understanding of its meaning in this time and place, followed by a concomitant challenge back to Christian traditions for refinement, purification, and possibly revision.

Testing the Theological Adequacy
of Culturally Contextualized Theology

While the approach to culturally contextualized theology at JST is defined, yet flexible, the customary three-step pattern as just described surfaces theological responses to cultural questions. However, less obvious are the means or criteria to test the adequacy of the answers. If one follows the steps, is that enough for good theology? Clearly, the answer is no; not every interpretation is adequate. Some understandings are beyond the bounds of the Christian revelation, and must be identified as such. Here, I am absolutely not suggesting that we privilege one theology over others, but there are important reasons to judge the adequacy of outcomes produced by doing theology from a cultural context.[12]

As a caveat, I want to separate out exploratory and private theological interpretations. Most of the time individual theological interpretations at JST are formulated for class discussions, student theses, academic investigation, and personal reflection. Beginning a reflection from culture can illuminate one's faith, supply meaning, and provide a range of insights for daily life. In some respects, like the practice of comparative theology,[13] the resulting personal and local meanings need not be subjected to exacting scrutiny against academic standards for cultural analysis or as doctrinally appropriate interpretations. Such scrutiny would crush the creative and faithful exploration of God's living presence in the

---

12. While Bevans's models are helpful for generating appropriate analytical questions and interpretations and he provides guidance for their use, he stops short of a robust critical test for the adequacy of these answers.

13. Francis Clooney, SJ, admonishes that the purpose of comparative theology is a return to one's own faith traditions refreshed and revitalized by glimpsing God's presence and grace in others' beliefs and faith practices, not to seek the conversion of the other or reconciliation of competing beliefs. Francis X. Clooney, *Comparative Theology: Deep Learning across Religious Borders* (Malden, MA: John Wiley & Sons, 2010).

world, antithetical to the most fundamental purpose of theologizing—faith seeking understanding.

On the other hand, because JST is preparing women and men to serve the Church through a range of vocational calls, there are occasions when we do need to assess our theological outcomes in an explicit and structured way. First, in terms of academic quality, Goal 2 of every degree program asserts that graduates will develop basic theological literacy in four foundational areas as well as "critical fidelity to the Roman Catholic tradition." This implies that students know and respect certain boundaries of the Catholic tradition. Second, in terms of culturally contextualized theology itself, the approach ought to function prophetically as a corrective for inherited traditions, challenging them to respond authentically to the signs of the times. As the times change, theological discourse and its practical applications must develop in step. Thus, faculty members and graduates as professionally trained theologians and religious scholars need an approach for evaluating the products of their work. In the remaining pages of this chapter, I will propose five criteria based on David Tracy's work for assessing JST's culturally contextual theology.

Theology's task has always been an interpretive and heuristic one: to "mediate between a cultural matrix and the significance and role of religion [that is, Christianity] in the matrix."[14] Questions of adequate theological expression are answered not by privileging a particular theological tradition as a canonical guide against heresy, but by sound method, by a process that articulates what information counts and what to do with it. Method describes a structured approach to get an answer to one's questions and to disclose a reality not available before. Lonergan writes:

> A method is a normative pattern of recurrent and related operations yielding cumulative and progressive results.

---

14. Bernard J. F. Lonergan, *Method in Theology* (London: Darton, Longman & Todd, 1972, rpt. 1996 in Toronto by University of Toronto Press for Lonergan Research Institute), 1.

There is a method, then, [1] where there are distinct operations, [2] where each operation is related to the others, [3]
where the set of relations form a pattern, [4] where the pattern is described as the right way of doing the job, [5] where
the operations in accord with the pattern may be repeated
indefinitely, and [6] where the fruits of such repetition are,
not repetitious, but cumulative and progressive.[15]

Significantly, a method must correspond to a person's own interior norms for cogency, rationality, responsibility, and commitment.
In the remainder of *Method in Theology*, Lonergan explains the eight
functional specialties of theological method, each aligning with one
of the conscious operations of an authentic human subject.

Effectuating Lonergan's method in theology for any discrete theological question would require teams of theologians and scholars
working in a coordinated and integrated fashion to mediate between
a culture and religion according to a path "from data to results."[16]
The first four operations (*research, interpretation, history,* and *dialectic*) develop revelation and its meaning; the second four operations
(*foundations, doctrines, systematics,* and *communications*) produce an
adequate understanding of content for communication. The goal
of theological method is ultimately to communicate or mediate the
revelation to particular cultures. While I am drawn to the disclosive
power of Lonergan's functional specialties, utilizing his method at JST
presents obvious challenges. Pragmatically, converting a whole school
to his theological method is not feasible. Such a project would not
only encounter challenges to its suitability and practicality, but would
delay the pressing need for critical evaluation. The adage "the perfect
is the enemy of the good" guides me in seeking a practical approach

---

15. Lonergan, *Method in Theology*, 4.

16. Lonergan, *Method in Theology*, 136. Lonergan succinctly summarizes the
eight functional specialties in chapter 5, "Functional Specialties," of *Method
in Theology*. See also Thomas Cattoi's essay in this collection (chapter 3),
which provides details on the eight functional specialties.

to evaluate the quality of students' theological formation. So I offer an approach that is methodological, rooted in Lonergan's conscious operations, but without using his functional specialties specifically.

A Proposal

A theological method should provide some structure for getting a reliable answer to a theological concern. Its two major moments, then, are a path to answering a question and a means for testing the adequacy of the answer. As I described in the prior sections, JST has a three-step approach for answering questions that emerge in particular cultures. Certainly, in many situations, faculty members have sufficient expertise as scholars and practitioners to judge the adequacy of the answers, especially given what is minimally at stake in a student paper or class discussion. However, at times one may need more exacting ways to test the theological adequacy of the answers that have surfaced.

Condensing Lonergan's definition of method and consolidating its points, (1) a robust method must have a prescribed set of operations (or conscious activities, which Lonergan identifies as experiencing, understanding, judging, and deciding) that constitute a unified pattern; and (2) the operations must yield cumulative and progressive results when practiced. This presumes that one is faithful to one's own interior standards for rational judgment, responsible action, and loving compassion. However, a problem arises when the theological answers offered fail to align readily with revered Catholic interpretations, or even challenge them. David Tracy articulates the likelihood well: "Most simply put, the present postmodern approach to beginning with culture elevates and focuses our attention on an apparently polarizing commitment between obedience to traditional, orthodox expressions of Christianity (especially doctrinal expressions) and obedience to the critical demands of one's own intellect and judgment."[17]

---

17. Tracy, *Blessed Rage for Order*, 23; and see chap. 2 generally.

Likewise, Robert Schreiter notes: "The whole issue of the development of local theologies devolves finally on one point: are the results faithful to the Gospel and consonant with the church tradition? And how is this fidelity and consonance to be ascertained?"[18]

With grateful respect to David Tracy, I will use the criteria he outlines in *Blessed Rage for Order* as the starting point for a critical method to test the outcomes of a culturally contextualized theology. These are (1) meaning as disclosive of experience, (2) meaning as internal coherence, (3) meaning/truth as adequate to experience, and (4) theological outcomes appropriate to tradition.[19] Building on the third criterion (adequate to experience) and fourth (appropriate to tradition), I add a fifth test to probe whether the implementation is workable in the cultural context and faithful to tradition. I have framed the tests according to Lonergan's conscious operations and formulated questions that track Lonergan's explanation of interiority.[20]

EXPERIENTIALLY MEANINGFUL (EXPERIENCING): *Does the theology resonate as disclosing something meaningful about human experience?* This question examines the experience at the center of the reflection and whether the interpretation focuses on elements of meaning and shared resonances across human traditions. Specifically, this might look for the points that draw our hearts into the joys and sorrows of human life, regardless of a cultural location.

---

18. Robert Schreiter, "Local Theologies in the Local Church: Issues and Methods," *Proceedings of the Catholic Theological Society* 36 (1981): 96–112, 109, https://ejournals.bc.edu/ojs/index.php/ctsa/article/view/3018/2637. Schreiter offers five criteria to evaluate local theologies: cohesiveness of the Christian symbolic network, worshipping context of the community, praxis of the community, openness to the judgment of other churches, and prophetic challenge to other churches and the world. Significantly, criteria 2 and 3 emphasize the local community, and criteria 4 and 5 emphasize the dialogue with other local churches. See 109–11.

19. Tracy, *Blessed Rage for Order*. See chap. 4.

20. Lonergan identified these four conscious operations: experiencing, understanding, judging, and deciding. See, generally, Lonergan, *Method in Theology*.

INTELLIGIBLY COHERENT (UNDERSTANDING): *Is there an internal logical coherence to the theology? Does the interpretation hang together when probed?* These questions test for the coherence of the interpretation, for understanding, and whether the theology demonstrates internal logic.

REALISTICALLY CONVINCING (JUDGING): *Does the theology correspond to reality? Is it adequate to our knowledge of how the world works?* These questions test for realism and accuracy. They examine the theology against other things that we know about the world as it works and demand a critical judgment for or against. This criterion prevents fantastical or inventive assertions about the culture examined; it invites interdisciplinary scrutiny from the natural and human sciences.

APPROPRIATELY ESTABLISHED (JUDGING): *How is this theology grounded in the Christian tradition? Is this an appropriate way to understand and apply the Christian understanding of existence?* These are questions for reflective judgment. They focus on whether the interpretation of the Christian tradition is adequate. All theologians, within their respective disciplines, test proffered interpretations in light of non-negotiable symbols of our Christian faith.[21]

At this point, Tracy calls for a "critical correlation," that is, for testing how the proffered theology navigates between the culture and Christian symbols in that culture. The test invites "obedience to the critical demands of one's own intellect and judgment."[22] Critical correlation might be understood as an exercise in balancing

---

21. Jack Mahoney suggests that examining traditional doctrines in light of scientific developments and evolving standards for textual interpretation may, conversely, require us to abandon traditional doctrines. Jack Mahoney, *Christianity in Evolution: An Exploration* (Washington, DC: Georgetown University Press, 2011, 154–55). His principal argument in *Christianity in Evolution* is that the Church must abandon the doctrine of original sin and related theologies such as concupiscence and sacrificial atonement.

22. Tracy, *Blessed Rage for Order,* 23.

the dipolar values inherent in the situation. "[T]he meanings discovered as adequate to our common human experience must be compared to the meanings disclosed as appropriate to the Christian tradition in order to discover how similar, different, or identical the former meanings are in relationship to the latter."[23]

I suggest that these four criteria do not go far enough in capturing the purpose of doing theology, which is to ascertain meaning *for living*. A local theology is necessarily an answer to a vital local concern. Therefore, I offer an additional test that looks forward by anticipating the situation into which the theology will be introduced and lived. It probes the eschatological promise of the proffered theology.

AUTHENTICALLY PROPHETIC (DECIDING): *Can this theology conceivably lead to a more just and loving society? Will its implementation foster a more authentic human community?* These questions extend Tracy's fourth criterion to probe the appropriateness of the theological position at the intersection of culture and Christian symbols. This creates the space for ethical reflection by asking how *this theological interpretation* might actually impact *this culture* if implemented. It diminishes the focus on doctrinal articulations of the past in favor of prospective responses.

Adding this fifth criterion makes sense because it rests on a fuller integration of the natural and human sciences into theological positions, and it looks toward the prophetic future that believers will co-create with God's grace. Real issues of injustice, despair, and human oppression call for actual responses. Brueggemann challenges theologians and ministers in *The Prophetic Imagination*: "It is the task of prophetic ministry to bring the claims of the tradition and the situation of enculturation into effective interface."[24]

---

23. Tracy, *Blessed Rage for Order*, 79, footnote omitted.

24. See Walter Brueggemann, *The Prophetic Imagination* (Minneapolis: Fortress Press, 1978), 12.

Theology's task, then, includes efforts "to nurture, nourish and evoke a consciousness and perception radically alternative to the dominant culture around us," that is, through the eschatological lens of God's promised justice.[25] Looking toward Christianity's eschatological future is essential to Tracy's activity of critical correlation between culture and tradition, so this addition respects the spirit of his work while also extending it.

Particularly for JST, this criterion is indispensable. For some time, the faculty members have been asking whether it is time to engage public issues more directly but still responsibly. This fifth criterion implicitly scrutinizes the morality of a theological response. It recognizes that there are situations for which action may be theologically adequate but morally offensive. Before advocating change or action, responsible human beings discern whether they have the necessary skills and resources to carry through any proposed response. Theologians and ministers of the church also study the extent to which a response respects the dignity and autonomy of that community and its self-understanding. Thus, the criterion raises questions from Catholic social ethics, such as those of subsidiarity, autonomy, cultural hegemony and privilege, human dignity, and charity versus justice.

Overall, the proposed adaptation of Tracy's work on a critical methodology offers important benefits. First, it provides a way to evaluate any contextual theology. It presumes there may be many approaches for offering imaginative theological assertions for individual appropriation or for local faith communities. It extends Tracy's criteria with a fifth inquiry that scrutinizes the impact of a response according to the Christian prophetic vision of what ought to be. The five criteria rest on Lonergan's transcendental method; they build specifically on the normative transcendental precepts. As with the general empirical method, these questions are iterative, each outcome leading to a deeper, more nuanced

---

25. Brueggemann, *Prophetic Imagination*, 13.

understanding that corrects prior errors and provides elaborations and meanings not disclosed formerly.

When I use these criteria to evaluate the outcomes from *Race, Theology, and Justice*, I find that they helpfully indicate areas for improvement. Most students' investigations into racism produced observations that were experientially meaningful, intelligibly coherent, and realistically convincing analyses of culture. Additionally, they were able to demonstrate theologically how sin, as a Christian symbol, disclosed the painful reality of White privilege and anti-Black racism. However, the final test of *authentically prophetic* makes an important contribution to the evaluation. Through discussions and assignments, students offered ways to resist racism in large and small ways and suggested how some Christian symbols (for example, Eucharist) might highlight the oppressions embedded in U.S. culture. However, I now realize that I did not provide sufficient critical feedback on their work; our discussions might have been more fruitful if I had asked students to explore more practically how Christian symbols (especially eschatological symbols) could, in fact, be developed for particular situations to resist racism or remediate a particular oppressive culture. This would have required them to engage their communities concretely and prophetically, which may have moved us all from ideas to response, from understanding to action. While my notes here are quite cursory, even this brief evaluation will help me revise the class for next year.

Conclusion

Theology's task has always been an interpretive and heuristic one: to "mediate between a cultural matrix and the significance and role of religion [i.e., Christianity] in the matrix."[26] As we deepen our appreciation of the fluidity of culture as a particular

---

26. Lonergan, *Method in Theology*, 1.

historical community's values-based solution to the problem of living together, we realize that Christian theology is likewise fluid. However, our work is not without its anchors. Theologizing cannot be shored up by privileging particular historical periods of the past, nor by canonizing specific language and concepts. Rather, its anchors must be embedded in the methods by which theologians practice their craft as they search for ways to live authentically as people committed to Christ.

For nearly twenty years, JST has chosen to begin its theological reflections with the sufferings, longings, and faith-filled convictions of specific communities. In this way, the faculty embraced the Society of Jesus's commitments from GC 34: "We commit ourselves to develop the dimension of inculturated evangelization within our mission of the service of faith and the promotion of justice." JST's questions interrogate the meaning and goodness of human life by examining how Christian symbols can provide hope for a more just future. As a school and as individuals, we would be less than compassionately human if we ignored the hard questions emerging from the suffering in the world or refused to discern meaningful, effective, and faithful responses. As JST continues to deepen its commitment to a "faith that does justice," this chapter offers a starting point to evaluate the fruits of culturally contextualized theology.

PART II

INTO THE FIELD

Chapter Seven

MAPPING THE SPIRITUAL EXERCISES ALONG THE *CAMINO IGNACIANO*

Hung Trung Pham, SJ, and Kathryn R. Barush

"Leave the Creator to act immediately with the creature, and the creature with its Creator and Lord."[1] With these words, Ignatius instructs those who are directing and giving the *Spiritual Exercises*, which he wrote as a roadmap to facilitate prayerful ascent toward God for the willing pilgrim. The goal of having a personal encounter with the Creator and Lord must remain the ultimate purpose of these exercises. Therefore, these exercises can vary, as long as the end goal is achieved. In fact, Ignatius identifies them to be a broad range of "*every way* of examining one's conscience, of meditating, of contemplating, or praying vocally and mentally" (*Sp Ex* 1).[2] In the same annotation, he further prescribes: "for as strolling, walking, and running are bodily exercises, so *every way* of preparing and disposing the soul to rid itself of all disordered tendencies... to seek and find the Divine Will... is called a spiritual exercise" (*Sp Ex* 1). Thus, the exciting challenge for a giver or director of the *Spiritual Exercises* lies in the ability to adapt and accommodate the various

---

1. Michael Ivens, SJ, *Understanding the Spiritual Exercises: Text and Commentary, A Handbook for Retreat Directors* (Leominster, UK: Gracewing, 1998), 15. This translation of the *Exercises* is used throughout this chapter unless noted otherwise. References to the *Exercises* are in the text.

2. Italics are ours.

exercises according to the person, time, and circumstances in order to maximize the space in which the sacred encounter between the Creator and the individual may occur. Taking these Ignatian tenets of embodiment and encounter as a starting point, the contextual learning and immersion experience of a pilgrimage along the Ignatian *Camino,* or Way, was developed.

During the spring semesters of 2015 and 2017 and then for two weeks in the summers of those years, Prof. Hung Pham, SJ, taught with Prof. Kathryn Barush and Prof. Alison Benders, respectively, and—in collaboration with Fr. Josep Lluís Iriberri, SJ, director of Oficina del Peregrino del Camino Ignaciano—led two groups of twelve graduate students in the *Camino Ignaciano* course at the Jesuit School of Theology at Santa Clara University in Berkeley.[3] The course was designed to give the students an opportunity to deepen their personal relationship with God, as well as to serve as part of their ongoing theological studies and formation. Envisioning the students as pilgrims and the classroom as a road, the course emphasized the importance of encountering sacred space and objects *in situ* and doing theology in the context of a *camino.* We intentionally engaged with Ignatius's use of pilgrimage metaphors and motifs throughout the *Autobiography* and the *Exercises,* and his emphasis on active embodiment through walking, which was formational to his own spiritual growth. It was the conjunction of journey and metaphor that Ignatius engages throughout the *Exercises* that would ultimately act as a catalyst for others to become open to an encounter with God. Our experience of traveling roughly 250 miles with the students across Spain engendered this kind of encounter and resonated with the conjunction of pilgrimage metaphor and praxis, the value of which we will describe in detail here. The theology that ensued was the grace that transpired from the experience of engaging the *Spiritual Exercises* along the *Camino.*

---

3.   This paper is based on the collective experiences of instructors and students who participated both in 2015 and in 2017.

Theological ideas and concepts emerge from experience of personal encounter with the transcendent. Faith formation and pastoral education have too often been relegated to the classroom or the pulpit, failing to immediately connect or to directly engage with concrete realities and, most often, the messiness of the daily human experience. The incarnational nature of the Christian faith insinuates an immediate and direct encounter between the Creator and the created. Therefore, when disassociated from the realness of encounter, theological doctrines run the risk of lacking depth and meaning, thus becoming something that can be construed as superficial. Advanced technology, when used to good advantage, gives students instant access to all the events and locations of the world without having to leave their rooms, but on an important level they are distancing themselves from personal and direct engagement with the potential associative value of such events or physical locations. In Ignatian spirituality, there is an important emphasis on the conjunction of physical journey and contemplation or mental travel, which work in tandem to facilitate a personal encounter with the divine. It is one thing to *watch* a live event. It is another to actually be part of the experience, to live it, and to then recall and reflect on it. It is one thing to *read* theology. It is another to wrestle with and to *live* theology.

One of the methods that Ignatius employs to assist the person entering such an encounter, or to *live* theology more effectively, is the composition of place. He instructs:

> When a contemplation or meditation is about something that can be gazed on, for example, a contemplation of Christ our Lord, who is visible, the composition will be to see in imagination the physical place where that which I want to contemplate is taking place. (*Sp Ex* 47)

Three important aspects that underpin the *Camino* course can be located in Ignatius's instruction. First, the composition of place is deliberately set up with "something that can be gazed on." Second, it has a specific focal point. Finally, using the imagination, the person is engaging in the act that is taking place. Most importantly, all three aspects interact with one another to form one spiritual dynamic leading the person to encounter what he/she contemplates. Thus, "being present" in the composition of place entails a "two-sided" movement. While the person who contemplates makes himself or herself present to what he or she contemplates, at the same time, what is being contemplated becomes present "here and now, and indeed in a unique way" engaging with and demanding responses from "the people who contemplate."[4]

This *Exercise* begins at a physical locus or sacred place that is later imagined or mentally called forth in the mind's eye as part of the process of spiritual ascent through meditative pilgrimage. In his own experience, Ignatius desired to make physical contact with the places in which Jesus had lived and taught; he deeply longed for an embodied experience of "kinship and connection" that would serve as an entrance to intimacy with the Lord.[5] Only after having failed to travel to Jerusalem with his companions did Ignatius compromise the geographical encounter by leading them to "experience Jesus in the flesh of the imagination" through the "composition of place" during the Second Week of the *Spiritual Exercises*.[6] Indeed, Ignatius often recalled moments on his pilgrimages to specific geographic locales—the landscape of Jerusalem, where the Gospels took place, an image of the Virgin Mary, and so on—that would ground him and act as a catalyst to his entry into this prayerful state of presence. The site-specific aspect of walking the *Camino* and encountering sacred objects likewise became an important stimulus for the students, especially when they reflected on their experiences after the fact: we heard again

---

4. Nicolas Standaert, "The Composition of Place: Creating Space for an Encounter," *The Way* 46, no. 1 (2007): 7–20, 10.

5. Robert R. Marsh, "*Id Quod Volo*: The Erotic Grace of the Second Week," *The Way* 45, no. 4 (2006): 7–19, 9.

6. Marsh, "*Id Quod Volo*," 9.

and again that the *Camino* did not end in Manresa or Rome, but continued to "work" for them in their prayer lives as they called forth their experiences on the road.

Detailed information plays a key role in Ignatian composition of place. Ignatian repetition demands that the person not simply repeat the exercise but focus or "zoom in" on the concrete details of the composition that caught the attention of the person through the exercises. For the "Contemplation on the Incarnation" point in the *Spiritual Exercises*, Ignatius directs the person to see various characters in the scene, paying close attention to their "dress" as well as to their "actions"; to their skin colors as well as their political states "in peace" or "in war"; to their emotional as well as their physical well-being; to their "birth" or their "dying," and so forth (*Sp Ex* 106). During the last contemplation of the day, the person is to exercise an Ignatian repetition of the earlier composition, applying all of his or her five senses. In other words, the person is immersed more deeply into the composition of place, moving from the more general to the more particular, from the imaginary to the more concrete. Therefore, material things (*cosas*) or physical places play a significant role in constructing a space for Ignatian contemplation. For that reason, Ignatius insists that the person darken the room to create a space for contemplating the passion of the Lord.

To those who have engaged in the *Spiritual Exercises*, particularly the Ignatian composition of place, it would come as no surprise that Ignatius focused on seemingly mundane details that he encouraged the pilgrim to bring to the fore. For Ignatius, nothing is profane. Since the Divine presence is enfleshed and imminently permeates all things (*Sp Ex* 230–37), so in all things (*todas las cosas*) the person can encounter God. In fact, the emphasis on the particulars does not stop with the exercises. Similarly, Ignatius, in his position as Superior General, keenly instructs missionaries in Brazil and the West Indies to carefully observe the natives' costumes, "food and drink" (*su comer y beber*), even the "bed they sleep on" (*las camas en que duermen*), as well as the temperature of the place, the kind of soil, the house in which they live, and other particulars.[7] Indeed, Jesuits in the old Society had studied and published widely on topics in botany, geology, map making, and geography, as well as natural history. In fact, their writings numbered nearly "eight hundred titles in geography and natural history." The scope of these interests and the fact that they were pursued by a religious order of clerks puzzled contemporary scientists.[8] However, given Ignatius's insistence on the sacredness of even so-called profane things, it is not surprising. Indeed, it underscores the value of the wide variety of encounters that occur on the road.

Following the Ignatian method of composition of place, the *Camino Ignaciano* course is structured and executed in a way that is firmly rooted in the Christian tradition of pilgrimage, or spiritual ascent, through contemplation in action. Hence, knowledge of what pilgrimage traditionally entails serves as a crucial composition. Throughout Christian history, earthly journeys functioned as reminders of the journey toward the heavenly Jerusalem and dwelling place of God. These notions, grounded in scripture (both in the Hebrew Bible and the New Testament) have fueled the Christian imagination and have been manifested in art and theological discourse. Works range from Augustine's *Civitas Dei* to Dante's *Divine Comedy*; from Michelangelo's magisterial Sistine ceiling to the humble and yet most-reproduced book after the Holy Bible, John Bunyan's *Pilgrim's Progress*. Outward pilgrimages function as a composition within which the interior journey and spiritual growth can take place. Therefore, it is important to keep in mind the multiple levels of the composition of place at work during the *Camino Ignaciano* course: the classroom preparation and awareness of the history of pilgrimage; the physical walk itself (with all of its trials and tribulations, and grace), which reflects the journey

---

7. *Sancti Ignatii de Loyola Societatis Iesu fundatoris epistolae et instrucciones*, 12 vols. (Madrid: Horno, 1903–1911 [reimp. 1964–1968]), V, 329–30.

8. Steven J. Harris, "Mapping Jesuit Science: The Role of Travel in the Geography of Knowledge," in *The Jesuits: Cultures, Sciences, and the Arts 1540–1773*, ed. John W. O'Malley et al. (Toronto: University of Toronto Press, 1999), 212–40, 213.

of Ignatius; and the fact that both of these are microcosms of the ultimate journey of the human pilgrim encountering God.

Keeping in mind this important conjunction of metaphor and practice, the students first study the various spiritual movements of conversion found in Ignatius's life journey as it is recorded in the *Auto-biography*. After having contemplated these movements on their own, they share with one another the fruit of their contemplation. As they have learned how God was working in Ignatius's life, they consider how God has been working in their own life journey. This preliminary preparation, which can be understood metaphorically as a sort of fur-rowing of a field in preparation for the planting of seeds, takes place in the classroom in Berkeley. As Ignatius often refers to himself as a *per-egrino* throughout the *Autobiography*,[9] the students, by proxy, and in studying, reflecting, and sharing their lives, have technically engaged in the pilgrimage and become pilgrims, too. Traveling from Califor-nia to the Basque country of Spain, they move from reading about Ignatian sites, as noted in the writings of Ignatius, to walking and breathing in their air. The composition of place is no longer a product of imagination or intellectualizing but a concrete and lived reality.

First Movement of Contemplation: In the Classroom

*We travel again the path taken by Ignatius. As in his experience
so too in ours, because a space of interiority is opened where God
works in us, we are able to see the world as a place in which God
is at work and which is full of his appeals and of his presence.*
(GC 35, DECREE 2, 8)[10]

---

9. More than thirty times. See *An Ignatian Concordance*, ed. Ignacio Echarte (Bilbao: Ediciones Mensajero, 1996), 937–38.

10. See Boston College, The Portal to Jesuit Studies, for the full text of the decrees of the 35th General Congregation, https://jesuitportal.bc.edu/re search/documents/2008_decree2gc35/.

As Ignatius's conversion was inspired by contemplating the lives of Saint Dominic and Saint Francis (*Au* 7),[11] students were asked to contemplate Saint Ignatius's experience and his *Spiritual Exercises*. Toward the end of February 1522, Íñigo of Loyola, a courtier descended from Basque minor nobles, left the Loyola castle and embarked on a pilgrimage to Jerusalem. After recovering from what had seemed to be a devastating, dream-shattering experience (he was immobilized after a cannonball struck his legs), he committed his life to the pursuit of holiness by imitating the lives of the saints and walking in the footsteps of Christ in perpetual penance (*Au* 35–48).

From Loyola, Ignatius (then still Íñigo) made an actual foot pilgrimage through Aránzazu, Montserrat, and Manresa before entering Jerusalem on September 4, 1323, spending nearly one-and-one-half years on the road. Trading his sword and knightly clothes for the simple garments of the pious pilgrim, Ignatius slowly learned not to run ahead but to allow himself to be led by the Spirit. Step by step, a *camino*—a road—was opened, leading him to ever deeper conversion and transformation. As the *peregrino* journeyed through various locations on the physical level, he experienced conversion in the inward journey of his soul. Ignatius reminisced that "On this journey something happened to [me] which it will be good to have written, so that people can understand how Our Lord used to deal with this soul: a soul that was still blind, though with great desires to serve him as far as its knowledge went" (*Au* 14).

The motivation and desire that inspired Íñigo López de Loyola to make a pilgrimage did not come easily. Had his leg not been struck and his bones not crushed during the battle in Pamplona, Íñigo would not have been confined to bed while convalescing in Loyola, but instead would have continued his pursuit of "vanities

---

11. The version of the *Autobiography* of Saint Ignatius of Loyola used in this chapter is taken from *Saint Ignatius of Loyola: Personal Writings: Reminiscences, Spiritual Diary, Select Letters Including the Text of the Spiritual Exercises*, trans. Joseph A. Munitiz and Philip Endean (London: Penguin Books, 1996), 13–64.

of the world and special delight in the exercise of arms with a great vain desire of winning glory" (*Au* 1). Only during this period of immobile convalescence, during which he was pushed to the border between life and death (*Au* 3), helpless on his own, removed from the world that he knew and was familiar with (*Au* 5), did life alternatives emerge. Possibilities were imagined, new life directions envisioned. The *Life of Christ* and *Lives of the Saints* helped Íñigo to pause and contemplate: "Suppose that I should do what Saint Francis did, what Saint Dominic did?" (*Au* 7).

Grappling with the choice between his former way of life and new possibilities, between "things of the world" and "going barefoot to Jerusalem and eating nothing but herbs and performing the other rigors he saw that the saints had performed" (*Au* 8), Íñigo learned to discern evil spirits from holy ones among the various interior movements that were being stirred up in his soul. Further, he came to realize that it was not he but God who had initiated the encounter ever so "gently and kindly," awakening holy desires within him (*Sp Ex* 7). Inflamed with divine love, Íñigo resolved to go on a pilgrimage to Jerusalem "as soon as he was restored to health undertaking all the disciplines and abstinences" (*Au* 9).

Second Moment of Contemplation: On the Road

Encounters in Context: Aránzazu, Montserrat, Manresa

Although none of the student participants on the *Camino* course had undergone dramatic, bone-crushing injuries or were pushed to the limit of immobile convalescence in the same way that Íñigo had, we—both as individuals and as a group—were wrestling with our own human limitations and vulnerability on our way to, and during our stay in, Loyola. The pilgrim groups during both *Caminos* (in 2015 and 2017) included students and immigrants who hailed from countries and cultures as diverse as Armenia, India, Kenya,

Korea, Mexico, the Philippines, the United States, and Vietnam, and included lay and religious women and men. Each student had his or her own reasons for embarking on this journey.

One student reflected on the difficulty of negotiating a delayed airline flight on foreign territory, becoming aware of his fear of uncertainty, which led him to pray and to rely on God's grace at work in the moment. For another Jesuit student, the sudden death of a good friend and Jesuit companion prior to the *Camino* had left him feeling somewhat helpless in his grief and sorrow. The *Camino* would serve as a way for him to contemplate life's mysteries in a deeper and more active way. For a Latina American student, the anticipation of entering yet another culture both widened and narrowed the space-in-between in her liminal intercultural identity, widening it by being enriched with the best values that each of her cultures offers, and at the same time narrowing it by being caught in the loneliness brought on by a realization of belonging to none.[12]

ARÁNZAZU

It was with much anticipation and varying expectations that we embarked on the journey in Spain, following the basic path of Ignatius's pilgrimage for approximately 250 miles—beginning in Loyola, the place of his birth, and ending at Manresa, where he began to formulate the *Spiritual Exercises* in a lonely cave on the bank of the River Cardoner. We stopped to eat, pray, and sleep at a number of

---

12. As instructors, we braced ourselves for our own pilgrimages as well. Especially on the inaugural and rather experimental 2015 journey, there was much to consider in terms of planning, transportation, and the pastoral care of a group of twelve students with diverse lifestyles, customs, and language. For a narrative of our personal experience as instructors, see our published travelogue: Hung Pham, SJ, and Kathryn R. Barush, "From Swords to Shoes: Encountering Grace on the *Camino Ignaciano*," *Practical Matters Journal* (June 28, 2016), https://wp.me/p6QAmj-KB. We are grateful to *Practical Matters Journal* for allowing some of the material published there to appear in this chapter in a different format.

other significant Ignatian sites along the way, including Aránzazu, where Ignatius had a devotion to Our Lady of the Thorn; Verdú, the birthplace of the modern saint Peter Claver, who fought for the rights of those who were enslaved; Montserrat, the ancient mountainous pilgrimage site dedicated to a miraculous Madonna, where Ignatius renounced the *caballero*, or sword, and truly became a *peregrino* (in his own words). We finished our travels in Rome, flying to the airport from Barcelona, and proceeding on foot to La Storta, where Ignatius had a vision of God the Father placing him into the service of Jesus, who was carrying the cross—an image that would bear much significance for the charism of the Society of Jesus.

To Íñigo, Aránzazu embodied a step in both familiar and unknown directions. Like other members of the Loyola family who had come to pray in front of the sanctuary of La Virgen María de Aránzazu (Basque for thorn; in Castilian, *espinar*), Íñigo knelt down, his eyes fixed on the smiling Virgin with the baby Jesus on her lap, where he sought the grace of confirmation in his discernment to move forward.[13]

We have already commented on the importance of the idea of the contemplation of space for Ignatius, or bringing to mind the sacred landscapes and objects he encountered on his own pilgrimage. At Aránzazu visual reminders not only of Ignatius's journey, but all the pilgrims who had come before (and who will proceed to enter the space come the fullness of time) were everywhere, and hence became places where communitas could be enacted. Here we borrow from cultural anthropologists Victor and Edith Turner, who coined the term *communitas* in part to encapsulate the idea of anti-structure, or the removal from the quotidian realm in order to describe spontaneous encounters with others, and to capture the possibility of renewal and transformation that occurs on the sacred journey. In addition to thinking about the community of

13. Ricardo García-Villoslada, *San Ignacio de Loyola: Nueva Biografía* (Madrid: Biblioteca de Autores Cristianos, 1987), 185.

those on pilgrimage, we mean to emphasize here an adaptation of the Turners' notion, that is, the fact that a built environment facilitates a tangible connection to all those who have come before and all those who will come again—not unlike the invitation to join one's voice with the choir of saints and angels during a Roman Catholic Eucharistic celebration.[14] The divine architecture of Aránzazu and the sacred objects within, and the other sacred loci along our pilgrimage, bring to mind the journey of Ignatius and, by proxy, engender the inherent link to the *civitas Dei* toward which all Christians proceed as "strangers and pilgrims."[15]

MONTSERRAT

Another site of this deep communitas was the image of Our Lady of Montserrat, where Ignatius prayed to the Virgin Mary and professed the life of a pilgrim. As we proceeded up the holy mountain, little mosaic stations depicting the Virgin Mary in her different global and cultural contexts (Our Lady of Fatima, Our Lady of Guadalupe) decorated the high mountain walls and began to prepare us for our prayerful journey into the shrine where Ignatius prayed and had an impactful encounter with Jesus. The enthroned statue of Mary, holding a great, golden orb with Christ seated on her lap, is attached to many legends and oral histories. Some say that the statue was carved by Saint Luke during biblical times and then carried to Spain by one of the apostles. During a

---

14. Victor Turner and Edith Turner, *Image and Pilgrimage in Christian Culture: Anthropological Perspectives* (New York: Columbia University Press, 2011), 13, 252–54, and passim. For more on this adaptation of the Turnerian notion of communitas, see Kathryn R. Barush, *Art and the Sacred Journey in Britain, 1790–1850* (London: Routledge, 2016), and "Material Culture and the Catholic Imagination: The Los Altos Labyrinth," in Chris Ocker and Susanna Elm (eds.), *Material Christianity: Western Religions and the Agency of Things* (Springer Academic Publishers / Sophia Studies in Cross-Cultural Philosophy of Traditions and Cultures, forthcoming 2019).

15. 1 Peter 2:11 and Hebrews 11:13, where followers of Christ are called strangers and pilgrims.

Saracen invasion, the statue was said to have been hidden from the enemy in a cave and was later discovered by shepherds who had been led to the hiding place by following mysterious lights and heavenly song. A later bishop wanted to move the statue to Manresa, but it miraculously became heavier and heavier—Mary apparently wanted pilgrims to come to her in the mountain of Montserrat. The shrine has since been the site of many miracles and attracts over one million pilgrims a year.[16]

Saint Ignatius of Loyola was one of those who found solace at the shrine of the Madonna of Montserrat. Earlier, during his convalescence in Loyola, Ignatius began to prayerfully reflect on "how would it be, if I did this which Saint Francis did, and this which Saint Dominic did" (*Au* 7). This paradigmatic imagining is central to pilgrimage practice, wherein the pilgrim often reflects and meditates on the life of Christ or the saints (as instruments of God). Ignatius's imagining of himself as the saints is important in understanding the value of the students not copying Ignatius but continuing his "work." His life and actions became catalysts for their own personal experiences: he imagined Dominic and Francis; the student pilgrims imagined Ignatius. In our usual sharing (within the context of an evening liturgy), many of the students mentioned Ignatius's moment of leaving behind the sword as framing their own experiences at Montserrat. They described a sense of renewal and change going forward, similar to a renewal of baptismal vows in a liturgical context, both on the pilgrimage and in their lives. This is consistent with the Turners' theory that myriad symbols and images engender a sense of rebirth and spiritual renewal. In this instance, the Virgin Mary, as Mother of God and a vessel of the incarnation, became another place of encounter during the pilgrimage. The representation of Mary and Christ in the

---

16. Michael P. Duricy, "Black Madonnas: Our Lady of Montserrat," March 26, 2008, https://udayton.edu/imri/mary/m/montserrat-black-madonna.php; and Sarah Jane Boss, *Empress and Handmaid: On Nature and Gender in the Cult of the Virgin Mary* (London: Bloomsbury, 2000), 5.

form of a statue in and of itself reminds us of the importance of matter—after all, Jesus himself took on a material body when he became human.[17] These representations, as Ignatius taught, are important components of the composition of place, and certainly took on this role for the students.

The experience of the students reflects, but also—and crucially—continues what Ignatius had encountered at Loyola, Aránzazu, and in the sacred mountain of Montserrat. The Turners posit pilgrimage as a liminoid phenomenon, that is, voluntary and non-routine, and distinct from a "liminal" experience, which is usually understood as tied to a rite of passage within the structure of a set religious system or ritual.[18] They point to the transformative effect of approaching the final grotto or shrine, where sins are forgiven and the pilgrim identifies with "the symbolic representation of the founder's experiences"—hence "'put[ting] on Christ Jesus as a paradigmatic mask."[19] This resonates with Ignatius's yearning to become more Christ-like, and with the student-pilgrims' framing of their pilgrimages as walking in the footsteps of Ignatius—an instrument of Christ—as a catalyst for their own ultimate growth and renewal. Ignatius symbolically (and literally)

---

17. As John of Damascus wrote, and as several modern papal documents have emphasized in relation to the art of the Catholic Church, "Either we must suppress the sacred nature of all these things, or we must concede to the tradition of the Church the veneration of the images of God and that of the friends of God who are sanctified by the name they bear, and for this reason are possessed by the grace of the Holy Spirit. Do not, therefore, offend matter: it is not contemptible, because nothing that God has made is contemptible" (*Contra imaginum calumniatores orations tres*, I, 16, ed. Bonifatius Kotter, 89–90, as cited by Benedict XVI, John Damascene, General Audience (May 6, 2009), https://w2.vatican.va/content/benedict-xvi/en/audiences/2009/documents/hf_ben-xvi_aud_20090506.html.

18. As Deborah Ross has stated, "[a]s modern pilgrimage in complex postindustrial societies is voluntary, [the Turners] described it as a 'liminoid' experience, rather than a liminal one in the rite-of-passage sense." Introduction, in Turner and Turner, *Image and Pilgrimage*, xxxi.

19. Turner and Turner, *Image and Pilgrimage*, 11.

cast off his knightly attire and sword and clothed himself as a pilgrim in sackcloth with a gourd to drink from. When he arrived at Montserrat he kept a vigil all night and decided to "clothe himself in the armour of Christ" (*Au* 17). While at Montserrat, Ignatius made a written confession for three days—hence compatible with the Turners' notion of the transformative effect of reconciliation during this phase of pilgrimage.

One of the students shared that "at Montserrat, [a] sense of identification with Ignatius deepened," and another affirmed that "as [he] walked in places like Loyola, Montserrat, and Manresa, [he] was permeated by the spirit of the Saint in a more radical way." The student who had wondered aloud where Mary was among the throngs of people had a moment of peace and consolation at the shrine, where she was able to leave behind burdens of her own:

> In little moments, when I paid attention to the grace around me instead of the pain of my feet and exhaustion, it was evident how the Spirit was at work. The interior work, along with the great consolation at Montserrat, brought me inner peace. I became in tune with my deepest desires and was graced with interior freedom. I was reminded through this transformation that the Christian vocation is about love. I am grateful for the grace of freedom that will enable me to love more deeply and healthily, beginning with myself.[20]

While this experience was one that emerged from her own personal pilgrimage, struggles, and contemplations, it was the act of following Ignatius's route that acted as a stimulus for this shift. She recalled: "As [Ignatius's] conversion story unfolded

---

20. A graduate student pilgrim reflecting on the experience of walking the *Camino Ignaciano* in June–July 2015.

before us, it drew me inward to the spiritual dynamics at play in my own story."[21]

Likewise, another student (a Jesuit scholastic) shared a moment of letting go of unhelpful burdens that were keeping him from being a good priest and a good Christian. His description is framed within the autobiography of Ignatius, even though the experience is entirely his own: "The moment in which Ignatius placed his armor and sword before Our Lady of Montserrat...illustrates the power and beauty of conversion and turning one's life around."[22]

The student goes on to describe a significant vision in which Mary helps facilitate a leaving behind of burdens; together, they stamped out the unhelpful "negative messages that lead...to darkness and isolation."[23] The theme of reflecting on letting go of negativity appeared in many of the students' narratives post-*Camino*. Another shared:

> As the scene unfolded, I wasn't before a statue of Mary. Instead, I was experiencing the real presence of Mary alive and well in my prayer.... I've found myself reflecting about what Ignatius had left behind, and I began to similarly ask myself if there is anything that I need to leave behind as I look ahead into the future.[24]

Again, the experience that Ignatius had and the imaginative putting-on of the paradigmatic "mask" of the saint (to borrow from the Turners) helped to facilitate a powerful, and very personal, moment that revealed the things holding back the students in their lives and in their relationships with God.

---

21. Graduate student, 2015.
22. Graduate student, 2015.
23. Graduate student, 2015.
24. Graduate student, 2015.

MANRESA

On the way from Montserrat to Manresa, the journey became even more physically difficult because of extreme temperatures and a scarcity of water sources between stopping points as we proceeded through the desert-like terrain. The earthly and physical discomfort became an important catalyst for reflection and a reminder of moments of spiritual desolation during life's pilgrimage. One student pilgrim wrote of "the physical pain of the *Camino*—and the inner turmoil that bubbled up and spilled out with such frequency and fervor as outer suffering called forth innermost wounds and fears." This is perhaps what the Puritan preacher John Bunyan had in mind when he wrote of the pilgrim's progress through the Slough of Despond, or allegorical swamp, where one encounters a burden of guilt for sins and shortcomings that form a real or imagined barrier to achieving a closeness with God.[25]

The physical challenges were not, however, without moments of spiritual revelation, one of the hallmarks of a walking pilgrimage. The student with the foot pain wrote that her "feet were a conduit, drawing pain out and bringing healing in." Like Ignatius's surrender at Manresa, she opened her vulnerability to an experience she described as "being cradled by Jesus."[26] Another student recalled a moment of grace and reconciliation:

> I remember [as we came close to arriving] at Manresa, [one of the pilgrims] struggled with each step, her knees swollen and giving out. I walked beside her trying to encourage her, but felt exhausted myself and wasn't much help. [Our guide] José came beside her, and without a word took her backpack onto himself, and supported her as she walked. When I saw him do this, I was deeply

---

25. John Bunyan, *The Pilgrim's Progress from This World, to That Which Is to Come* (1678).

26. Graduate student, 2015.

moved. I chose that moment as my "icon" of José: him walking with [the pilgrim's] bag, letting her rest her hands on his shoulders.

I felt like Jesus said to me in that moment, "you are seeing him as I see him. This is who he truly is." At the same time, I knew in a deep and interior way that Jesus looks at me the same way, "as I truly am," not as I see myself and not as others see me. This moment was a moment of deep forgiveness for me, an icon of José, an icon of forgiveness, and a window into the compassion of God. If only I could see like that, with the eyes of Jesus all the time. How wonderful life would be.[27]

Ignatius did not wish for the Jesuits to become known as "the Ignatians" (as in the orders eventually named after their founders, such as the Franciscans, after Saint Francis); rather, he referred to them as the *Compañía de Jesús*, or the Society of Jesus, to emphasize the importance of all Jesuit life and mission, such as teachings, compassion, humanity, and divinity, to be centered in Christ. The student's experience again transcends Ignatius's to focus on Jesus, and then on his own life. It again marks an example of the moments when his journey was not being copied by modern-day pilgrims such as ourselves; rather, we were continuing it (to borrow from the Thomist notion, which makes sense in this context, too, that "artistic creation does not copy God's creation, it continues it").[28]

Besides the heat, we faced several more difficulties on the way to Manresa. At one stage our way was blocked by barbed wire. Then some students became sick with heatstroke, and there was an incident involving a stolen bag. All of this seemed to prepare us for what we would encounter in the cave in Manresa, where Saint

---

27. Graduate student, 2015.

28. Jacques Maritain, "From 'Art and Scholasticism,'" in *Theological Aesthetics: A Reader*, ed. Gesa Elsbeth Thiessen (Grand Rapids: Eerdmans, 2005), 327.

Ignatius of Loyola experienced mystical revelations and enlightenments near the River Cardoner for most of the year 1522 while fasting, praying, and meditating on the Gospels. In reflecting on his experiences there, he would ultimately write the *Spiritual Exercises*, which, as we have said, is a compendium for pilgrims desiring to deepen their faith. In the words of one of the students:

> Many of us had almost yielded to fatigue, heat, and thirst, which indeed overstretched our capacities to the point that we…felt the frailty of our humanity. Experience of human weakness and failure is an experience of our true self, our true identity. In my fatigue, I was reminded that I am a limited creature and God is the almighty and unlimited creator. I view this as a call to rely on God more rather than rely on my strength and wisdom.[29]

The ornate narrative sculptures in roundels affixed to the cave had been stripped off in a recent renovation to reveal the smooth, bone-white walls, giving a sense of the bareness where Ignatius would write about the "composition of place" in the *Spiritual Exercises*. He encourages the individual retreatant to see where, through the gaze of the imagination, the "physical place" of a scriptural scene or any passage or topic that she or he wants to contemplate is situated. He teaches that "by 'material place' I mean, for instance, a temple or a mountain where Jesus Christ or our Lady happens to be, in accordance with the topic I desire to contemplate" (*Sp Ex* 47). In a compelling reversal, we first imagined Ignatius in the cave, with his thoughts and prayers, as he was imagining mountains and temples several hundred years before. Again, the experiences of composition and *Camino* were deeply interconnected, transcending temporal boundaries and facilitating spiritual growth through *both* contemplative prayer and physical place.

---

29. Graduate student, 2015.

Conclusion:
"To Make an End Is to Make a Beginning"[30]

> *Our mode of proceeding is to trace the footprints of God ev-*
> *erywhere, knowing that the Spirit of Christ is at work in all*
> *places and situations and in all activities and mediations that*
> *seek to make him more present in the world.*
>
> (GC 35, Decree 2, 8)

There was a distinct sense that the students' *Camino* experiences were not ending at the cave, but were, in fact, just beginning. One pilgrim's thoughts reflect those that were shared while we prayed at Manresa, aloud and in silence:

> I continue to have a sense of Jesus's presence near me, and I feel that this has been the point of the Camino for me. Jesus is real; he is near; he is present. I have come to realize that the Camino didn't end at Manresa. In a genuine way, the Camino continues, and I have been assured by Jesus that he is with me. I am reminded of the words of the resurrected Jesus to his disciples: "And behold, I am with you always, until the end of the age" (Mt 28:20, NRSV).[31]

To another, the experience of the *Camino* helped him to get in touch with the voice of Christ calling him into solidarity with those who walk not out of freedom but of necessity, not as a privilege of choosing, but as a result of being marginalized—the migrants and immigrants, the displaced and the homeless. The student describes how physical tiredness and hunger plunged him into a deep contemplation of the struggles of migrants, and how

---

30. T. S. Eliot, "Little Gidding," http://www.columbia.edu/itc/history/winter/w3206/edit/tseliotlittlegidding.html.

31. Graduate student, 2015.

Ignatius's exercises address these issues of justice. For this particular student, it was the physical process of walking that allowed these ruminations to emerge. In a very real sense, communitas was enacted—in this case, through the contemplation and *composition*, in the Ignatian sense we have outlined throughout this essay, of the immigrant struggle. He was, in a very real sense, walking in solidarity with those people as he physically walked through Spain. The discomfort of the road was a catalyst for an internal dialogue, consisting of two voices that took place in his imagination:

Voice 1: "We'll soon get to eat at the shelter."

Voice 2: "Imagine that you did not have a place to rest and to eat."

Voice 1: "That will not happen because José Luis has everything organized."

Voice 2: "But there's always something we cannot control...."

Voice 1: "I do not think that happens. That should not happen."

All of a sudden, a third voice began talking:

Today you have walked almost thirty kilometers, and you know that you will have a place to eat and rest, but those African migrants that you have seen in the cities of this country have traveled thousands of kilometers and have nowhere to rest. They have nothing. In Mexico, you have also seen migrants walking the streets hungry and without a place to rest. They are everywhere. Remember them! They have always been there! Where else have you seen them?

After the delirium and more than thirty kilometers walked, we arrived in Jorba. I rested for a couple of hours, and when I approached the table for dinner I began to remember all the African migrants I had seen in Spain. Then the ones I had seen in Mexico. The images that came to my mind were many. I remembered the migrants I saw in

Tijuana, Guadalajara, Tabasco, Palenque, Torreon, Mexicali, Tecate, etc.

I automatically asked myself: What have I done for Christ? What am I doing for Christ? What ought I to do for Christ? (*Sp Ex* 53). I remained without answers for several minutes until gradually I began to remember that the Christ I have come to know through St. Ignatius is the poor, humble, and humiliated Jesus of the Gospels, who walks the streets of the cities without having anything to eat nor a place to rest, as well as the migrants I saw in the previous days and who continued to appear in Manresa, Barcelona, and Italy.

I understood at that point that the inner self, which in the previous days insisted I continue on my spiritual path, was the one that now told me my vocation acquires meaning by loving and serving the poor, humble, and humiliated. When I have the sensitivity to look and listen to others—from them, for them, and with them—my formation and life as a Jesuit make sense.[32]

This meditation emerged through the act of pilgrimage and the student's encounters with the migrants both in his life and those he saw on the road. In reflecting on the words and images that were drawn forth through walking, there is recourse to the *Spiritual Exercises* of Ignatius and the Gospel of Christ that underpins them. The fullness of his experience, where the walk became a catalyst for theological reflection and (in this case) an understanding of his vocation, serves to encapsulate the goal of our efforts in facilitating this course of study at JST.

The ancient pathways that our *Camino* students traveled served as roads not only to and from sites and shrines, but inward. The multi-sensory pilgrimage experience—the pain of blisters, the

---

32. Graduate student, 2015.

sweat, the smell of incense in ancient churches, the feel of the cool water in mountain passes, the salted tears in those silent prayers—is something that cannot be taught through books or slides. Students no longer read about those experiences, but are living them. History blossomed in living color all around us pilgrims, students, and teachers, in Spanish polychrome altarpieces from Ignatius's time to the ancient trees along the route we traversed. As we walked, the ancient pathways transcended time and space as they mapped onto and continued onto our own experiences and stories. And in engaging and interacting with what seems to be ordinary and mundane—things such as rocks and trees—from dusk to dawn we experienced the extraordinary by encountering at a most personal level the Creator, who is immediately acting, intensely laboring, and unceasingly loving the world.

Chapter Eight

FIELD EDUCATION
AT A SHARED PARISH
NAVIGATING CONTEXTUAL AND
PASTORAL OPPORTUNITIES

Deborah Ross

In the late 1990s, the Jesuit School of Theology (JST) sought a ministerial praxis site to enable the practicing of contextual theology with a local parish community. St. Patrick Parish, in Oakland, California, was selected, initiating mutual engagement between the school and the parish community.[1] Thus began the relationship between a theological school of the Graduate Theological Union in Berkeley, California, situated on what is affectionately known as "Holy Hill," and a parish in the West Oakland Deanery.

St. Patrick Parish historically served an African American community alongside a smaller Latino/a community. This demographic ratio has reversed in recent years, and the parish currently serves a congregation consisting of a Latino/a majority and an African American minority. St. Patrick, a "shared parish," consists of two distinct cultural groups, each representing unique pastoral and cultural needs.[2] The shared parish creates an opportunity for the parish

---

1. St. Patrick became a Jesuit-affiliated parish under this arrangement. As JST was seeking a ministerial praxis site, it simultaneously explored initiating international immersion experiences for students.

2. A shared parish is a community "in which two or more languages or cultural contexts are an integral part of the ministerial life and mission of a particular parish." See the U.S. Bishops' *Best Practices for Shared Parishes:*

to minister to both communities while navigating the inevitable tensions occurring as the groups share the same physical space. The parish, located in an economically challenged neighborhood in Oakland, is subject to gang culture and gun crime. Yet the neighborhood is also experiencing gentrification fueled by the rising cost of housing in the San Francisco Bay Area.

JST's present-day collaboration with St. Patrick Parish is primarily through JST Jesuit community involvement, with the community providing the pastor on staff and JST students undertaking field education placements at the parish. The contours and expressions of a lived contextual theology as embodied in the school-parish relationship are explored in this chapter. Contextual theological themes, specifically those experienced in JST student field education at the parish, are featured. A "guest-host" hospitality motif provides a culminating theological reflection theme.[3] The contextual engagement within the school-parish relationship aims to be one of hospitality and dialogue.

Field Education at the Jesuit School of Theology

Field education at JST forms an integral part of students' ministerial formation.[4] During the second year of the Master of Divinity (MDiv) degree, Jesuit scholastic seminarians, other religious, and lay students minister at several locations in the San Francisco Bay Area. Students select from parish ministry in diverse parishes; educational placements, including teaching in high schools, or campus

---

So That They May All Be One (Washington, DC: United States Conference of Catholic Bishops, 2014), 1.

3. See Luke Bretherton, *Hospitality as Holiness: Christian Witness amidst Moral Diversity* (Abingdon, UK: Routledge, 2016), 135–38, for an exploration of this theme.

4. In my role as director of ministerial formation at JST, I direct the school's Field Education program.

ministry work, for example, at Santa Clara University or the University of San Francisco; health care ministry at Sojourn Chaplaincy at Zuckerberg San Francisco General Hospital and Trauma Center; or prison ministry at San Quentin State Prison for men and the Federal Correctional Institution, Dublin, a low-security prison for women. JST enjoys a special relationship with St. Patrick Parish and San Quentin State Prison, with students regularly committing to field education placements at these sites. Students from various degree programs opt to work at social agencies such as the Catholic Worker in Berkeley and Oakland.

JST students are shaped by the people to whom they minister and the ministerial and cultural contexts within which they serve. Working to develop context-specific practical skills related to a new or familiar ministerial craft, students may participate in, for example, hospital clinical pastoral care, retreat leadership, spiritual direction, ministry to those on death row, or faith formation for children, teenagers, and adults. The practice of collaborative ministry, and the observation of ministerial and ethical boundaries, augment students' contextual learning. In a spirit of collaboration, students support one another's growth in leadership, ministerial identity, and personal vocation as Jesuit, religious, or lay ecclesial ministers.

Field education ministry requires the development of practical wisdom or a *habitus*. A *habitus* is a disposition of the heart and mind leading to a natural flow of action prompted by the Spirit dwelling within us, becoming a "way of life."[5] As students navigate the social, economic, and religious realities of their field education sites, they manifest growth in practical wisdom, and they display ministerial virtues comprising compassion, dedication, humility, and a willingness to learn. I am frequently reminded of the students' generosity as they exercise discipleship and serve the local San Francisco Bay Area community.

---

5. Terry Veling, *Practical Theology: On Earth as It Is in Heaven* (Maryknoll, NY: Orbis, 2005), 16. Veling describes practical wisdom and *habitus* as features of practical theology.

JST students integrate personal learning at their ministerial sites with their theological studies and spiritual lives. MDiv students utilize the "Pastoral Circle" model of theological reflection as an aid in this process. The Pastoral Circle has four moments of reflection—"insertion, social analysis, theological reflection, and pastoral action"—as developed by Joe Holland and Peter Henriot, SJ. The model directs attention to the context of the ministerial location, specifically emphasizing "social analysis," or reflection on social, economic, religious, ecclesial, and other factors influencing a community.[6] The Pastoral Circle has been the signature theological reflection model at JST, with students structuring their theological reflection papers according to the four elements of reflection.

Students undertaking field education have weekly conversations in theological reflection groups, based upon their theological reflection papers. This creates the opportunity for students to reflect on the lived or operant theology (the theology evident in pastoral practice) at their field education sites. Students bring this lived theology into conversation with normative theological sources (scripture, church teachings, or Ignatian spirituality) and formal theological sources (the work of individual theologians).[7] Field education embodies Stephen Bevans's "praxis" model of contextual theology and "faith seeking intelligent action."[8] In reflecting theologically, and as

---

6. See Joe Holland and Peter Henriot, *Social Analysis: Linking Faith and Justice* (Maryknoll, NY: Orbis, 1984). JST students prepare papers utilizing the Pastoral Circle. Second-year MDiv students also use the "Shared Wisdom" model of theological reflection, a case study approach for theological reflection. See Jeffrey H. Mahan, Barbara B. Troxell, and Carol J. Allen, *Shared Wisdom: A Guide to Case Study Reflection in Ministry*, 2nd ed. (Nashville: Abingdon Press, 1993).

7. See Helen Cameron et al., *Talking about God in Practice: Theological Action Research and Practical Theology* (London: SCM Press, 2011), 53–56, for references to the "Four Voices in Theology" model of reflection, including operant, espoused, normative, and formal theological sources.

8. See Stephen Bevans, *Models of Contextual Theology*, rev. and exp. ed. (Maryknoll, NY: Orbis, 2002), 70–87.

they navigate complex lived theological realities, students acquire a "practical theological agency."[9] As they foster the "pastoral action" dynamic of the Pastoral Circle, students learn to advocate for others, and sometimes for themselves.

The JST MDiv degree program's emphasis on Ignatian spirituality prompts students to interpret ministerial experience through an Ignatian lens. They reflect on how God is working both within them personally as ministers and in their chosen ministerial and cultural contexts. As students reflect on where God is in their field education experiences, they are invited to discern the movement of spirits, in the Ignatian sense. Students are invited to focus on God and what God is calling them to do in their ministries rather than focusing disproportionately on themselves, a dynamic reflecting the conversion movement of the first week of the *Spiritual Exercises*.[10] Multifaceted realities inform theological reflection, and God's revelation is often encountered in unexpected places.

MDiv students participate in spiritual direction for the duration of the degree. This practice assists students with integrating their field education experiences and their spiritual lives, paying attention to the discernment of spirits, and serves as an important act of ministerial self-care. Given the often challenging and unpredictable demands of the ministerial context, students may find God calling forth latent or undeveloped gifts from them during their experiences. Oftentimes, students continue to hone ministerial gifts they developed prior to coming to JST.

In recent years, field education at St. Patrick Parish, with its shared parish reality, has required JST students to serve the African

---

9. M. Shawn Copeland, "Weaving Memory, Structuring Ritual, Evoking *Mythos*: Commemoration of the Ancestors," in *Invitation to Practical Theology: Catholic Voices and Visions*, ed. Claire E. Wolfteich (New York/Mahwah, NJ: Paulist Press, 2014), 125–48, 130.

10. See David L. Fleming, ed., "Ignatian Exercises and Conversion," in *Ignatian Exercises: Contemporary Annotations* (St. Louis: Review for Religious, 1996), 72–85, 77.

American community, referred to in the parish as the "English-speaking community," and the Latino/a community, referred to as the "Spanish-speaking community." Students have participated in youth ministry, confirmation catechesis, adult faith formation, liturgical ministries, spiritual direction, and other projects. Second-year MDiv Jesuit scholastics participating in field education placements at the parish often engage in transitional diaconate ministries at the parish during the third year of their MDiv degree. International Jesuit STL students also serve at the parish.

History of the JST–St. Patrick Parish Relationship

JST has a long-standing relationship with St. Patrick Parish, forged under the leadership of Fr. Joseph Daoust, SJ, former president of the school.[11] Prior to Joe Daoust's appointment, the faculty decided to adopt "culturally contextualized theology" as a way of doing theology. St. Patrick Parish, selected as a contextual praxis site because it would require ministering to an African American ecclesial community, at the time consisted of a 75 to 80 percent African American population and a smaller Latino/a population. The African American cultural engagement was important because the Jesuit School of Theology at Berkeley, or JSTB, as it was then known,[12] sought to participate in ministry to African American Catholics, a cultural group contrasting with the Euro-American cultural background of

---

11. I am grateful to Fr. Joseph Daoust, SJ, who provided the historical details of the JST–St. Patrick Parish relationship in an interview on May 15, 2015. Fr. Joe Daoust served as president of JST from 1998 to 2008. In addition, I am thankful to JST faculty members William O'Neill, SJ, and George Griener, SJ, for providing various historical facts and information.

12. The Jesuit School of Theology of Santa Clara University was known as the Jesuit School of Theology at Berkeley (JSTB) prior to its merger with Santa Clara University in 2009.

many JST faculty and staff members. Working with the African American parishioners would require ministering to a community with historical experience of slavery and racism in the United States. Ministering to a culture outside of one's own experience would potentially provide a vital opportunity for a minister to examine his or her own personal cultural contextual experience and learn from this encounter. In addition, St. Patrick was chosen because it had experienced economic challenges. The Parish Pastoral Council was informed that JSTB was "coming here because our students want to learn from you how to be good ministers."[13] The parish welcomed and invited JSTB's partnership.

Fr. Timothy Godfrey, SJ, served as pastor for the first five years of the school-parish collaboration (1999–2004). He worked with Sean Carroll, SJ, a scholastic student at the time, who continued to serve the parish after ordination. Faculty member William (Bill) O'Neill lived and served at the parish for four years, and Fr. Mark Ravizza, SJ, served for one year while a scholastic student. All four Jesuits lived in the rectory and participated in the daily life of the parish.[14] Bill O'Neill recalls how, under Timothy and Sean's leadership, the relationship between the school and St. Patrick Parish flourished. Timothy and Sean won the trust of the African American community and initiated ministry for the Hispanic community.

---

13. Daoust, interview.

14. Bill O'Neill, SJ, email to author, May 12, 2018. The second Jesuit pastor was Fr. Gregory Chisholm, SJ (2005–2011). As George Griener, SJ, explained in a May 17, 2018 email to the author, in 1999 JST received a five-year, $1.2 million Lilly Foundation grant for a JST project entitled "The Enhanced Contextual Ministry Program." The program assisted with the implementation of the culturally contextualized study of theology and ministry at JST. The grant sponsored a trio of three-year scholarships for JST lay MDiv students participating in field education placements at parishes in the West Oakland Deanery. One program initiative included the then–Jesuit Community Rector, Charlie Moutenot, SJ; the president, Joe Daoust, SJ; and some Jesuit scholastic students living in a community within the parish.

These Jesuits exemplified the utilization of the Pastoral Circle in their ministry and service of the parish. They also directed a major architectural renovation of the church, built in the 1950s, to emphasize the presence of both cultural groups.[15] For example, as one faces the sanctuary, there is a statue of Our Lady of Guadalupe on the left-hand side of the altar and an image of an African Madonna on the right-hand side, created by a local artist. Gilbert Sunghera, SJ, a Jesuit architect and JSTB student at the time who worked on the renovation, and the late JSTB professor Anne Brotherton, SFCC, facilitated dialogue between the African American and Latino/a communities concerning the re-design of the church.[16]

Historically, as part of the JST–St. Patrick Parish relationship, JST students, administration, faculty, and staff all contributed to parish liturgies and activities.[17] Over the years, JST faculty have worshipped at the parish, with Jesuit faculty and staff regularly presiding at parish liturgies. JST faculty member Professor Gina Hens-Piazza facilitated Bible study groups for parishioners. Bill O'Neill described how his living and working at the parish had a profound influence on his own theology, leading him to give a presentation at the 2002 Annual Convention of the Catholic Theological Society of America (CTSA) entitled "Theology and the Politics of Privilege: A White Theologian's Response to Black Theology."[18]

For a period of six years, as part of the school-parish collaboration, Fr. George Quickley, SJ, the St. Patrick's pastor and JST

---

15. O'Neill, email.

16. Griener, email.

17. As George Griener, SJ, explained in an email to the author, when he served as dean of JST, he and Eduardo Fernández, SJ, occasionally met with those living in the rectory to help discern how the parish involvement would change the school, including its curriculum and pedagogy. As Daoust referenced during his interview, Peter-Hans Kolvenbach, SJ, former Superior General of the Jesuits, visited the school and presided at a liturgy at St. Patrick Parish. At a later date, Fr. Robert McChesney, SJ, who at the time was director of Intercultural Initiatives, served as an advantageous bridge between JST and the parish.

18. O'Neill, email.

adjunct faculty member, facilitated a second-year MDiv field education theological reflection group and study groups for sacramental and liturgical studies courses.[19] St. Patrick parishioners have attended JST liturgies and events at the school, including Advent *Las Posadas* celebrations. Children of the parish have reenacted the story of Our Lady of Guadalupe at the school during her feast day liturgy in December. Parishioners have also volunteered to be directed by JST students training to be spiritual directors during the JST summer Spiritual Direction Practicum.

A JST research project conducted in 2010–2011 under the direction of former staff member Rob McChesney, SJ, required student research assistants to survey and interview St. Patrick parishioners. The survey identified the strengths of the parish, as well as areas for improvement. It also assessed the JST-parish relationship. Eighty-eight percent of St. Patrick parishioner survey respondents stated that the JST-parish relationship was good for the long-term future of the parish, and 100 percent of interviewees affirmed that the relationship had been positive.[20] As the research project findings attest, the St. Patrick Parish–JST relationship has been a mutual blessing and fostered a reciprocal encounter between the school and the parish. The level of school-parish collaboration has varied more recently, perhaps due to the challenging nature of such a relationship. As Joe Daoust recalled, the St. Patrick Parish–JST relationship is unique.[21] A theology school–parish collaboration is a rarity, and a relationship of this kind is difficult to sustain.

---

19. George Quickley, SJ, recently completed his term as pastor and has been replaced by David Masikini, SJ.

20. The research, partially sponsored by the Lilly grant, consisted of twenty-one face-to-face interviews (including ten with participants from the English-speaking community, ten with participants from the Spanish-speaking community, and one with a parishioner who participated in both communities). In addition, 110 English speakers and 108 Spanish speakers participated in surveys distributed during parish Sunday liturgies during the fall of 2010.

21. Daoust, interview with author.

The following contextual theological themes, arising from JST student field education experiences, yield operant models of contextual theology. These insights illustrate how the school-parish relationship assisted the parish and developed the school's contextual imagination.

Contextual Field Education at
St. Patrick Parish

St. Patrick Parish has proven to be a rich context for JST student field education experiences. The contextual field education experiences of JST students at the parish, including data from interviews of five MDiv students and alumni/ae, provide source material for this chapter. The students' ministerial activities encompassed confirmation catechesis and youth ministry, participation in adult education, and liturgical responsibilities.[22] The students' contextual-ministerial skills were enhanced through intercultural encounter and theological reflection within the shared parish context.

The St. Patrick shared parish reality is complex, given the various cultural groups represented by the African American and Latino/a groups. The Latino/a community includes parishioners from Mexico, El Salvador, Guatemala, Honduras, Peru, and Venezuela. The African American community also includes parishioners from Nigerian, Ghanaian, and Kenyan backgrounds. The shared parish reality yields distinct styles of worship and devotional prayer and unique communication patterns and conflict styles. The parish has

---

22. Interview transcripts were coded and categorized using Grounded Theory, a qualitative research method. See Kathy Charmaz, *Constructing Grounded Theory*, 2nd ed. (Thousand Oaks, CA: Sage Publications, 2014). For further information on Grounded Theory, see Deborah Ross, *Research Report on Lay Ecclesial Formation at the Jesuit School of Theology of Santa Clara University* (unpublished report, 2018), 12–13.

celebrated bicultural liturgies encouraging participation of both the African American and Latino/a communities.

JST students and alumni/ae have spoken fondly of the various worship and devotional styles exemplified by parishioners at St. Patrick. The Spanish-speaking community has the tradition of *Las Mañanitas*[23] for Our Lady of Guadalupe, as well as sharing an image of Our Lady of Guadalupe among Latino/a homes in the parish. The English-speaking community embraces unique liturgical practices emphasizing preaching and music. One student recounted parish celebrations for the feast of All Saints Day. This included a display for the Latino/a *Dia de Muertos*, or the Day of the Dead, featuring pictures of dead loved ones and gifts of bread or other food. The parallel English-speaking community liturgical display at the parish featured a cross with an image of Martin Luther King placed in the center.

The vibrant liturgical celebration of cultural diversity at St. Patrick's spoke to students on a personal level. A JST alumna, who worked at the parish for the duration of her MDiv degree, recounted how the intercultural parish dynamic assisted with her ministerial formation:

> These were such strong experiences for me. Going to *Las Mañanitas* for Our Lady of Guadalupe.... Getting there at 5:00 A.M. and the church is packed and there is this Mariachi band blasting music and I was like [laughs], "Oh my gosh, what is happening here?" And always, when I think of St. Patrick, the first thing I think of is the joyful celebration of their faith. It was very new to me, in terms of my white very stoic mid-western [background] who would never be at something like this, and yet you're all here at 5:00 A.M. And I think here, at the time, I was struggling to figure out my own role in the

---

23. *Las Mañanitas* is a morning serenade on a birthday or feast day celebration.

Church and my own understanding of my faith and I felt really drawn to Mary and so being around people who so openly love Our Lady of Guadalupe was really kind of fun to be around them, and inspiring, and kind of helped me, I think, to not be so caught up in my bigger issues with the Church.... To just be with people who seemed so genuinely like they wanted to be there, who wanted to celebrate their faith, who wanted to do it so much they are willing to be there three–four hours before anyone else is up. That is a really important image for me of my experience there.

The African American community at St. Patrick also celebrates its identity and cultural diversity through Black Catholic History Month, the Kwanzaa cultural festival, Martin Luther King, Jr., Day, and Mother's and Father's Day celebrations centering on the roles of African American parenthood. In addition, the African American community organizes parish socials and community-building activities, and participates in political events in the Oakland area.

Given its shared nature, the parish called on JST students and alumni/ae to serve in a variety of ways. One Jesuit student spoke of the ministerial flexibility and adaptability required by the shared nature of the parish, observing that he sometimes felt he prepared homilies for two distinct communities. The cultural reality of the parish created a steep learning curve for students and alumni/ae, given their own cultural backgrounds. A Jesuit alumnus, conscious of his own cultural heritage growing up as an affluent white American, embarked on his ministry at St. Patrick by asking, "So do I know anything about the hood?" Aware that he was from neither the African American nor Latino/a parish cultural group, and having no experience of being an immigrant to the United States, he acknowledged being "out of his comfort zone." While engaging in confirmation group ministry he also interacted with parishioners through a ministry of presence, listening, friendship, and "just spending time." This included his befriending the adult parishioners: "I would get into the kitchen with the African American group when they were doing the fish drive, run the deep fryer, cook with them, and also with the Latinos as best I could, trying to spend as much time as I could with them." This ministry of presence would also include this Jesuit speaking from his own experience and integrating personal experience into homilies when appropriate.

JST students acquired various skills while ministering at St. Patrick Parish. These included classroom management techniques, leading confirmation retreats utilizing minimal resources, and adapting Ignatian spirituality to age-appropriate activities for confirmation classes. Given intercultural and social challenges, students adapted their catechetical styles and content. Observing generational and cultural differences between confirmation teenagers and their parents, students were sensitive to the social and cultural pressures affecting the young adults. Another Jesuit, a Nigerian international student who spent two years ministering at the parish, narrated how he brought ideas and lesson plans to the confirmation group only to quickly learn the group would teach him otherwise. Conscious of the social pressures the teenagers were experiencing, he established a countercultural space where they could safely explore faith issues.

The social and economic challenges experienced by parishioners often required the appropriation of experiences of poverty into students' ministerial praxis. The cultural and social reality of the parish neighborhood made for powerful field education experiences for JST students. Students sometimes faced serious issues of gun violence and gang crime, a lived reality of the parish's geographical context. The American Jesuit alumnus mentioned above ministered at the parish for two years, and recalled a murder taking place outside the parish just as he arrived to lead the weekly confirmation class:

> One time I went out there in the morning to do catechism class; I come around the corner and there was a body in

the street, on the sidewalk, that had been covered and the police were all there. There was a murder that had just happened. So, I go to class and the kids were on their way to class when this happened, and they had actually seen it happen. But the thing that I remember about that was, for the kids, it was like, "Yeah, a guy got shot, you know he was probably doing drugs." Just matter of fact, another day, another murder. And I thought, and I asked them, "Well, you just saw someone get killed, are you OK?" "Yeah." Part of their life. And I just remember thinking to myself, what kind of effect would that have on you as a kid. To live that way every day.

This Jesuit alumnus planned a retreat, hosted at JST, for the confirmation group. During the retreat, he led an exercise for students, inviting them to construct a graph depicting their lives. Despite this Jesuit's extensive prior ministerial experience, he stated that nothing could have prepared him either for confirmation ministry with teenagers at the parish or their stories. He recounted listening to the teenagers' personal experiences of immigration, trauma, violent crime, and on occasion difficult family backgrounds. He commented that "it was like one horrendous thing after another," and the stories were "completely beyond anything I have ever heard before.... [H]ow does that then shape how you would approach something like catechism class?" This alumnus employed sensitive accompaniment skills, consciously trying to "tap into where God is in their very difficult life." As they reflected on their life stories, the confirmation candidates unanimously recognized God being closest to them at their lowest points, a poignant moment of reflection during the retreat. All the retreat participants subsequently attended the sacrament of reconciliation. This unexpected level of participation led to the Jesuit alumnus's realization that "a certain grace opened up there." He was reminded in both ministering to the youth, and in witnessing lay and Jesuit students' collaboration and leadership skills on the retreat, "that God is in control."

The St. Patrick Parish shared reality gave rise to insightful theological reflection on behalf of JST students as they developed their theological reflexivity. The Jesuit alumnus mentioned above spoke of the Ignatian discernment of spirits. He identified the need for parish awareness of the work of the "evil spirit" possibly causing division and turmoil between the two parish communities. The Nigerian Jesuit student shared observations about the distinct Christologies in operation at the parish. He observed that members of the African American community would often identify with Christ as liberator, as they had endured experiences of oppression and racism in the United States. The Latino/a community, by contrast, identified with Christ as suffering servant, a Christology popular in Latin American liberation theology. This student brought awareness of these two operant Christologies into his ministerial work, including confirmation ministry. He also observed the Latino/a community's appreciation of devotional worship and sacramentals, while the African American community emphasized scripture. By establishing a media center at the parish comprising a religious bookstall and library, this student provided faith-formation resources to assist both cultural groups.

Reflection on Doing Contextual Theology with St. Patrick Parish

The JST–St. Patrick Parish relationship provides an operant example of Stephen Bevans's "synthetic" model of contextual theology as described in *Models of Contextual Theology*.[24] The synthetic model is a composite model incorporating Bevans's translation, anthropological, praxis, and countercultural models. The translation model acknowledges adaptation of the Gospel message to a culture. This is manifest at St. Patrick Parish in the bilingual masses and

---

24. See Bevans, *Models of Contextual Theology*, 88–102.

celebrations and in the renovation of the church. The anthropological model seeks to preserve cultural identity and is operative as the parish respects and serves the needs of various cultural groups. The countercultural model is active as the parish, in exercising its social justice initiatives, seeks to stand against the violence in the neighborhood. Parishioners regularly participate in local peace walks. The praxis model expresses "faith seeking intelligent action"[25] and is evident in the parish-school relationship over the years, as well as the parish's outreach to the local community. JST's collaboration operates out of a desire for reflective praxis, especially ministry with a diverse and economically disadvantaged community in the East Bay, and the sharing of faith and cultural perspectives.

A central feature of the "synthetic" model is its emphasis on dialogue. St. Patrick Parish embodies dialogue by catering to the needs of parishioners in a shared context. Dialogue is fostered through shared community life, inculturated devotional and liturgical practices, and collaboration in the everyday operations of the parish. According to Steve Bevans, practitioners of the synthetic model claim that true human growth occurs when human beings are in dialogue.[26] The everyday vicissitudes and demands of shared parish life at St. Patrick, and the necessary ongoing dialogue this invokes, inevitably requires human growth and partnership.

JST, through its St. Patrick Parish relationship, seeks dialogue as it learns from the parish community. The parish community seeks dialogue through the ministerial presence of JST community members. Dialogue also occurs when parishioners and JST students reflect on contemporary culture from a faith perspective, as the previously referenced confirmation ministry demands. A recent JST-led research project involving St. Patrick Parish identified a desire for Ignatian spirituality on behalf of lay ministers at the

---

25. See Bevans, *Models of Contextual Theology*, 70–87.

26. Bevans, *Models of Contextual Theology*, 91.

parish.[27] As part of an ongoing dialogue, JST students and the JST community may share knowledge of Ignatian spiritual practices with interested parishioners. The research also suggested that Ignatian spirituality may act as a bridge between St. Patrick's African American and Latino/a communities, bringing the two communities together as they are continually made aware of, and invited to live, the same spirituality.

As I have reflected on students' field education experiences, the shared nature of the parish, and the JST–St. Patrick Parish relationship, I have considered the importance of the theme of hospitality. Theologian Luke Bretherton, in *Hospitality as Holiness: Christian Witness amidst Moral Diversity*, explores the theme of hospitality and the motif of "guest-host." Bretherton identifies Jesus Christ acting as both guest and host in Luke-Acts. Jesus embodies in his life and ministry a "journeying guest/host" theme. For example, Jesus acts as a guest in the Emmaus story, only to become the host as he breaks bread with his companions. Cleopas, one of the featured guests at the meal, moves from being a guest at the Eucharistic celebration to becoming a host, as he proceeds to proclaim the message of the risen Christ.[28] Hospitality is central to Christian practice. Ultimately, we learn from Jesus serving as both guest and host.

---

27. This JST project led by the Office of Ministerial Formation explored a "spirituality of ownership" at the parish. Lay parishioners from both the African American community and the Latino/a community were invited to participate in focus groups and interviews as the research sought to explore how parish lay ministerial participation could be enhanced. The research findings revealed that the parish has an organic sense of a "spirituality of ownership," as parishioners described highly valued experiences of belonging and commitment. The research recommended exploration of the theme of stewardship as providing a way forward for increased lay participation.

28. Bretherton, *Hospitality as Holiness*, 135–36.

When students embark on their field education placements at the beginning of the school academic year and establish themselves in their placements, I encourage them to reflect on the process of *moving from guest to host*. Students are initially guests in the parish, school, prison, or other ministerial settings of their choosing. Through acquaintance with, and service to, their host communities, students often become ministerial hosts and leaders. The students, as they navigate the sometimes delicate movement from guest to host, are invited to be mindful of those to whom they minister and their new cultural surroundings. The movement from guest to host encompasses listening and observing, the asking of many questions, and engaging in dialogue at the ministerial site.

Encountering and practicing hospitality assists students in their formation as ministerial leaders. One of JST's international Kenyan Jesuit students, assisting with the St. Patrick Parish confirmation group for two years, described his own intercultural engagement at St. Patrick. As he began ministering at the parish, he experienced the challenges of assimilating into a new culture. These included both his unfamiliarity with American culture and the shared cultural dynamics of the parish. The student initially felt out of place, yet he later began to thrive as parishioners were compassionate toward him. He, in return, exercised compassion toward parishioners, and this mutual hospitality enabled him to, in his words, "experience God in what I was doing."

The role of student host in field education situations is varied, involving welcoming the stranger, proclaiming and living God's word, exercising justice and compassion, and ministering in challenging situations, as the examples from St. Patrick Parish demonstrate. Students have responded to God calling them to be servant leaders for their chosen field education communities. Through the exercise of various ministerial practices, students become hosts and Christ-bearers to others while being prompted and guided by the Spirit. These practices are trinitarian and missionary insofar as they are relational, involve dialogue, and are an expression of God's communion in the world.[29] Field education involves *ad-extra* missionary activity in the local community.

St. Patrick Parish's shared structure is illuminated by the guest-host hospitality motif. The shared parish demands that distinct cultural groups host one another and learn to engage in mutual dialogue. The act of journeying from guest to host involves a lived *habitus*, a way of participating in parish life. As the parish navigates from being a predominantly African American parish community to one that is mainly Latino/a, the shared host dynamic will evolve. The African American community at St. Patrick is part of the larger African American Catholic community practicing "uncommon faithfulness"[30] to the Catholic tradition, despite experiences of slavery, oppression, and racism. This group has welcomed the Latino/a community, a powerful example of one cultural group hosting another. A group of African American matriarchal figures, holding long-cherished memories of their lives in the parish, have been central to the parish's lay leadership. These parishioners will continue to guide the parish during its current change in community dynamics. Awareness of the guest-host theological theme may assist the various cultural groups in transition.

The JST–St. Patrick Parish relationship is illuminated by the guest-host theme. St. Patrick Parish hosts JST students for their field education. The students assume leadership positions and become hosts for those to whom they minister. Similarly, JST at times hosts parish retreat days and liturgical celebrations in Berkeley. Hospitality is essential to this school-parish shared dialogical experience. The JST–St. Patrick Parish relationship has reflected

---

29. Stephen B. Bevans and Roger P. Schroeder, in *Prophetic Dialogue: Reflections on Christian Mission Today* (Maryknoll, NY: Orbis, 2011), 24–26, describe missionary practice as trinitarian. The authors state: "God in God's deepest triune nature is a communion-in-mission," 26.

30. See M. Shawn Copeland, "Introduction," in *Uncommon Faithfulness: The Black Catholic Experience*, ed. M. Shawn Copeland (Maryknoll, NY: Orbis, 2009).

"prophetic dialogue"[31] as JST has pursued its mission with the parish and each community has learned from the other. A central facet of both prophetic dialogue and mission is the sacred art of being present to another and listening.[32] The relationship with St. Patrick Parish has encompassed an integral component of JST's contextual-theological narrative and journey. Through engagement with the parish and other field education sites and agencies, JST will continue to exercise its mission with the local community through pastoral accompaniment, dialogical encounter, and shared hospitality.

31. See Bevans and Schroeder, *Prophetic Dialogue*.
32. Bevans and Schroeder, *Prophetic Dialogue*, 20.

Chapter Nine

BECOMING A CONTEXTUAL THEOLOGIAN

DOING ETHICS FROM BELOW

William O'Neill, SJ

When I first went to Africa as a young Jesuit, to the town of Tabora in Tanzania, I found myself charged with the care of young refugee children. Having just completed my language studies, and more naïve than noble, I thought I must simply love the children and all would be well. A fond illusion! For almost immediately, two of the boys began to fight, and as the fighting escalated, I knew I must intervene. To my chagrin, however, I could not remember the word for "stop." So I rushed into the house, found my large dictionary, looked up the Kiswahili for "stop," and with mounting apprehension, thought how to put it in the imperative plural. I recognized then the hard grace of what Dorothy Day, quoting Fr. Zossima in Dostoevsky's *The Brothers Karamazov*, called "love in practice," so different from "love in dreams."[1]

In this chapter I will first say a word about being a contextual theologian, less a state achieved, certainly in my case, than a vocation incrementally realized. I will then consider the fruits of doing contextual theology, touching particularly on the wisdom of "rights talk" from below in the postcolonial African context. Finally, I will

---

1. Dorothy Day, "Our Country Passes from Undeclared to Declared War; We Continue Our Christian Pacifist Stand," *Selected Writings*, ed. Robert Ellsberg (Maryknoll, NY: Orbis, 1998), 264.

explore the pedagogical implications of adopting such a hermeneutic in a curriculum devoted to the practice of contextual theology.

Setting the Stage

As I noted above, my primary responsibility in my years in Tabora was the care of young Hutu refugees from Burundi who had fled ethnic cleansing and the massacre of their parents. Little by little, I came to feel at home in the language, learning its poetry in the mundane work of nurturing children who had suffered such great loss. At the time, we worked closely with Mother Teresa's sisters, whose African novitiate bordered our parish; they had assumed similar responsibility for young girls from the refugee camp. Living in the city offered these children the opportunity to be educated under the generous refugee policy of Julius Nyerere, the first president of Tanzania. Yet the trauma of the children went deep, and often I was overmatched by the demands of their care. It was love in practice, harsh and dreadful at times, but love nonetheless.

I was invited to teach religion in neighboring government secondary schools. Nyerere believed that the pan-African dream of *Ujamaa* required the distinctive religious contributions of Christians, Muslims, and traditional believers alike. In the political literature, *Ujamaa* is often described as "African socialism," but this, I believe, is a misnomer too beholden to Western Cold War polemics. *Jamaa* is the Kiswahili word for extended family, and *Ujamaa* signifies a political philosophy of familyhood extended, analogically, to the nation, African states, and global community.

Writing just as Gustavo Gutiérrez was pioneering liberation theology, Nyerere drew deeply from his Christian African heritage and, in particular, the emerging conciliar and encyclical tradition of his Catholic faith. Long before I began a systematic study of modern human rights rhetoric in the West—the heritage of Locke, Kant, and J. S. Mill—I drew on Nyerere's political wisdom in my teaching. For me, the "first language" of rights was embedded in the wisdom of *Ujamaa*; only later would I learn to translate rights talk into the idiom of Western political thought.

Later doctoral studies at Yale allowed me to explore the differing uses of rights, deepening my sense of the distinctive African contributions to the discourse. My appointment at the Jesuit School of Theology in Berkeley in 1988, following my doctoral studies, coincided with the opening of our school to international students, many seeking ecclesiastical licentiate (STL) or doctoral (STD) degrees. Our students hailed from many countries in the Global South, and their scholarly pursuits reflected the richness of their own traditions as they addressed contemporary crises such as ethnic cleansing, genocide, the gendered reality of HIV/AIDS, and the plight of refugees and forced migrants. My appointment likewise permitted me to teach as a visiting professor at our sister theology school in Nairobi, Hekima (the Kiswahili for "wisdom").

While teaching there in the winter term of 1995, my former rector at Hekima, Augustin Karekezi, SJ, invited me to join him in Rwanda, not long after the horrific genocide that left in its wake over 800,000 massacred. At first I hesitated, since I did not speak French and recognized how little I could contribute in the face of such great suffering. Yet I went, visiting church after church still filled with bodies where victims had sought refuge. At our Jesuit residence in Kigali, the bullet holes were still visible where Jesuit priests and others had been murdered, among the first victims of the genocide for their role in seeking to broker peace.

The horror, the sorrow, the endless tales of suffering compelled me to reimagine my teaching and writing in human rights—how we speak the unspeakable. How we say "never again," yet again. I learned, then, that ethics must begin with witness, with bearing testimony. The following academic year at Berkeley I offered a course I have taught many times since on the ethics of social reconciliation in witness to what Walter Benjamin once called "anamnestic solidarity," the solidarity of remembrance. (I will say more about the course in the final section.)

Later still, while teaching once again at Hekima in 1998, I was offered the opportunity to travel throughout South Africa, attending the amnesty hearings of the Truth and Reconciliation Commission (TRC). Here, too, victims found voice: in the TRC, "our nation," writes Archbishop Desmond Tutu, chair of the TRC, "sought to rehabilitate and affirm the dignity and humanity of those who were cruelly silenced for so long, turned into anonymous, marginalised victims." Here, testimony evokes what was systemically effaced. "Now through the Truth and Reconciliation Commission," writes Tutu, victims "would be empowered to tell their stories, allowed to remember and in this public recounting their individuality and inalienable humanity would be acknowledged."[2]

And yet, as Primo Levi reminds us, there is finally no "price of pain."[3] "This inside me...fights my tongue," says one witness in the Human Rights Committee. "It is...unshareable. It destroys...words"—even in speaking.[4] Perhaps it must be so, this talk of rights where language halts. Yet speak we must, in flawed words and stubborn sounds of witness. This is the burden of anamnestic solidarity; it is, I firmly believe, the place (rhetorical *locus*) of contextual ethics.

Rights Talk

These and kindred experiences have shaped my sense of rights, claims that, in Edward Said's words, bring to word what has been "silenced or rendered unpronounceable."[5] And it is the word of victims we first must hear. Again and again, I am reminded of the

---

2. Desmond Tutu, *No Future without Forgiveness* (London: Rider, 1999), 32–33.

3. Primo Levi, "The Symposium on Simon Wiesenthal," in *The Sunflower: On the Possibilities and Limits of Forgiveness*, rev. ed. (New York: Schocken Books, 1998), 191.

4. Antjie Krog, *Country of My Skull* (Johannesburg: Random House, 1998), 26.

5. Edward W. Said, "Nationalism, Human Rights, and Interpretation," *Raritan* 12, no. 3 (Winter 1993): 45–46.

limits of my understanding; how little I have suffered, how my own privilege—white, male, educated—blinds me. I can never be fully free of prejudice, those tacit prejudgments (what Hans-Georg Gadamer calls the "infinity of the unsaid") that define the horizon of my understanding; but recognizing prejudice little by little is surely the first fruit of contextual theology.

Such prejudices, moreover, are "writ large" on our body politic and its rhetoric of rights. The academy follows suit as, for critic and partisan alike, rights are treated as a mere stepchild of Enlightenment rationalism—the idiom, for Richard Rorty, of "post-modernist bourgeois liberalism."[6] Yet contextual theology teaches us to imagine otherwise; for what we say of rights need not be fixed by Western genealogy. Indeed, I will argue that in popular mobilization "from below," the notion of rights "lives on and transforms itself" in the passionate remembrance of those who suffer and endure.[7]

Let me first say a word about our regnant rhetoric of rights so as to bring into relief the distinctive inflections of contextualized interpretation. For though the origin of modern "subjective rights" may be traced to late twelfth-century canonical jurisprudence, the liberal philosophic tradition has prevailed, fixing our meanings and determining our use. To be sure, many variations are worked on within the tradition, but we may discern a certain family resemblance. For liberalism, as a philosophic doctrine, is typically marked by individualism, abstract formalism, and what we might call methodological agnosticism.

---

6. Richard Rorty, "The Priority of Democracy to Philosophy," in *The Virginia Statute for Religious Freedom: Its Evolution and Consequences in American History*, ed. Merrill D. Peterson and Robert C. Vaughan (New York: Cambridge University Press, 1988), 259.

7. See Jacques Derrida, "*Des Tours de Babel*," in Joseph F. Graham, ed., *Difference in Translation* (Ithaca, NY: Cornell University Press, 1985), 188. Commenting on Walter Benjamin's "The Task of the Translator," Derrida writes: "The translation will truly be a moment in the growth of the original, which will complete itself *in* enlarging itself," 188.

With the eclipse of the traditional ethical ideal of the common good in the sixteenth and seventeenth centuries, the sovereign self reigns supreme. Emancipated from all tutelage of traditional mores and natural social relations, subjective rights emerge as the coin of the realm. No longer does political obligation rest in the civic friendship of the perfect community (*koinonia teleios / communitas perfecta*), but rather in the legal device of a social contract—whether Hobbes's imperious Leviathan, or the more peaceable kingdom of Locke. In modern liberal theory, individual rights precede social duties and constitute the ground of mutual obligation, which, as A. P. d'Entrèves observes, "would not otherwise exist by the law of nature."[8]

Indeed, divested of intrinsic finality (formal and final causality), nature ceases to tell a moral tale.[9] Natural law is "de-theologized" as natural, and later human rights become the currency of a thoroughly disenchanted realm—a lingua franca for religiously pluralist or secular polities. Not surprisingly, then, negative liberty—the liberty in J. S. Mill's words "to pursue our own good in our own way," becomes the foremost right, parsed as our several immunities or negative rights, limited principally by (negative) duties of forbearance. Under the banner of negative freedom, positive delimitations of liberty, for example, that claim rights to adequate nutrition, potable water, education, or healthcare are relegated to an inferior sphere, if not dismissed as mere rhetorical license. Our negative liberties, says Robert Nozick, "fill up the space of rights."[10]

Even as the banner of rights was raised, however, the modern doctrine itself was called into doubt.[11] The "rights of man," wrote Edmund Burke, were a "monstrous fiction" spawning anarchy—

---

8. A. P. d'Entrèves, *Natural Law* (London: Hutchinson, 1970), 55–56.

9. In Aristotelian and Thomistic metaphysics, formal causality refers to the perfected essence of an artifact or natural kind; final causality to its end or *telos*.

10. Robert Nozick, *Anarchy, State, and Utopia* (Oxford: Basil Blackwell, 1974), 238.

11. John Donne, "An Anatomy of the World," in *John Donne: The Complete English Poems*, ed. A. J. Smith (New York: Penguin Books, 1976), lines 205–18, 276. "And new philosophy," says Donne, "calls all in doubt.... Prince, subject,

"false ideas and vain expectations," bringing "ruin" in their wake. For Burke, rights were an "entailed inheritance," resting in the "prejudice" or "latent wisdom" of Englishmen.[12] Jeremy Bentham, too, regarded rights as "the child of [positive] law." For "from real law come real rights," wrote Bentham, "but from imaginary laws, from 'law of nature,' come imaginary rights." "Natural rights" were but "simple nonsense," and "natural and imprescriptible rights, rhetorical nonsense, nonsense upon stilts."[13] For Bentham, as for Burke, natural rights were a dubious progeny, exciting "a spirit of resistance to all laws—a spirit of insurrection against all governments."[14] Still others deplored the want of such a spirit; for Marx, the modern doctrine of rights merely enshrined the proprietary interests of the bourgeoisie.

This dubious heritage of modernity poses a dilemma for contextual theology, for the thin "metanarrative" of *universal* rights preserves the possibility of critique in pluralist polities, but only by abstracting from particular cultural systems. The thick communitarian appeal to *particular* narrative traditions, conversely, enshrines not only our native wisdom, but also our latent "local and ethnocentric" prejudices. Does decrying rampant poverty, gender, race, or ethnic bias, or homophobia imply the liberal "view from nowhere," or can a truly *contextual* theology allow for *theological* critique?

Each of the models of contextual theology developed by Stephen Bevans, I would argue, adopts, to differing degrees, something of a *via media*. None, that is, forsake the possibility of ethical critique

---

father, son, are things forgot, For every man alone thinks he hath got to be a phoenix, and that then can be None of that kind, of which he is, but he."

12. Edmund Burke, *Reflections on the Revolution in France*, 1790, in *Works*, vol. 2 (Bohn's British Classics, London, 1872), 305–6, 412; See also Burleigh Taylor Wilkins, *The Problem of Burke's Political Philosophy* (Oxford: Clarendon Press, 1967), 59–60, 109–10.

13. Jeremy Bentham, "Anarchical Fallacies," in *Works*, vol. 2 (Edinburgh: William Tait, 1843), 523.

14. Bentham, "Anarchical Fallacies," 501.

in acceding to epistemic or moral relativism. Why we attend to those consigned to the margins of society, choose a particular context in comparative studies, or seek to understand in terms of internal validity claims (not imposing our cultural pre-judgments), bespeaks *our* ethical commitments. Can we make sense of them without thoroughly decontextualizing our theology?

Giving Voice

Just here, I believe, we see the originality of non-Western rights talk—rights in the spirit of *Ujamaa* or *Ubuntu*. For neither Nyerere nor Archbishop Desmond Tutu begin with sovereign selves, emancipated from tradition. Neither is "negative" liberty ceded pride of place in a rights regime. Rather, rights are "thickened," even as appeals to a particular narrative tradition are "thinned." Both, as we saw above, look to the concrete universality of dignity that each person, as a moral agent, and not merely a passive recipient of others' agency, is owed equal respect and recognition. Yet such respect and recognition are directed not to a "generalized" other (as in philosophic liberalism), but always to a concrete other enmeshed in an ensemble of social relations. Indeed, the subject in the TRC is less the abstract, sovereign self of classical liberal philosophy than the discursive "we" of *Ubuntu*—that, in Tutu's words, we are persons in and through other persons.

As we saw in the previous section, victims' testimony in the TRC evokes what was systemically effaced. In telling their stories, victims' "individuality and inalienable humanity" was publicly acknowledged.[15] Lukas Baba Sikwepere, blinded in a brutal attack by police in Cape Town and later tortured, testifies:

> I feel what—what has brought my sight back, my eyesight back is to come back here and tell the story. But I feel

---

15. Tutu, *No Future without Forgiveness*, 32–33.

what has been making me sick all the time is the fact that
I couldn't tell my story. But now I—it feels like I got my
sight back by coming here and telling you the story.[16]

Telling the story is, at once, part of Baba Sikwepere's story, what
is woven into collective memory.[17] And so, too, the converse: in
Jean Baudrillard's words, "forgetting the extermination is part of
the extermination itself."[18]

Such a rich, solidaristic conception of dignity enlarges our conception of basic human rights. For if we respect the moral agency
of persons like Baba Sikwepere, we necessarily respect the basic
conditions (or capabilities) of its exercise—not only civil liberties,
but no less, security and subsistence claims. Elaborating African
usage, Julius Nyerere argues eloquently that "those who control a
(person's) livelihood control a (person); his freedom is illusory and
his equal humanity is denied when he depends on others for the

---

16. Testimony of Lukas Baba Sikwepere, at Human Rights Commission hearing in Heideveld, Cape Town; as reported in Krog, *Country of My Skull*, 31;
South African Truth and Reconciliation Commission, *Final Report*, vol. 5,
chap. 9, par. 9.

17. Charles Villa-Vicencio writes: "'Scream as loud as you want; no one will
hear you,' torture victims in apartheid jails were often told by tormentors
who were confident that knowledge of the crimes would never go beyond
the cell walls. The defeat of the apartheid regime offers the opportunity
for the suppressed anguish of these victims to be heard. 'Now there is a
chance for the whole world to hear the victims scream,' Marlene Bosset of
the Cape Town–based Trauma Centre for Victims of Violence and Torture
told The South African Conference on Truth and Reconciliation organized
by the Justice in Transition Project" ("Telling One Another Stories," in
The Reconciliation of Peoples: Challenge to the Churches, ed. Gregory Baum
and Harold Wells [Maryknoll, NY: Orbis, 1997, 37–38]. Villa-Vicencio cites
Marlene Bosset in *Democracy in Action* 8, no. 5 [August 31, 1994]: 16). Villa-
Vicencio led the Research Department of the TRC.

18. Jean Baudrillard, quoted in James E. Young, *The Texture of Memory: Holo-
caust Memorials and Meaning* (New Haven, CT: Yale University Press, 1993),
1; see Martha Minow, *Between Vengeance and Forgiveness: Facing History
after Genocide and Mass Violence* (Boston: Beacon Press, 1998), 118.

right to work and to eat." Such rights, says Nyerere, are not the fruit of noblesse oblige, but of the "equality and human dignity of all those involved. For human dignity involves equality and freedom, and relations of mutual respect among men and women."[19]

The richer conception of basic rights likewise thickens our conception of duties. For basic human rights, as a "morality of the depths," imply not only duties of forbearance, but "positive" duties to protect persons against systemic deprivation, and duties of provision, both personal and systemic. For both Nyerere and Tutu, instantiating a rights regime bids us to ask how best duties of forbearance, protection, and provision can be realized in a given context. But attending to such systemic realization compels us to ask first whose equal dignity and rights have been systemically denied or threatened. It is thus the very equality of persons that enjoins our "preferential option for poor," where the poor are understood to comprise not only those suffering from economic deprivation, but from any systemic violation of basic human rights.

Ethics, as in the TRC, thus begins with victims' testimony, giving voice. And indeed, counting prominently among basic rights (rights presumed for the fulfillment of agential rights) is that of "effective participation." In the rights' theorist Henry Shue's words, those most affected by public policy should have the greatest say. The suasive force of basic human rights thus appears when those consigned to society's margins speak, when they bring to word what has been "silenced or rendered unpronounceable." And it is thus that we speak of the hermeneutical privilege of the poor, for example, in the testimony of victims.

The instantiation of a rights regime will always, then, be contextual, tailored to the particular conditions or context of both social

---

19. Julius Nyerere, *"Kanisa na Maisha ya Watu,"* in *Binadamu na Maendeleo* (Dar es Salaam: Oxford University Press, 1974), 97–98. My adaptation of the English translation, "The Church's Role in Society," in *A Reader in African Christian Theology,* ed. John Parratt (London: SPCK, 1987), 121, in light of the *Kiswahili* text.

and interpersonal redress. In the spirit of *Ujamaa* or *Ubuntu*, then, rights appear as less a metanarrative or the culturally specific narrative of the Western bourgeoisie than a narrative grammar. As in the Human Rights Committee of the TRC, rights talk is less talk about rights than the talk—for example, victims' testimony— that rights make possible. Rights, that is, function performatively, letting victims' stories be heard *as* testimony, evoking anamnestic solidarity of those testifying with those who hear their stories.

In victims' testimony, the TRC revealed the systemic distortions and evasions of apartheid; no mitigating redescription of apartheid would henceforth serve.[20] But the disclosure of atrocity is a clearing for new stories to be told—in Martha Minow's words, "a new national narrative."[21] In the "uniquely public testimony" of the TRC, memory speaks.[22] Testifying of being tortured at the age of sixteen, says Mzykisi Mdidimba, has "taken it off my heart":

> When I have told stories of my life before, afterward I am crying, crying, crying, and felt it was not finished. This time, I know what they've done to me will be among these people and all over the country. I have some sort of crying, but also joy inside.[23]

---

20. See Kader Asmal, Louise Asmal, and Ronald Suresh Roberts, *Reconciliation through Truth: A Reckoning of Apartheid's Criminal Governance* (Cape Town and Johannesburg: David Philip, 1996), 7. "It is simply shortsighted, not canny *realpolitik*, to ignore or suppress the moral distinctions between the battle to preserve apartheid and the battle to abolish it. South Africa cannot afford this brand of playground relativism, so what might seem obvious needs meticulous re-emphasis: Apartheid was evil. It was a crime against humanity."

21. Minow, *Between Vengeance and Forgiveness*, 78.

22. Wilhelm Verwoerd, "Continuing the Discussion: Reflections from Within the Truth and Reconciliation Commission," *Current Writings* 8, no. 2 (1996): 70.

23. Tina Rosenberg, "A Reporter at Large: Recovering from Apartheid," *New Yorker* (November 18, 1996), 92.

What Wole Soyinka calls "the burden of memory" is borne in such testimony.[24] Wounded memory,[25] "trauma's *lived* memory," in Gobodo-Madikizela's words, speaks "among these people and all over the country."[26] Such storied use of rights, as the grammar of narration, privileges those like Baba Sikwepere and Mzykisi Mdidimba, "who were cruelly silenced for so long, turned into anonymous, marginalised victims."

As in the TRC, basic rights and correlative duties must be embodied or schematized in testimony and in the body of testimony, forming what Charles Villa-Vicencio, research director of the TRC, calls "the greater story that unites." For rights, we argued, are neither abstract metanarrative nor the particular narrative of the "postmodernist, liberal bourgeoisie," but the grammar of "telling you the story." And, as in the TRC, the story may be godly. We need not trim Nyerere's speeches or Tutu's homilies of all religious reference—there is room for re-enchantment of the world.

In December 1992, Mandela himself acknowledged the role the "confessing" churches played in opposing apartheid and urged them to act "as a midwife to the birth of our democracy."[27] The maieutic

---

24. Wole Soyinka, *The Burden of Memory, The Muse of Forgiveness* (New York: Oxford University Press, 1999).

25. See Judge Ismail Mahomed of the TRC, "Constitutional Court of South Africa, Case no. CCT 117/96 (July 25, 1996), Azanian Peoples Organization (AZAPO) and Others vs President of the Republic of South Africa and Others"; as cited in Tutu, *No Future without Forgiveness*, 29. Judge Mahomed was then deputy president of the Constitutional Court. Pumla Gobodo-Madikizela observes that the "narratives of trauma…are not simply about facts. They are primarily about the impact of those facts on victims' lives and about the painful continuities created by the violence in their lives.… The lived experience of traumatic memory becomes a touchstone for reality…" (Pumla Gobodo-Madikizela, *A Human Being Died That Night: A South African Woman Confronts the Legacy of Apartheid* [Boston: Houghton Mifflin, 2003], 86, 90).

26. Gobodo-Madikizela, *A Human Being Died That Night*, 90.

27. Nelson Mandela, speech delivered to the Free Ethiopian Church of Southern Africa, Potchefstroom, December 14, 1992, as cited in John W. de Gruchy, "The Dialectic of Reconciliation," in *The Reconciliation of Peoples*, 23.

role of the churches appears not only in the religiously integrated critique of apartheid, but (re)constructively, in the "narrative project" of the TRC. "[F]rom the beginning," says Antjie Krog, Tutu "unambiguously mantled the commission in Christian language."[28] The TRC was supported by major religious groups, and religious symbolism (tropes, ritual, etc.) permeated the hearings. The Commission, said Tutu, "accepted my call for prayer at the beginning and end of our meetings, and at midday when I asked for a pause for recollection and prayer." Religious motifs of reconciliation and forgiveness were sounded in the Human Rights Violations Committee when

> we agreed that when victims and survivors came to our victim-oriented hearing to testify about their often heart-rending experiences, we would have a solemn atmosphere with prayers, hymns and ritual candle lighting to commemorate those who had died in the struggle.[29]

Not only does Tutu's *Ubuntu* theology ground his rhetoric of rights and critique of apartheid as "heresy," but the TRC itself becomes a rite of public reasoning—the *locus/topos* of rights "on holy ground." Rights rhetoric is framed or schematized in Christian narrative. At the very first meeting of the Human Rights Violations Committee (December 16, 1995), Tutu announced: "We will be engaging in what should be a corporate nationwide process of healing through contrition, confession and forgiveness."[30] Of such "nonpublic" religious reasons, Tutu writes: "Very few people objected to the heavy spiritual, and indeed Christian, emphasis on the Commission.[31]

---

28. Krog, *Country of My Skull*, 153.

29. Tutu, *No Future without Forgiveness*, 72.

30. Tutu, as quoted in Susan V. Gallagher, *Truth and Reconciliation: The Confessional Mode in South African Literature* (Portsmouth, NH: Heinemann, 2002), 118.

31. Tutu, *No Future without Forgiveness*, 72.

Conclusions and Application

In the previous section, I've adumbrated a modest contextual interpretation of rights, in the spirit of *Ujamaa* and *Ubuntu*. In either case, the performative practice of rights, incorporated in both personal and national narrative, is deeply contextual. In victims' testimony, rights talk loses the patina of individualism, abstract formalism, and methodological agnosticism it has acquired in Western liberal theory, inviting us to reimagine rights from below.

In the first section, I touched on several of the formative experiences that have and continue to shape me, little by little, as a contextual theologian. In the second section, I explored the fruits of doing contextual theology in giving voice to rights from a postcolonial African perspective. Let me now reflect briefly on the pedagogical implications of such a contextual theology of rights. For if we are, as Gutiérrez urges, to take the victims' side, we must begin with their questions. This is the first hermeneutical desideratum: what questions inform our study, guide our reading, nourish our scholarship? And the second follows closely: what resources do we draw on? Have we incorporated the richly textured stories of those "silenced for so long"? Does their wisdom temper our scholarship? And finally, and most critically, to whom are we accountable? In the course on the ethics of social reconciliation I have taught since my time in Rwanda, I have sought as best I could to heed these questions.

As I traveled through Rwanda in the wake of the genocide, I began to think of my teaching and scholarship as bearing witness, as testimony. How do we imagine evil, bring to word what Levinas says is the first command against killing, and the first transgression? In a course I have offered regularly, The Ethics of Social Reconciliation, we begin with Wiesenthal's harrowing autobiographical tale of the *Shoah* in *The Sunflower*. Wiesenthal introduces his readers to a symposium on the nature and limits of forgiveness from a variety of religious traditions, and our students add their voices, reflecting on the Rwandan genocide, apartheid and the TRC, ethnic cleansing in Bosnia, and endemic racism in the United States. The students "read" the assigned texts from the perspective of their own experiences and against the backdrop of ecumenical and interreligious dialogue (including traditional or indigenous religious wisdom, for example, *Ubuntu* in South Africa and *gacaca* in Rwanda).

In the years I've offered the course, a Rwandan student who had lost most of his family wrote a remarkable paper on the theology of reconciliation and forgiveness, a Vietnamese student wrote of the reconciling role of the Vietnamese church, and a Filipina American student drew on postcolonial criticism in exploring the reconciliation of Christian churches with Native American and First Nation peoples. Other African and Malagasy students considered strategies to redress civil strife in their home countries, and several American students wrote tellingly of the heritage of White privilege and racism. One, a Jesuit theologian, recounted the troubled history of Jesuit slaveholding and the need for reparation. Our seminar ends by revisiting *The Sunflower* as the students share the fruits of their research. They too have borne witness, often more eloquently than I, teaching their teacher what it means to become a contextual theologian.

Chapter Ten

MEETING OTHERS
ON HOLY GROUND
THE INTERCULTURAL CONTEXT OF
INTERRELIGIOUS EDUCATION
Anh Q. Tran, SJ

Introduction

Nepal, January 2014. After an exhausting flight from San Francisco via Seoul and Thailand, our group of ten students and a faculty member from Berkeley, California, arrived at the snow land of the Himalayas to begin our interreligious immersion among Tibetan Buddhists. For the next three weeks, we stayed in a guest house attached to a Tibetan monastery in Boudhanath, a center of Tibetan Buddhism in Kathmandu, eating vegetarian food and engaging in theological and spiritual exchanges with Nepalese and other Western expatriates who were interested in Christian-Buddhist dialogue. This educational trip was one of the many immersions that the Jesuit School of Theology of Santa Clara University (JST) has organized for its students of theology and ministry since 2003, as a way to implement contextual learning in theological education, which has been a feature at JST for the past two decades or so.

In 1995, the most authoritative deliberative body of the Society of Jesus met in Rome to conduct its 34th General Congregation in the 455-year history of the Jesuits. One major recommendation to come out of the ensuing decrees by the Jesuit delegates from around the world was a call for greater emphasis on interreligious dialogue.

As a way to implement the recommendation of Decree 5 of the 34th General Congregation on *Mission and Interreligious Dialogue*, the Jesuit School of Theology—a member school of the Graduate Theological Union (GTU)—began to revise its master of divinity curriculum to include ecumenism and/or interreligious learning as a specific requirement for future priests and lay ecclesial ministers.

This essay is an attempt to share the experience of interreligious learning that has taken place at JST in the past decade and that has shaped our evolved understanding of ministerial formation for Jesuits and lay ecclesial partners in ministry.[1] A recent Association of Theological Schools (ATS) study on the need for multi-faith competency in church ministry highlights significant features of the contextual theological model that contributes to successful interreligious encounters.[2] This goal is to be achieved in one of several ways: (1) taking a class in world religions or specific traditions, (2) involvement in some local interfaith ministry as part of a student's field-work, or (3) participation in an interreligious immersion program. These initiatives are designed to ensure that future pastoral ministers and priests will have some exposure to non-Christian religious and cultural traditions that have been very much a part of the American social fabric over the past fifty years or so.[3] The emphasis on collaborative learning, local and

1. A portion of this essay reflects the contribution of Rev. Robert McChesney, SJ, of JST, and Prof. Marianne Farina, CSC, of the Dominican School of Philosophy and Theology (another member school of the GTU) following the 2015 Indonesia Muslim-Christian immersion. See Marianne Farina and Robert W. McChesney, "A Contextual Model for Interreligious Learning," in *Teaching Interreligious Encounters*, ed. Marc A. Pugliese and Alexander Y. Hwang (Oxford: Oxford University Press, 2017), 276–96. The author is grateful to Prof. Farina, who co-led this immersion experience and shared her perspective on Christian/Muslim dialogue.

2. Stephen R. Graham, "Christian Hospitality and Pastoral Practices in a Multifaith Society: An ATS Project 2010–2012," *Theological Education* 47, no. 1 (2012): 1–10.

3. Since the Immigrant Act (1965), there has been an increased flow of immigrants from Asia and Africa that bring with them diverse religious traditions. See a survey by Diana L. Eck, *A New Religious America: How a*

global encounters, and a holistic process underline how JST's interreligious immersions draw on developments in contextual theology.

Our Context

The Jesuit School of Theology located in Berkeley, California, has been an integral part of the ecumenical GTU since 1969, long before its recent affiliation with Santa Clara University.[4] Joining the GTU allowed JST to increase its exposure to other Christian denominations and their theologies. Throughout the years, the GTU has expanded to include centers of religious learning in addition to Christian schools of theology. At the present time, in addition to the eight member schools,[5] four of the eleven affiliated centers provide classes and programs for the study of non-Christian traditions.[6]

Interreligious learning at the GTU has been an integral feature for decades. Given the diverse religious backgrounds of member schools and affiliated centers, the GTU offers a variety of classes

---

"*Christian Country*" *Has Become the World's Most Religiously Diverse Nation* (San Francisco: HarperSanFrancisco, 2001).

4. In response to Vatican II's direction on priestly formation, the Alma College of the Jesuit California Province relocated from the rural Los Gatos to the college city of Berkeley. Alma College was renamed the Jesuit School of Theology at Berkeley (JSTB) and eventually became one of the two Jesuit pontifical theological centers in the United States (now one of three in North America, counting Regis College in Toronto, Canada) that provide graduate theological training for ministry and research.

5. They are: American Baptist Seminary of the West, Christian Divinity School of the Pacific (Anglican), Dominican School of Philosophy and Theology, Jesuit School of Theology, Pacific Lutheran Theological Seminary, Pacific School of Religion (ecumenical), San Francisco Theological Seminary (Presbyterian), and Starr King School of Ministry (Unitarian). The Franciscan School of Theology also was a member of the GTU from 1968 to 2013.

6. They are the Richard S. Dinner Center for Jewish Studies, the Institute of Buddhist Studies, the Center for Islamic Studies, and the latest addition, the Mira and Ajay Shingal Center for Dharma Studies.

that can lead to an MA in interreligious studies (and a PhD in the foreseeable future) in addition to the existing MA/certificate in specific religious traditions such as Buddhism, Islam, Judaism, and Hinduism, or a general course on Asian religious traditions. In addition to classes on interreligious dialogue for Christians with Buddhist, Muslim, or Hindu partners offered at the GTU, JST faculty also offer coursework in missiology, the theology of religions, and, recently, comparative theology/religion. The richness and diversity of our faculty and students facilitate interreligious learning within the classroom. Many GTU faculty team-teach a class, or give lectures derived from their own religious background and research interest, in each other's schools.

Generally, interreligious learning coursework includes the comparative theological study of one or more religious traditions from a Christian perspective. Because the majority of our students are seminarians, religious brothers and sisters, and lay men and women who are in training for ministry and teaching, the experiential component is frequently emphasized. Often in a class on world religions, missiology, or interfaith dialogue, students are required to engage another tradition not of their own, learn from each other, and then report back their own learning to the class. In addition, community engagement outside of the classroom is encouraged. To facilitate the interfaith engagement, fieldwork in a local interfaith initiative is also available. For example, the student can be trained in Buddhist chaplaincy or in another form of ministry to meet the religious needs of the non-Christian population in the Bay Area—in a hospital, social center, or prison.

Judith Berling, one of GTU's former academic deans, devised an academic guidebook for interreligious education that helps facilitate the learning process and approach to other religious traditions.[7] Berling developed a "beyond-the-classroom" approach, advocating

---

7. Judith A. Berling, *Understanding Other Religious Worlds: A Guide to Interreligious Education* (Maryknoll, NY: Orbis, 2004).

that religious knowledge is constructed through conversation rather than receiving information. She proposed that students should "speak from their own experiences and to hear and understand others across the line of differences," rather than relying on "theories that offer a monocultural perspective on 'objective' knowledge."[8] By providing a praxis-based involvement in an interfaith ministry or initiative, the desired learning outcome of these experiences is mutual understanding, enrichment, and possible peaceful coexistence. Hospitality and bridge-building are often emphasized.

Although these approaches are valuable, they tend to operate within the greater American context where Christianity is still the major player. Most interreligious learning takes place in the classroom or in exchanges with the local religious bodies in the San Francisco Bay Area. Students, therefore, have not had the opportunity to experience world religions in their native cultural settings and, more importantly, to understand and feel what is it like to be a religious minority.

Interreligious Learning through the Immersion Program

In 2004, the Jesuit School of Theology was awarded a multi-year grant by the Lilly Endowment to pursue an initiative entitled "Making Connections." One of the goals of the initiative's successful proposal was to "institutionalize our curricular offerings of theological immersion experiences in Pacific Rim cultures." The proposal went on to note the institutional optimism "that these exchanges and immersions can become an integral part of our pastoral education in the cultures shaping the American Church." The proposal language centered on Pacific Rim cultures and did

---

8. Berling, *Understanding Other Religious Worlds*, x. She elaborates on this approach in chapter 7 of the book, 110–26.

not specifically identify the international immersions envisioned as "interreligious." However, shaped by the subsequent emphasis of the Jesuit 34th General Congregation, JST moved to establish an interreligious focus for its program.

The JST interreligious immersion program provides students with a unique opportunity to study a religious tradition other than their own in native settings. Particular courses examine the teachings and historical developments of a tradition, as well as selected sacred texts and spiritual practices. During the immersion, students also have opportunities to experience interfaith relations in their native, contextualized settings through interaction with host communities and institutions. Additionally, opportunities are provided to experience ritual, devotional, and spiritual practices of these traditions. Each immersion has three basic components—interreligious learning through theological exchange, interreligious encounter through visiting and meeting others, and interreligious spiritual experience through participation in worship and retreats.

The annual program begins with coursework during a semester in Berkeley, California, followed by a three- to four-week immersion in a country during the school intersession. Recent destinations have included India, Indonesia, the Holy Land, and Nepal.[9] In preparation for this theological exchange, the students learn the basic beliefs and practices of a tradition by examining selective passages from the tradition's sacred texts and history. This is explored in coursework at JST. In addition, students learn about the social, cultural, and political setting of the country wherein the immersion will take place. Often the coursework is designed around a theme

---

9. JST's immersion sites between 2004 and 2018 have been South India (2004, 2005, 2007, 2017), North India (2009, 2010, 2013), Yogyakarta, Indonesia (2006, 2008, 2011, 2015), Kathmandu, Nepal (2009, 2012, 2014), and Jerusalem, Israel (2014, 2016, 2018). There have also been immersion or pilgrimage trips to Mexico or Spain, but not necessarily with an interreligious focus. For an experience of interreligious learning in Nepal led by my colleague Prof. Thomas Cattoi, see "Reading Ignatius in Kathmandu: Toward a New Pedagogy of Interreligious Dialogue," in *Teaching Interreligious Encounters*, 208–19.

that can be explored further during the actual immersion trip. For example, the 2015 immersion to Indonesia was an exploration on "A Common Word"—a topic inspired by the open letter written by 138 Muslim scholars and religious leaders to Christians in 2007 as a response to Pope Benedict XVI's Regensburg address.[10] By using a Muslim document rather than Catholic magisterial teachings, the students were prepared to dialogue with Muslims on their home ground, using their methodology and approach.

In the immersions, academic learning continues in the host country. In Kathmandu or Yogyakarta, for example, the students joined fellow students from other traditions, mostly from the host country's universities or learning centers, for a short course taught by local teachers, religious leaders, or professors, and our Christian faculty. Topics ranged from theoretical concerns—the principle and meaning of interfaith dialogue, interpretation of sacred texts, comparative perspectives on doctrinal beliefs—to practical issues in ethics and society and theological reflections on interfaith relations. Lectures, group discussions, and meals shared between JST students and their fellow classmates broke down barriers and suspicion, and allowed interreligious friendship to emerge.

The goals of the interreligious encounter are met by various pilgrimages and visitations to holy sites, as well as meetings with local peoples. For example, while in Yogyakarta, Indonesia, the students visited the Prambanan Hindu temple complex, Borobudur Buddhist temple compound, Tembayat Muslim shrine, and Catholic shrines of the Sacred Heart in Ganjuran and of Mary in Sendangsono (Muntilan). Cultural exchanges included trips to the Royal Palace of Yogyakarta, a farm commune in Ganjuran, and various local mosques, Islamic boarding houses, and churches. Going to these sites was a kind of pilgrimage for JST students in that they connected to the history and culture of the local people. An important encounter

---

10. "The ACW Letter," A Common Word (2007 CE, 1428 A.H.), http://www
.acommonword.com/the-acw-document/.

involved students living with a host family for a short-term overnight or weekend stay, which provided an opportunity to experience hospitality and friendship. Cultural exchanges often took place around food, entertainment, and learning about day-to-day life.

Another important aspect of an immersion is the opportunity for our Christian students to experience what it is like to be a minority in a non-Christian country. For some, it is an eye-opening experience. Through working with the Sisters of Charity and serving the poorest of the poor in Kathmandu, one student described God challenging her to recognize the reality of poverty in her own country and not to be afraid to touch this reality. The experience helped to solidify her desire to be an advocate for the poor and the needy. The encounter with local Christians also helps students to grow in their own faith. Another student recalled his experience of attending Mass at the local cathedral. The spiritual encounters with Buddhist and Hindu rituals were wonderful and enriching, but his heart felt full when he saw a Catholic Church and worshipped with fellow Catholics, all of whom had stories to share about why they were there.

Direct spiritual or religious experience of the other takes place when one is encouraged to participate in his or her worship or rituals. The students enter a house of worship on a regular basis to observe how the religious faithful carry out their daily and weekly rituals. One student engaged in a prayerful daily walk around the Buddhist shrine (*stupa*) in the neighborhood. On several occasions he went to pray in the *stupa*, and there experienced God's presence in the gazing eyes of the Buddha. For him, though professing a different faith than that of the local Nepali, he realized that people are looking for the same experience, that is, a relationship with the transcendent that raises them from their sense of emptiness.

Depending on timing and availability, participation in a local religious festival is also an eye-opening experience. Immediately upon their arrival at Yogyakarta, our students were invited to a local festival, and they participated with enthusiasm along with the local people. Laughter and sharing were common in such activities.

Further, the students integrate this experiential learning by making a five-day group retreat in a local ashram (India), Buddhist monastery (Nepal), or a religious center (Indonesia). Jointly guided by a faith leader of that tradition and a Catholic director, the students learn to meditate on the words of wisdom from scriptural texts and spiritual writings from both traditions. It is a time to integrate the immersion experience into their own spiritual lives. At other times it is an opportunity to learn a new way of prayer—for example, yogic practice or Buddhist meditation.

Interreligious Learning as a Form of Contextual Learning

Interreligious pedagogy through direct contact with the religious other fits well within the culturally contextual approach to theological studies and reflection advocated at JST. According to the Catholic missiologist Steven Bevans in his *Model of Contextual Theology*, all theologies are "contextual theologies."[11] Bevans argues that what makes contextual theology *contextual* is that it takes the present experience and situation of individuals and communities as the point of departure for theology (*locus theologicus*). If theology is an interpreted response of the revelatory message—in particular of the Christ event—then every generation of Christians, in different eras and locations, will express the content of faith using the language and thought pattern of their space and time. As such, there is no theology without a context.

In a culturally contextual pedagogy, theological reflection takes seriously the culture, history, and social location of oneself and of individuals and groups as sources of theological reflection. During interreligious immersions, students develop intercultural and

---

11. Stephen B. Bevans, *Models of Contextual Theology*, rev. and exp. ed. (Maryknoll, NY: Orbis, 2002), 4.

interreligious competency through their engagements with members of other faiths, either at home or abroad. Our immersion experience has shown that it is not enough to learn *about* a religion or culture; we must learn *with* those active in it. It broadly involves both teaching and learning about the process of crossing all kinds of boundaries, especially overcoming cultural and religious barriers.

Each immersion course includes opportunities for comparative studies, direct dialogue, religious experience, theological reflection, and engagement with multi-religious communities and institutions both in the San Francisco Bay Area and abroad. The goal is to make these courses into interreligious encounters between JST students and their peers from other religious traditions, as well providing the opportunity for similar interreligious encounters for participating faculty. Ideally, the interreligious encounter begins at home and from the outset, in the fall semester classroom and in the planning for the subsequent in-country experience. Using this approach, students develop a deeper understanding of various religious traditions, interreligious dialogue, and the complex realities of these traditions in their local settings. And in this way they learn to deconstruct grand schemes of a religious tradition while awakening in themselves a critical awareness of the need for a construction of local theologies in their own tradition.

This contextual approach contributes positively toward growth in a graduate student's interreligious learning and ministerial training. Throughout the immersion in a host country, JST students and faculty have opportunities to experience the fourfold dialogue promoted by the Church—the dialogues of life, of common action, of theological exchange, and of religious experience.[12] This approach to interreligious learning thus allows the student to engage the religious other in various settings:

---

12. This fourfold dialogue approach is suggested by the Pontifical Council for Interreligious Dialogue in *Dialogue and Proclamation* (1991), http://www.vatican.va/roman_curia/pontifical_councils/interelg/documents/rc_pc_interelg_doc_19051991_dialogue-and-proclamatio_en.html.

- As a *dialogue of life*, students share their lives by spending time with their hosts in meals and recreation. This is also where they will learn the culture of the host country.
- As a *dialogue of action*, students learn about the socioeconomic conditions of the host country and, where possible, engage in volunteer charitable work led by a social agency at home, by one in the host country, or both.
- As a *dialogue of conceptual or theological exchange*, students study the other's religious texts, histories, and issues—both at home before the immersion and in lively on-site discussions with students and teachers from other traditions. It is one thing to learn Buddhism from a Christian teacher and another to learn it from a Buddhist practitioner, lay or monk.
- As a *dialogue of religious experience*, students undergo three- to five-day retreats conducted by a practitioner or adherent of the other religious tradition. This includes experiencing mysticism and spiritual practices present in unique religious traditions. One assumes this would include openness to certain ritual and liturgical practices.

For students and faculty, the dialogue is not about acquiring information or discussion but about formation and transformation. Each encounter with the other, great or small, is an opportunity for the heart to become more loving and more caring. This fourfold dialogue solidifies the student's experience of the religious other and prompts him or her to engage in an interior or introspective dialogue that may lead to a change in attitude toward members of other religions. In doing so, students (and even faculty) acquire a degree of "cultural/religious intelligence" that helps dispel fear, prejudice, or misunderstanding.

At the debriefing back in Berkeley, most students agreed that the immersion had been a life-changing experience for them. Not only did they gain insight into their own identity, but also into how to deal with otherness. They deepened their religious commitment and became open to others' ideas, faith, and devotion. They were aware of the uneasy yet liberated tension in their hearts during the immersion. This tension was attributed to a Western, conservative, and doctrinal approach to Christianity, one that potentially isolates Jesus Christ from others, in contrast to a more Eastern approach to Christianity, that is open to other faiths and embraces religious diversity. The lessons from an encounter with the religious other will be with them beyond their ministerial formation and academic learning.

Interreligious Friendship

In JST immersions, we recognize that religions are living realities, not simply objects for study. The theological approach of religious learning through direct encounters can loosely be identified as a "friendship model," a model that could date back to the time of Matteo Ricci in sixteenth-century China. Ricci himself advocated for creating the necessary space for a mutual witnessing of faith and practice.[13] James Fredericks has eloquently shown that interreligious friendship is itself a virtue enhancing our capacity for lifelong learning about God and others.[14] We design our courses so that engagement with local communities is a vital source of theological learning.

The JST's 2015 Indonesian immersion course is a good case in point.[15] The immersion began in Berkeley during the fall semester

---

13. One of his first Chinese books and the best seller of its time was *Jiao-yu lun* [On Friendship]. For an English translation, see Timothy Billings, *On Friendship: One Hundred Maxims for a Chinese Prince* (New York: Columbia University Press, 2009).

14. James L. Fredericks, "Interreligious Friendship: A New Theological Virtue," *Journal of Ecumenical Studies* 35, no. 2 (Spring 1998): 159–60. Also see James L. Fredericks and Tracy Sayuki Tiemeier, eds., *Interreligious Friendship after* Nostra Aetate (New York: Palgrave Macmillan, 2015).

15. I have written about this immersion for the Jesuit Asia Pacific Conference. See "A Common Word: An Interfaith Experience of Islam," March 25, 2015, http://www.sjapc.net/2015/03/common-word-interfaith-experience-islam/.

by connecting the participants in the course with Bay Area Indonesian communities, both Catholic and Muslim, and through classroom discussions and participation in social events and prayer exercises. Engagement with these communities enhanced our understanding of Indonesia's reality. Prior to our trip, we already knew something about Indonesian cultures, religions, and politics, as well as the challenges and concerns that awaited us on the trip.

Academic study is enhanced by students participating in group discussions and informal gatherings with Indonesian students and faculty, both at home and in the host country. These experiences provide an important forum for our students and their fellow interlocutors to share their histories, cultures, and concerns, the critical context for theological study. The diverse types of encounter complement the interdisciplinary character of the course itself, which in the context of the immersion includes textual study, retreat/prayer days, visits to the host country's families and groups, as well as formal dialogue events. Throughout the immersion, JST students continue to learn about Indonesia through encounters with Christian, Muslim, Buddhist, and Hindu communities and visits to their villages and sacred sites. Finally, back home, the JST and GTU communities, as well as the public, are invited to a presentation by and conversation with the cohort. The 2015 immersion presentation featured an original short video narrative shot in-country by one of the JST students.[16]

As noted above, our methodology links interpersonal visits in both the home and host country's communities with formal study. These are opportunities for spiritual sharing and dialogue about various issues, especially the challenges facing religious communities in these settings. Such collaboration with social and religious community leaders in different countries is an essential aspect of studying texts contextually. This curriculum connects two types of

---

16. This video may be seen at "Interreligious Dialogue Yogyakarta 2015," May 19, 2015, https://www.youtube.com/watch?time_continue=8&v=hqac OuOGggY.

contextual approaches: the ethnographic, which emphasizes respect for a cultural identity, and the liberation approach, which is devoted to uncovering the "forces of oppression, struggle, violence, and power" in a culture.[17] We engage in a process that "gives voice to the theology of the community" to enhance its self-understanding—that is, what God calls the community to be and to do and the community's response in a particular place and time.[18]

Lifelong Learning

The learning experience in Berkeley extended to Indonesia and continued with the partnerships that were formed during the immersion. Ideally, immersion experiences continue to bear fruit once participants are back home—for example, in later interreligious encounters that flow from these experiences, such as initiatives for comparative study and interreligious cooperative projects in students' ministry settings or academic programs. In this way, the time spent at the immersion site constitutes only the initial experience of the interfaith learning process. Interreligious engagement is the whole of the course, from application through evaluation, and eventually into pastoral ministry, subsequent studies, and civic participation.

The interreligious engagements resulting from these immersions contribute to a culture of respectful dialogue. Students typically report that they return home from the interreligious retreat more knowledgeable about, and sympathetic to, the religious practice, cosmology, and sacred texts of other believers, and experiencing more dedication to their own religious traditions and rituals.[19] Such

---

17. Robert J. Schreiter, *Constructing Local Theologies* (Maryknoll, NY: Orbis, 1985), 14–15.

18. Schreiter, *Constructing Local Theologies*, 20.

19. This common experience undercuts fears that such interreligious encounters might diminish identification with one's own tradition. The reverse is evidently more likely.

comparative interreligious experiences deriving from this close encounter with other believers are a special feature of interreligious immersions. Through the continuation of interfaith experiences on returning home, interreligious encounters are a path to greater harmony and peace within the global community in religious, political, civic, and cultural arenas.

When students engage in an interreligious relationship, they are open to encountering the sacred reality mysteriously present. In the written reflections and evaluations of the immersion trip, students speak favorably of their experiences on interreligious retreats, for in them they have entered the realm of the sacred guided by the religious other. Obviously, religious seekers returning home will need ongoing formation in their intrinsic religious traditions, as well as guided practice in discernment. The spiritual breakthrough is found not only during these interreligious retreats but in the very experience of mutual dialogue and encounter itself. Perhaps this is because such encounters are more or less intrinsically mystical or sacred. Students sense that they have in some fashion experienced the sacred in meeting, praying, and living with members of other faiths. The pedagogical goal of these encounters is to expose the students to firsthand experience of the sacred dimension of the religious other and, one hopes, to make such encounters a lifelong habit.

The experience of recent years has convinced us that thoughtful, effective assessment of interreligious encounters is essential. We employ an evaluation tool, tested and refined over the years, as well as some of the research that underlies the model. Following a consistent procedure, the first evaluation is given in-country, typically on the last full day of the immersion. JST recommends a standard array of assessment questions but also encourages individual faculty leaders to adapt it according to course goals and preferred pedagogic modalities.[20] Experience has shown the importance of

---

20. JST Professor of Religion and Society Jerome Baggett, a specialist in survey research, helped draft the questionnaires for our evaluation. For some years,

undertaking an evaluation in-country. Once back home, it is difficult to identify an adequate time for debriefing, and the immediacy of the reflective experience diminishes.

The second assessment involves students sharing their experience with the wider learning community at home. This usually takes the form of an evening of presentation and sharing, often accompanied by video or pictorial footages of their immersion experience. Sights and sounds can help students to relive and savor those encounter moments, as well as to allow the rest of the learning community—other students and faculty—to join in the experience. Often students from past immersions also participate in the presentations and have an opportunity to relive their experiences, both similar and different, and thus enhance their interreligious learning experience.[21]

Conclusion

The Jesuit School of Theology's goal of contextual learning through interreligious immersions has found success in keeping the dialogue of life, actions, religious experiences, and theological beliefs grounded in and animated by such on-site encounters. Since interreligious education is integral to a contemporary theological and ministerial preparation for church leaders today, an interfaith competency should move beyond a comparative study of religions, often undertaken in an armchair setting, toward real engagement with the religious other in their own setting. These face-to-face encounters help us to engage with other faithful in

---

the data were collected by Rev. Robert McChesney, the coordinator of the international programs at JST from 2010 to 2017.

21. McChesney conducted another survey approximately ten weeks after the students' return home. This survey was used to assess the effectiveness of the program from an administrative perspective and to help plan future immersions.

ways that have constructive consequences for our understanding of our own faith. Seeing one's own religion, and the faith of others, with greater nuance has fostered in our programs respectful and honest dialogue and learning.

The experiential learning here, of course, does not supersede the academic learning of religions. The lived encounters, however, enhance studies and through them facilitate dialogue in the host country, as well as at home. The experiential interreligious learning is not done when the immersion is over; rather, it is a jump start for ongoing learning about one's own tradition, as well as developing effective pastoral ministry within our communities. Moreover, friendly interreligious encounters provide an opportunity for self-transformation that includes a deeper appreciation of the religious tradition of the other for students and teachers alike. The experience of "walking in the other's shoes" challenges one's own cultural and religious assumptions and helps to break down prejudice and build friendship, and leads to collaboration and mutual enrichment.

The immersion program at JST has helped our students come to a deeper theological understanding of our multicultural and religiously pluralistic world, especially when our encounter with the religious other turns into our willingness to collaborate and live our faith *for* and *with* others. Mutuality of relationship, or friendship, emerges as the foundation. Students report that they have in some sense encountered the sacred, fostering qualities that will contribute to ongoing learning from the religious other. The interpersonal encounters experienced during the immersion can sustain their efforts to seek out other religious partners for dialogue and collaboration. In this way we hope to train a new generation of theologically informed leaders and ministers who will be committed to building bridges among religions and will foster cordial relationships that transcend religious boundaries and lead to societal transformation.

Chapter Eleven

WOMEN, WISDOM, ACTION
CONTEXTUAL THEOLOGY IN THE
KEY OF MEMORY AND NARRATIVE

Julia D.E. Prinz, VDMF

The hunger for bread can be satisfied. The hunger for beauty is endless.[1]

The Beginnings

In the remote region of North India, at the local diocesan St. Albert's Seminary, a religious sister, Rashmi Kiro, was listening to a recent doctoral alumnus of the Jesuit School of Theology (JST) talking about Christ as the Supreme *Adivasi*. It was in this context that I got to know Sr. Kiro while being part of a JST delegation that had been traveling extensively through Asia for weeks to review the formation process, especially the theological education of women religious. Sr. Kiro shared later with Valan Anthony, SJ, another alumnus of JST and a professor of sacred scripture at Vidyajyoti College of Theology, Delhi, where Kiro is presently pursuing her doctoral studies, that she was surprised by the interest shown in tribal culture by both the young Jesuit doctoral graduate and the delegation of JST. Sr.

---

1. This epigraph is quoted by Dorothee Sölle, "Dresdener Stollen," in *Loben ohne Lügen* (Berlin: Wolfgang Fietkau Verlag, 2000), 65.

Kiro, herself of tribal descent and belonging to one of the few tribal communities in the northern part of India, grew up in a Catholic family in Jharkhand and has personally witnessed the suffering of the Tribals (*Adivasis*) all her life: "I didn't connect it with my faith," she shared in an interview with Valan Anthony, SJ.

Sr. Kiro began her studies in 2008 in the local seminary to enhance her education as novice mistress. She knew "how theological studies would change my life, my faith, and my understanding of the people I am serving," she shared in the interview cited above. She affirmed:

> Jesus was my savior and the center of my life, but while doing theology, I realized that he is also the center of the very suffering I have been witnessing all my life passively. He is immersed in who I am, in the most vulnerable and suffering people and in my tribal novices who can't make sense, at times, of the Roman Catholic rituals. Our faith is not written in a separate place and time of salvation but is the story of my people.[2]

One thing she felt was painfully missing in her nearly decade-long excellent and challenging theological education was networking with other religious women theologians. Another was being taught by women religious who would have given her the confidence to speak her own mind as a woman in front of others.

Seven years after Sr. Kiro began her studies in rural Ranchi, the opportunity to fill that gap arrived on her doorstep. The Women of Wisdom and Action (WWA) Initiative, which was founded as a response to the JST faculty research journey in Asia, gave sisters the opportunity to receive full scholarships for tuition and living expenses while studying for advanced theological degrees at JST.

---

2. Interview of June 15, 2018, St. Peter's Seminary, Bangalore, India. Recorded with permission by Valan Anthony, SJ.

Moreover, this arrangement provided the opportunity for sisters having worked at the grassroots level in Asia to receive leadership formation in an international and inter-congregational community of women religious that has been organized by members of the international Verbum Dei community.

Furthermore, WWA was active in various countries (China, India, Vietnam, and Myanmar), and it was at a seminar organized by Vidyajyoti College of Theology and in the sessions conducted by WWA that Sr. Kiro discovered her ability to articulate her thoughts and gained the confidence to speak. A year later she was invited to be part of a lively first encounter of young women religious theologians at Navjivan Renewal Centre, New Delhi, November 17–21, 2017, which made her dream come true: to be connected with other women religious theologians throughout the country.[3]

WWA developed in 2012 at JST through a close collaboration between the Verbum Dei Missionary Fraternity (USA) and the international Society of Jesus with JST. It has made a small yet unique contribution to the global reality of contextual theology and prophetic dialogue. The initiative has (1) provided advanced theological leadership training in Berkeley for twelve religious sisters from Asia, (2) offered an opportunity for the sisters to know the local Church, and (3) supported and/or built theological networks in the home countries of the sisters who studied for postgraduate degrees at JST or elsewhere in the world.

The work overseas and in Berkeley connected six constituencies: (1) the global Society of Jesus and the Verbum Dei Missionary Fraternity, (2) the alumni of JST/WWA, (3) the theological institutes in each country, (4) the local sisterhood of the congregations in each country, (5) the General Superior Conferences of the various countries, and (6) the local bishops.[4] By January 2019, twelve

---

3. L. R. Arun, SJ, Vidyajyoti College of Theology, New Delhi, India. The fifteen-minute video is archived there and may be viewed in the archive.

4. This initiative was made possible through the generosity of both the Henry Luce and Conrad N. Hilton Foundations, in collaboration with the Jesuit

sisters from China, India, Malaysia, the Philippines, and Vietnam will have graduated with advanced theological degrees from JST and received parallel leadership formation at Sophia House, the residential program for the sisters coming to Berkeley. Hundreds of other sisters in China, India, Myanmar, and Vietnam have participated in theologically oriented conferences and seminars; some were published through WWA networks. Congregations received support with their constitutions or with leadership development programs. UISG (Union Internazionale Delle Superiore Generali) gatherings (675 in attendance in May 2016) and AMOR (Asian Meeting of Religious) gatherings (460 in attendance in February 2017) were platforms for WWA to encourage the holistic theological formation of sisters. Conferences of Superiors in the corresponding countries have invited WWA to facilitate sessions and workshops, and countless superiors, priests, and bishops have been involved in dialogues about the importance of women's voices in the local church. Networks supporting sisters with theological education were founded or strengthened. In all these developments I learned with awe how much the communal reflection on one's faith experience across diverse forms of Asian Christianity, academically and otherwise, was a key narrative component of all WWA endeavors.

The Role of Memory for Contextual Theology

The theological framework of "weak categories," specifically those of memory and narrative (concepts pioneered by Johann Baptist Metz), provide a structure for the concept and development of the WWA initiative. "Weak categories" is a terminology developed by Metz as a corrective to the nineteenth- and twentieth-century scientific understanding of theology, its methodologies, and

---

School of Theology of SCU and the Verbum Dei Missionary Fraternity Community (USA).

metaphysical categories. The metaphysical and the scientific are both strong categories: unmovable and "proven." Weak categories, on the other hand, try not only to liberate faith from such strong categories but to liberate the ecclesial authority of the community of the faithful from such a supra-context.[5]

Taking memory and narrative as a hermeneutic for contextual theology, this chapter argues that the WWA initiative is an embodiment of text-context dialogue. I attempt to remain close and faithful to the incarnate, remembered, and lived experience of particular sisters in the shared community. The experience took place in diverse locations in Vietnam, India, China, and Myanmar, as well as Sophia House in Berkeley, one that I was privileged to witness. However, this communal sharing, which was particular and unique, arising as it did from differing contexts, revealed broader Asian sensibilities. The hope is that this approach subverts a merely conceptual understanding and leads the reader herself into a fuller "feel" for the questions and challenges evoked by the text-context relationship at the heart of WWA.

Memories and narratives are not simple tools but complex hermeneutical approaches that support a contextual theology emerging from "the place of encounter" modeled by the sisterhood. It is the sisters' experience of suffering and hope, and their mutual encounter informed by their "place of origin," that contributes to the female perspective shaping the ground of theological academies in Asia and throughout the globe.

---

5. Johann Baptist Metz, inspired by Jewish tradition and influenced by Walter Benjamin and Theodor Adorno, tries to break out of the enlightenment dichotomy between emancipated reason and authority by turning to the history of suffering and its implicit call for a just world. This turn to history—more specifically, a remembered history of suffering—demands both an openness to learn from any authority or dogma and a critical questioning toward emancipated knowledge. In doing so, memory becomes philosophically the primary category of reason, connecting it indissolubly with history. Johann Baptist Metz, "Memory," in *Faith in History and Society*, trans. Mathew Ashley (New York: Herder & Herder, 2007), 169–85.

The following diagram (Figure 11.1) shows a complex hermeneutical approach coming into being through listening to, sharing,
and tapping into memory. It is memory that makes each "place of
origin" unique, and in its uniqueness it becomes a "place of encounter," while sharing life and conversing about it. Without the process
of opening the memory to community, there cannot be a learning or network process. This very model exemplifies how every text
that holds and transmits the memory of the place of origin "grows,"
"learns," and "changes" when it becomes a place of encounter, where
it meets other texts of origin. The dichotomy between text and context is challenged by the communitarian experience of sisterhood.

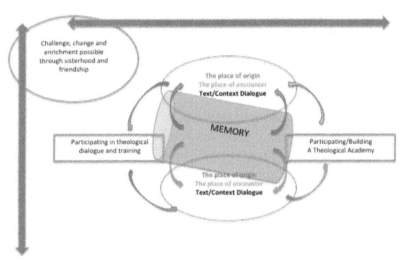

Figure 11.1. Memory as Place of Encounter and Origin

Memory is located at the core of human existence and in a specific way at the center of the Jewish-Christian tradition.[6] It is not

---

6. Juan Luis Segundo develops a similar idea by grounding faith in what he
   calls "referential witnesses" who have told communally—since Abraham—
   the stories of memory of salvation. Thus the essence of the Creed is not the
   formula but the retelling of the memory. Juan Luis Segundo, *Faith and
   Ideologies* (Maryknoll, NY: Orbis, 1984), 79ff.

a coincidence that the scriptures of these traditions primarily retell memories in narratives, poems, and aphorisms or proverbs. Following Metz's emphasis on the centrality of memory for both Christian existence and for human reason and learning, how might we imagine building academic relationships around the globe informed by such memory? In what way is it possible to create a theological academy in which the narrative-poetic foundations of reason and experience constitute central theological categories? What, then, happens to the memories of the marginal voices that are deemed by some to be irrelevant because of their distance from the centers of power?

Narratives That Delineate Memory

When I was Sixteen
I think back and remember
I cannot think forward about you
a friendship as an overgrown courtyard
the grass grows out of the windows
and the lilac is still in blossom, too.

what was not promised to us
under the five wild swans
often we were called sisters
and then you were a bit embarrassed
but I, the little one, was proud
I still taste the humidity of the cellar at school
there were teachers who wanted to keep us from singing
and parents who found sisterhood exaggerated
a big brother straightened us out.

that was in the time of the bombing
you crashed through the burning city
looking for your parents

I want to remember this until that
burning city's smoke is on my tongue
resisting the stupid: long, long it's over and forgotten—
in my book it says that memory
walks with us and shows us the way into tomorrow
a dark cloud by day
a fiery one by night
my sister do you remember our cloud
come let us look for it.[7]

The German theologian and writer Dorothee Sölle invokes memory as a bridge into the future. Her poetic narrative recalls a friend, an icon of life, during the Third Reich and the Second World War, a person whose prophetic response involves a constant recourse to the memories of the healing cloud, a powerful memory from the Exodus. Sisterhood then is constituted by friendship, bound by choice, commitment, and solidarity. In the fascist era of Sölle's childhood, this sisterhood is seen as something excessive, something to be suppressed. Instead, sisterhood provides for Sölle precisely the place for future hope and mutual support amid the destructive experience of death and oppression. This kind of sisterhood was the reason why JST asked the Verbum Dei Missionary Community to collaborate in the WWA project.

The above poem, with its celebration of sisterhood and memory, could be said to characterize WWA and the life at Sophia House from 2012 to 2018: singing together, breaking open bread and memories, eating snake, curry and noodles, all amid global contradictions, wars, suffering, and injustice. The laughing, fighting, frustrations, play, and forgiveness broke forth from unbelievably complex memories and have been a gifted witness for me. The following collective narrative emerges from those who helped create

---

7. Dorothee Sölle, "Als ich sechzehn war," in *Spiel doch von Brot und Rosen* (Berlin: Fietkau Verlag, 1981), 54. My translation.

this sisterhood of friendship at Sophia House. WWA participants from various countries provide an impressionistic glimpse of backgrounds that the sisters cannot forget, as Sölle puts it, "Until the burning city's smoke is on our tongue" again. It is the taste of smoke that created this sisterhood and influenced the development of its theology. This desire to taste the smoke reveals the role of memory in dialogue: How does memory become prophetic? How is narrative a key to the poetic theological depth-structure of this dialogue? Obviously, this is not about romanticizing fantasies of the past. It is also not narcissistic. It is, rather, the memory of persons who have been silenced or forgotten, along with ones who have died. It is especially remembering the One, Jesus Christ, who has died for them. Making memory of their beauty as well as their suffering—remembering them as the "community of the beautiful," brings out the prophetic aspect of Eucharist.[8] Prophetic memory needs this narrative process of anamnesis, in breaking the bread, to unfold its healing and salvific character. It is a prophetic memory that situates itself not from one center but from various centers in the reality of global Christianity.

How is anamnesis, this prophetic memory or special way of remembering, celebrated in the local coming together of women, girls, and boys who have been left behind by their parents on the streets of the dusty villages, or by girls who were orphaned as soon as they were born, or by the elderly alone in the remote countryside who hardly make enough to sustain life?[9] We might also ask, how is

---

8. I draw from the central idea of Alejandro Garcia-Rivera, who understood the community of individuals as "the beautiful" in contrast to the philosophical understanding of beauty one may find in Hans Urs von Balthasar. Alejandro Garcia-Rivera, *The Community of the Beautiful: A Theological Aesthetics* (Collegeville, MN: Liturgical Press, 1999).

9. For a more detailed description of my experience of these realities, please see Fang Chang et al., *Understanding the Situation of China's Left Behind Children: A Mixed-Methods Analysis* (Stanford, CA: Stanford REAP, 2017), https://fsi-live .s3.us-west-1.amazonaws.com/s3fs-public/315_-_understanding_the_situation _of_chinas_left-behind_children.pdf; Zhai Zhenwu, *Aging in China: Trend,*

anamnesis celebrated in the glamorous city centers that are ringed by this poverty? Or by students, intellectuals, middle-class workers, teachers, or pastoral agents in China? Where does the dangerous and prophetic memory of the Sophia-Logos find its place?[10]

In India, the sheer number of religious sisters studying theology is breathtaking. The numbers in Bangalore and Kerala together are in the hundreds; add to these several hundred more sisters studying at the Jesuit theology centers in Pune and New Delhi, and, of course, also at Mater Dei in Goa (for sisters only). At first I was speechless and thought that the female theological academy must be vast. But after multiple visits and interviews, I discovered that many of the sisters are only studying in short certificate programs—lasting from three months to a year—connected to their formation, renewal, or, for some, extra qualification. Most of these sisters are not in the pontifical cycles of theological training that the diocesan and religious priests undergo.

However, there is a smaller group of sisters who do study for their master's degrees or first-cycle pontifical degrees (baccalaureate degree). Despite the fact that these women religious are running schools, health care centers, orphanages, and other social services, not to mention innumerable pastoral programs, these sisters have had to learn to deal with the reality of being the gender minority, often being the only female students in classrooms, seminars,

---

Process and Character (Beijing: Renmin University, 2015), https://www.unes cap.org/sites/default/files/Session1_Mr.ZhaiZhenwu_China.pdf; and Alice Yan, "The Forgotten Farm Families in Beijing's Anti-Poverty Campaign: How China's Rural Poor Fall through the Cracks," *South China Morning Post* (2018), https://www.scmp.com/news/china/society/article/2149994/forgotten-farm-families-beijings-anti-poverty-campaign-how-chinas.

10. Interpreting anamnesis in the Roman Catholic Eucharist from a Johannine perspective, as being one centered on Jesus as the incarnated logos who was with God before all creation, is more deeply connected with the understanding of the Old Testament characteristics of Sophia (Wisdom) than the dominant Platonic and Aristotelian interpretation of logos. Sophia incorporates justice and human loving and living within notions of the divine logos.

and within the larger philosophical and theological environment. There are approximately forty to sixty sisters spread out over the different years of the first-cycle MA programs (BTh—bachelor of theology) in all of India. Far fewer sisters go on to study for licentiates or doctorates. However, taking all institutes in India together, approximately twenty sisters are enrolled annually in various doctoral programs.

Memory & Narrative: The Warp Threads to a Theological Academy

These background notes show some of the political, economic, and cultural frameworks with which the WWA initiative is in dynamic relationship. The women religious are esteemed for their pastoral labor in the poorest areas of the countryside and in areas where no diocese yet exists. With the memory of the suffering shared in these pages, how does one envision the emergence of a theological academy? What can horizontal-feminist communication add to theological discourse?[11] How can such an academy build on the narratives of resistance, beauty, and courage that these women are articulating? Might there be a theological academy built by women with the weft of hope weaving through the warp of suffering?

---

11. The situation of analyzing the structures in which we are bound as religious, in the congregation, church, and society, has been a long-standing discourse at the LCWR. It is with the help of systems thinking that the Leadership Conference of Women Religious (LCWR) tries to encourage communities to enter into a more horizontal and feminist way of relationship, breaking out of hierarchical and dualistic ways of communication. See *An Invitation to Systems Thinking: An Opportunity to Act for Systemic Change* (Silver Spring, MD: LCWR, 2004), https://solidaritywithsisters .weebly.com/uploads/1/2/2/3/12230470/systems_thinking_handbook.pdf. For more discourse on the situation in India, see Pauline Chakkalakal, dsp, "Theologizing in India: Contribution of Feminist Theology," presented at the ITA 2017 (publication forthcoming).

If memory, not knowledge, is the first step into reason, then what academy are we building among women? The narrative understanding of theology, with its central category of memory, opposes a theology effectively geared to maintaining the status quo. The study of theology needs to be a praxis of change on behalf of the memory of the suffering.

Dialogue is a second step in the creation of a theological academy that is sufficiently sensitive to the cry of injustice that weaves through our memories. Being equal participants in a dialogue means that we have listened to each other's memories. Hence WWA developed a circular theological process[12] in the countries of China, Vietnam, India, and Myanmar.

Memory becomes the place of encounter in dialogue with others (see Figure 11.1). The place of encounter will change through the process of remembering and sharing both the cry and the awe experienced by other women. Memory, in this depiction, is understood as the heart of the Christian mystery; we remember the One who suffered in all who suffer. This memory will be celebrated and enacted distinctly in the places of origin and encounter, but the focus is on equality in the possibility of diverse locales for the Christian memory. One memory has no priority over another. There is no movement from the center to the margin or from margin to center. The movement is between different places of origin that, as original places of Christian memory, become places of encounter. No place of origin, with its memory of suffering incarnated in the Christian memory, receives a priority standing over another place of origin, and no one needs to measure up to the centrality of one specific place. Instead, all are equal in the incarnation of the Christian memory in their places of suffering as the "community of the beautiful." This was the foundational idea of the weaving loom called WWA.

---

12. In the first grant application to the Henry Luce Foundation, the idea of a "dynamic theological model" was articulated as the driving force of the WWA initiative.

The Experience of Women of Wisdom and Action

The process of creating the WWA initiative opened by paying attention to the memory of those who suffer and who are made whole through the sharing of their narratives and communal memories. Consequently, the first step in the initiative was to visit, listen, and learn from the women religious in their places of origin: China, Vietnam, India, and Myanmar. We aimed to share in their cry in solidarity and silence, and to experience being part of a place of encounter. We learned from and about local communities, including their memories and claims for a future, and we learned from the individual sisters who inhabited each locale.

Receiving the first women religious in Berkeley to study for an advanced degree in theology at JST as part of the leadership formation in the Sophia House community finally became a reality. These women would learn from each other and partake in a specific Sophia House curriculum. The curriculum focused on building awareness of various places of origin, understandings of religious leadership, self-awareness, the critical apprehension of cross-cultural enhancement, deconstruction of colonial and victimization structures, and specific experiences of Christian memory, of the ones who suffer and are forgotten.

Parallel to working with the few sisters who came to Berkeley, sustained support was also given to the networks in the home countries that supported theological formation for individual sisters. The learning process of the women religious who came to Berkeley included navigating the expectations and standards of U.S. academic degree programs. To facilitate this encounter, we discovered that it was crucial to develop the leadership formation curriculum of Sophia House, so that the personal (the individual/communal memory of the place of origin) and the academic (U.S. graduate university educational system) overlapped and were complementary.

After two years, the first graduates returned to home environments in the Philippines and Vietnam. Soon after, others returned to Taiwan and China. There they began participating in networks supported by WWA during their absence. At the same time, they began to build up their own networks and projects, often connecting pre-colonial resources with Christian memory. They became anamnestic agents of social and ecclesial awareness. These Sophia House alumnae thus began to make connections within their own countries, and some began to enter the international exchange of a growing global theological academy. A reciprocal, ongoing learning relationship was thereby initiated. This international exchange continues to be rooted in the community of origin and the memory celebrated within it. Bit by bit, the alumnae have made contact with those of WWA programs in other countries for mutual support. Special attention is being given to writing and publishing and teaching and research, since these are the biggest lacunae for Asian religious women.

Looking Forward

To the question of how to create an international theological academy grounded in the memory and narratives of women, this chapter has not offered an "answer" but a direction and an intuition grounded in the experience of the WWA initiative. The chapter has referenced the anamnestic moments where WWA narratives and memory have been integrated into the paschal mystery. These overlapping memories of suffering and wholeness are brought into a place of encounter where each equally represents a different place of origin. Memories may hold a prophetic quality leading us toward a vision of a world (church) that does not favor one place of origin over another but takes seriously the reality of the incarnation of Sophia-Logos in all places of origin.

WWA had to learn as it moved through the years; some things did not work out as planned, and sometimes national, cultural, and personal differences seemed bigger than shared memories. Yet WWA nonetheless represents a unique attempt to incarnate the endless hunger for the "community of the beautiful" in this world and gifted me with the surprise of theologizing in a sisterhood of friendship. Twelve sisters have graduated in Berkeley since we began in 2012; various congregations have joined new networks through their sisters, and many sisters have resolved to remain connected to a theological network and/or academy in their countries. In a certain way, after finishing the foundation cycles from 2012 to 2018, the work has just begun: the work of believing that, at the places of origin and at the places of encounter, the prophetic memory of our Christian faith is leading us to the memory of the "community of the beautiful." To return to the words of Sölle, friendships are like overgrown courtyards, and sister-friends do not forget until they taste the smoke: because the hunger for beauty is endless.

Chapter Twelve

IMPRISONED THEOLOGY

George T. Williams, SJ

John and Lori Rainwater's infant son was seven days old when his parents were murdered. He and his fifteen-month-old sister were found alive and sheltered under their slain mother's naked body in the parking lot of their apartment complex in Atascadero, California.

The night before, on Wednesday, February 4, 1987, Dennis Webb, a parolee from the Utah State Prison system, out of prison just two months, broke into their home with the intention of robbing them.[1] The Rainwaters managed an apartment complex and were responsible for collecting the rent from their tenants, so Webb planned to steal whatever cash they had on hand. He had scoped out the place a few days before, claiming to be looking to rent an apartment.

The last person to see the Rainwaters alive reported seeing them around 8 P.M. speaking to a tall, stocky man at their front door. The witness said that he remembered this because he noticed Lori, usually a positive person with a sunny disposition, had an uncharacteristic frown on her face. Both John and Lori were devout Christians. They worked hard and were saving money to move to a larger place for their growing family.

---

1. *The County Telegram-Tribune*, San Luis Obispo, CA, July 16, 1988, http://sloblogs.thetribunenews.com/slovault/2009/04/dennis-duane-webb-sentenced-to-death/.

Lori may not have known, though she undoubtedly sensed, that she was looking into the face of radical evil that evening. The next ten hours were to be a scene of nightmarish savagery and suffering for her and her husband.

Dennis Webb was a thirty-five-year-old tenth-grade dropout from West Texas who from the age of twenty had spent several years in the Texas prison system for burglary. By his mid-twenties, as an aimless drifter full of rage and racist ideas, he joined an outlaw motorcycle gang in North Texas. By his thirtieth birthday, he had by his own account killed five people. His first victim was a gay man he selected at random because, in his own words, "I don't like homosexuals." His second victim was murdered because he was black. He admitted to having killed three others who caught him burglarizing their homes.

His cocaine-amplified violence landed him in the Utah prison system in 1981, where he would serve five-and-a-half years for robbery and aggravated kidnapping. He was released from prison in Utah in December 1986—two months before he met and murdered the Rainwaters.

The robbery was well planned. Dennis went to a local Kmart earlier that Wednesday afternoon and purchased duct tape to bind his victims. One of his bloody fingerprints on a piece of this tape would be evidence used to convict him.

Dennis forced his way into their home, pistol-whipping both John and Lori and splitting their scalps open. John was hit at least five times in the back of the head, his wife four times. Dennis then tied them up with the tape and belts and used nylon stockings to gag them. During the next eight hours, he would strip them, beat them, and rape both of them.

It is hard to imagine the horror, fear, and pain this young couple endured. No doubt they cried out to God many times. Their infant children were nearby—their cribs spattered with their parents' blood. Police reported finding blood spattered all over the apartment.

At some point, around 6 A.M., it seems Webb must have fallen asleep or passed out, because the couple were able to free their legs from the restraints and ran screaming for help into the parking lot of their building. Dennis, awakened, was right behind them. He shot John in the back and, when he fell, killed him with an execution-style shot to the back of the head. He then ran after Lori and killed her the same way. She was holding her two children, running with them to protect them.

In August 1988, Dennis Duane Webb was sentenced to death. It is reported that he laughed when the verdict was read.

The Context of Our Prison System

For the last seven years I have worked as the Catholic chaplain at San Quentin State Prison. I spend much of my time ministering to the 750 men on California's death row. Ministry on death row, or in any prison, occurs within the shadow of violent crimes laced with cruelty and indifference to human life. Cruelty and indifference to human life are not limited to the crimes of the inmates. Prison ministry must be seen in the context of the larger picture of the American prison system. To understand this context, it would be helpful to describe how the American penal system has evolved over the last forty years.

Beginning in the 1970s, the United States entered a period of mass incarceration. Capitalizing on public anxiety about crime, policymakers vied to outdo one another to appear "tougher on crime." Criminal justice policy rapidly shifted away from the pursuit of rehabilitation of offenders and toward the incapacitation of criminal offenders.[2] Federal and state legislatures, reacting to public fears about crime and economic uncertainty, enacted ever more punitive laws resulting in a mushrooming population of prisoners in the United States.

---

2. Craig Haney, *Reforming Punishment: Psychological Limits to the Pains of Imprisonment* (Washington, DC: American Psychological Association, 2006).

Today the United States manages the largest penal system in the world. Americans incarcerate a greater proportion of their citizenry than any other contemporary industrialized nation. The American "prison-industrial complex"[3] costs over $200 billion a year to maintain and employs more people than the nation's two largest private employers combined.[4] As of April 2016, the U.S. incarceration rate was four times the world average, with 2.2 million people in American prisons and jails.[5]

With the shift in policy from reformation to incapacitation, a new narrative was constructed around the metaphors of a "war on crime" and a "war on drugs," a conservative backlash to the liberal Great Society experiments in social engineering begun in the 1960s as a "war on poverty."[6]

The result was not only a "war" on crime and drugs, but also a war that disproportionately targeted poor and minority urban communities. Within our massive prison system, one does not have to look too hard to find evidence of structural racism, violence, and oppression. The unprecedented wave of prison construction was seen by some as an attempt to control "the dangerous classes"—the poor, urban underclass in contemporary society.[7]

For others, prison construction was seen as a boon to economically depressed rural communities, providing both construction employment and then steady work for workers who no longer

---

3. Eric Schlosser, "The Prison-Industrial Complex," *Atlantic Monthly* 282, no. 6 (1998), 51–77.

4. Robert Perkinson, *Texas Tough: The Rise of America's Prison Empire* (New York: Metropolitan Books, 2010).

5. Jason Furman and Douglas Holtz-Eakin, "Why Mass Incarceration Doesn't Pay," *The New York Times* (April 20, 2016), A29. Also found at: https://www.nytimes.com/2016/04/21/opinion/why-mass-incarceration-doesnt-pay.html.

6. Lyndon Johnson, "The War on Poverty," *The Annals of America* 18 (1964): 212–16.

7. Loïc Wacquant, "Deadly Symbiosis: When Ghetto and Prison Meet and Mesh," *Punishment & Society* 3, no. 1 (2001): 95–133.

had the opportunity for well-paying, blue-collar manufacturing jobs. In 1971, there were fewer than 60,000 correctional officers employed in U.S. jails and prisons. In 2017, the total number of correctional officers in the United States (in both state prisons and local jails) was 475,000.[8]

As with any war, the "war on crime" has generated its own cadre of traumatized veterans and victims. Similar to a battle zone in a war, prisons pose the challenge of having to subdue, manage, and secure a large number of unwilling and potentially dangerous people.[9] But it is not only inmates who are traumatized by the harsh conditions of confinement. There is ample empirical evidence that correctional workers are also traumatized by what they experience at work.[10]

Prisons are by their very nature places of punishment and manifestations of institutionalized violence.[11] Nowhere is this more obvious than on the thirty-five death rows in the United States today. The death row apparatus is a demonstration of the power of the state to kill those deemed unworthy to live in society. At the time of this writing (2017) it is very possible that California will resume executing prisoners in accord with the will of a slim majority of voters.[12]

---

8. U.S. Bureau of Labor Statistics, *Occupational Outlook Handbook*, 2017, https://www.bls.gov/ooh/protective-service/correctional-officers.htm.

9. Gaylene S. Armstrong and Marie L. Griffin, "Does the Job Matter? Comparing Correlates of Stress among Treatment and Correctional Staff in Prisons," *Journal of Criminal Justice* 32, no. 6 (2004): 577–92.

10. George Williams, "Resisting Burnout: Correctional Staff Spirituality and Resilience" (PhD diss., Northeastern University, 2017).

11. Michel Foucault, *Discipline & Punish: The Birth of the Prison*, trans. Alan Sheridan (New York: Vintage, 2012).

12. California Proposition 66 was approved by 51 percent of voters on November 8, 2016. The ballot initiative called for a limit on the time allowed for Death Row inmates' appeals. The intention behind the initiative was to speed up the execution process in California.

Doing Contextual Theology in Prison

We must ask ourselves, "What does a theology school have to say to these harsh realities?" This is the context, steeped in violence and suffering, that forms the backdrop for ministry for those who are willing to enter the gates of the modern American prison. What happens when we send our students from the classroom into prisons to minister? How do we equip our students to work in this alien, violent environment with its unique culture? Do we talk about our complicity in institutionalized racism in our theology classes? How do we help our students make sense of the suffering they encounter behind the walls of the prisons and still hold on to hope?

These are not just interesting questions worth pondering. The contemporary American prison poses a dramatic challenge to the relevance of our theology training. It is imperative that North American theological schools attempt to understand and respond to this harsh reality in our own culture.

If Stephen Bevans is correct, there is no such thing as theology—only contextual theology.[13] There are few places in the United States that allow theology students to enter into such a real and starkly challenging context of human suffering as the prison. How does one articulate a "vital, coherent theology"[14] or attempt to understand one's faith in the prison context described above?

This context is radically different from anything most of our theology students have encountered. Yet it touches in a concrete way the universal mysteries of human suffering and evil, as well as healing, redemption, mercy, and forgiveness. In other words, it offers, in a very tangible way, a theology of the cross of Christ.

Since 1996, the Jesuit School of Theology in Berkeley has highlighted contextual study of theology and ministry as a central

---

13. Stephen B. Bevans, *Models of Contextual Theology,* rev. and exp. ed. (Maryknoll, NY: Orbis, 2002).

14. Bevans, *Models of Contextual Theology,* 98.

pedagogical strategy. Contextual theology requires students to move beyond the classroom into the lived experiences of the marginalized poor. It is grounded in the Jesuit ideal of living a faith that does justice. Students have engaged in ministry at both San Quentin and the nearby federal women's prison in Dublin, California, for many years, but until 2011 they never had the opportunity to take a pastoral ministry course devoted specifically to prison ministry.

Beginning in 2011, JST students, along with other theology students from the Graduate Theological Union in Berkeley, have had the opportunity to take a course in contextual prison ministry offered by me, the chaplain at San Quentin. The course presents both the theoretical and practical skills needed for successful prison ministry, with an emphasis on the unique theological, psychosocial, and ministerial needs of the incarcerated. Students are introduced to the pastoral challenges of work in prison by spending a minimum of two hours per week outside the class engaged in ministry at a prison or jail.

This is more than "field education." It is an immersion in and an engagement with very real suffering that unites praxis with theory outside the safe spaces of the academy, inside the walls, fences, and barbed-wire barriers of the prison. It provides our students the opportunity to do practical theology, which Karl Rahner argued must be the "critical conscience" for the Church today.[15] Students are empowered to reflect theologically on the very real and challenging experiences they have in interacting with prisoners.

In any ministry, all the theologizing in the world is of no use unless one can truly be present with another suffering human being. This is especially true in prison ministry. When the heavy metal gates and barred doors swing shut and lock behind them, our students must still be able to "give an explanation to anyone

---

15. Karl Rahner, "Practical Theology within the Totality of Theological Disciplines," in *Theological Investigations* 9 (New York: Herder & Herder, 1972), 104.

who asks you for a reason for your hope" (1 Pt 3:15 NAB). Perhaps more important than helping them make sense of the suffering they encounter is how we help our students decide what they want to do about it. Given the harsh and unique challenges of the prison environment, it is surprising that there are not more academic courses devoted specifically to prison ministry offered to Catholic theology students in the United States.

For a Jesuit school of theology, prison ministry affords a unique opportunity to invite students into the charism of the Society of Jesus. The mission of Jesuits, since the beginning of the order, has been to go to the margins, to the places where the church was not being served. As the founding documents of the society state:

> Whoever desires to serve as a soldier of God beneath the banner of the Cross in our Society . . . should show himself ready to reconcile the estranged, compassionately assist and serve those who are in prisons or hospitals, and indeed, to perform any other works of charity, according to what will seem expedient for the glory of God and the common good.[16]

Ministry to the imprisoned is emblematic of the mission of the Society of Jesus, and the ministry of reconciliation is at the heart of Jesuit ministry to the imprisoned. Since the 32nd General Congregation in 1975, the Society of Jesus has clearly articulated its mission as "The service of faith, of which the promotion of justice is an absolute requirement. For reconciliation with God demands the reconciliation of people with one another."[17]

---

16. *The Constitution of the Society of Jesus and Their Complementary Norms* (St. Louis: Institute of Jesuit Sources, 1996), 3.

17. Thirty-Second General Congregation of the Society of Jesus, "Decree 4: Service of Faith and the Promotion of Justice," *Documents of the Thirty-Second General Congregation of the Society of Jesus* (Rome: Institute of Jesuit Sources, 1975), 2.

Suffering and Redemption through the Lenses of the Translation, Praxis, and Countercultural Models of Contextual Theology

There are three models of contextual theology presented by Bevans that are particularly helpful approaches to the challenge of educating our students for prison ministry: the translation, the praxis, and the countercultural models.

The Translation Model

What is unique to Catholic prison ministry? What is the message of the Gospel we bring with us into the prison? What is the message of the Gospel we are confronted with when we meet the prisoners? How do we remain faithful to our tradition in a post-Christian, even anti-Christian, environment? What exactly about our faith are we trying to "translate" in prison? What do transformation, redemption, and mercy look like in a system that actively discourages transformation, redemption, and mercy?

One learns quickly in prison that much of what you learn in theology classes doesn't get much traction in the cellblocks. Generally, the inmates I encounter do not want theory. They want concrete, sharply defined answers to their suffering-induced questions. They need some clear hope to hold on to. But the questions we ask in theology classes are often quite different from the ones prisoners usually ask.

In a practical way, this does not mean that our students should not ask the difficult, nuanced questions about injustice, racism, mass incarceration, human suffering, reconciliation, and forgiveness. But these questions must be asked in language that is accessible to men and women in prison, who usually lack a theological vocabulary. And our students must be willing to allow the prisoners to teach them. That means they need to learn the vocabulary of the prisoners. And that is something that cannot be done in a classroom of a theology school.

Even more important than this, the prisoners I have met over the years all desire to be listened to. Each one has his or her own story, yet they experience in prison the negation of their uniqueness.

Another challenge for our students is to find a way to engage men and women in prison who do not possess the cultural or catechetical knowledge of Catholicism that most of us take for granted. Not only do many prisoners lack knowledge of our faith tradition; many operate under false impressions of Catholicism instilled by other Christian volunteers or inmates who often present a very negative image of Catholicism.

Historically, Catholic prison ministry has taken a rather simplistic, naïve approach that stresses devotional practices over scriptural literacy. What is needed is a better balance of knowledge of devotional practices along with the ability to place them in the context of Christian life informed by both scripture and church tradition. Often our American theology training poses questions from a position of educated privilege beyond the theological vocabulary of prisoners. This problem of translation requires our students to become familiar with the prison culture, the worldview, and the existential needs of prisoners before they can hope to meaningfully provide words of encouragement and hope.

When I began working as a chaplain I tended to react skeptically to inmates' desire for "sacramentals"—holy water, rosaries, holy cards, blessings. These were not part of my spirituality, and I tended to look on them as vestiges of pre–Vatican II piety. I see now how arrogant that attitude was. I learned, slowly, that many inmates see these sacramentals as tangible signs of God's presence. Well over half of U.S. prisoners suffer from drug or alcohol addiction and major mental illnesses.[18] Addicts tend to see the world in

---

18. Jacques Baillargeon, Joseph V. Penn, Kevin Knight, Amy Jo Harzke, Gwen Baillargeon, and Emilie A. Becker, "Risk of Reincarceration among Prisoners with Co-Occurring Severe Mental Illness and Substance Use Disorders," *Administration and Policy in Mental Health and Mental Health Services Research* 37, no. 4 (2010): 367–74.

very black-and-white categories. Abstract theological concepts are a luxury of well-educated, comfortable people like myself. People in crisis, whose lives are chaotic and often violent, need the comfort of something solid they can touch and see. This brought home for me a part of my own tradition that I was not in touch with, and it showed me that the Jesuit ideal of finding God in all things requires an open mind and heart.

What is the practical theology our students need to have to enter into prison ministry? Are they equipped to remain focused on hope when confronted with the depths of hopelessness often found in prisons? Or perhaps more accurately, are they equipped to look for the hidden hope already present among the prisoners? Do they know what such hope looks like? Do we teach them to listen carefully to the stories and concerns of those they might encounter in the prison?

This is not a ministry of words and ideas; it is a ministry of presence—of truly being present in the raw human suffering, dirtiness, smells, and messiness. Do our classroom theology lessons address the problem of suffering? Do our students know how to stand before suffering people and listen to them without trying to fix them? In other words, do our students encounter the cross of Christ in their years of theological study?

Recently I was speaking with a man in solitary confinement. His cell was barren except for a small image of the Sacred Heart of Jesus that I had given him, along with a Bible, when he was put in "the hole" for breaking prison rules.

While in solitary he had nothing to do all day in his five-by-eleven-foot cell. He only got out of this cell four times a week for a few hours in a "recreation" cell that looks like a large cage in a kennel. The food offered to inmates in solitary is adequate but not really enough to prevent a grown man from feeling hunger most of the time. The man described being so hungry that he could have eaten the apple that Jesus was holding—pointing to the image of Jesus holding his sacred heart.

While amusing on one level, it also was, to me, a poignant reminder of how theologically unlettered most prisoners are. It was also an opportunity to acknowledge that this man was hungry both spiritually and physically and realized that Jesus could offer him some comfort, even if he misinterpreted the Catholic iconography.

The Praxis Model

> *Intellectual work does not begin or end within the walls or programs of the university.*[19]

How does JST provide a forum for its students to learn how to function in the unique culture of prison? As described earlier, students at JST have been able to take a three-credit prison ministry course since 2011. No other Catholic theology center in the United States is offering such a course today. Given the centrality of this kind of radical witness to the vision of Pope Francis, this lack of professional training for Catholic prison chaplains is, frankly, shocking.

Since its inception in 2011, the prison ministry course at JST has continued to evolve. Beginning in 2017, JST offered a one-credit course for students who wish to learn about prison ministry. Unlike the original prison ministry course, which had a requirement for at least two hours per week of on-site ministry at a jail or prison, this new course radically shifted the locus of the course. The course is taught entirely on location at San Quentin State Prison. This allows both inmates and correctional officers to participate in the classes. It is a major shift both symbolically and practically, an attempt to literally contextualize the course by situating it in the prison environment itself. While sociology of religion and social ethics courses have traditionally been taught in classrooms, this course and this approach allow students to be participant observers in the field. Instead of studying *about* prisoners and the prison system, students have the opportunity to both

---

19. Arturo Sosa, "On the Intellectual Apostolate: Speech at the University of Antonio Ruiz de Montoya, Lima, Peru" (March 2017), 2, http://www.sjweb .info/documents/assj/2017.03.23_Peru_ENG.pdf.

question and be questioned by both prisoners and correctional professionals within the walls of the prison itself.

In a speech at the University of Antonio Ruiz de Montoya in Lima, Peru, in March 2017, Jesuit Father General Arturo Sosa outlined his own contextual theological vision of the "Intellectual Apostolate" of the Society of Jesus: "What we call the intellectual apostolate is central to the mission of the Society today as it has been from its inception.... The Society of Jesus, from its birth, has been associated with spiritual depth, the intellectual apostolate, closeness to the poor and an intellectual understanding of human processes."[20]

What is radically Jesuit about Sosa's vision is the idea that our intellectual life does not occur in the isolation or silos of the academy. Instead, our curiosity, our passion, our hunger for knowledge need to emerge from our experience of being with real, suffering human beings.

The JST has provided a creative way to do this. Our students have the opportunity to come to know prisoners' names and their issues firsthand. They converse with these men and women and engage in weekly group theological reflection both in the prison and then again in weekly theological reflection groups back in Berkeley. This form of doing theology empowers our students to think critically about their experiences and how their theological education can be used as a tool for social justice. Invariably the students involved in prison ministry bring to their theological reflections a deep and rich direct and personal experience that helps them clarify and grow in their own practice of our Catholic religious tradition. As an action-reflection process, the theological reflection shared by our students is an example of how doing theology requires the integration of both theory and praxis. It allows for both critical theorizing about our religious systems and assumptions as well as a critical appraisal of the implicit patterns of injustice in our criminal justice system. The action-reflection process sets the

---

20. Sosa, "On the Intellectual Apostolate," 2.

stage for real discernment for our students and hopefully encourages a lifelong process of engagement and concern for justice work. "Whenever we examine what is creative or destructive about life and relationships, we are theologizing. Whenever we struggle with sin and human limitation, we are theologizing. Whenever we hunger and thirst to care and be cared for, we theologize. Whenever we attempt to bridge separation and cutoff, we do theology."[21]

The Countercultural Model

> *The task of prophetic ministry is to nurture, nourish, and evoke*
> *a consciousness and perception alternative to the consciousness*
> *and perception of the dominant culture around us.[22]*

A few years after he published *Models of Contextual Theology*, Bevans added a sixth model to his list—the countercultural model. At the turn of the millennium, many perceived that secularization in Western culture was increasingly at odds with their Gospel values. Bevans writes: "Some contexts are simply antithetical to the Gospel and need to be challenged by the Gospel's liberating and healing power."[23] The growing American prison system is a good example of this counter-Gospel trend. For our students, training for prison ministry is an invitation to encounter head-on the mystery of the cross and the power of reconciliation. The theology student entering prison ministry enters a totalitarian system based on power, control, and violence. Jon Sobrino, describing liberation theology, writes, "The most truth-filled place for any Christian theology to carry out its task is always the suffering of our world, and in the crucified people of our world, theology receives a light that it can

---

21. John Trokan, "Models of Theological Reflection: Theory and Praxis," *Journal of Catholic Education* 1, no. 2 (1997): 145.

22. Walter Brueggemann, *The Prophetic Imagination* (Philadelphia: Fortress Press, 1978), 13.

23. Bevans, *Models of Contextual Theology*, 118.

receive nowhere else...."[24] In the contemporary United States, this light shines brightly in the darkness of the prison system where prisoners are certainly among the crucified people of our culture.

The steel bars and the concrete walls of our prisons are not accidental things; they are the product of human hearts. They represent our common fears poured out in concrete and steel. The problems of crime and prisons and human brutality will not be solved through legislation because they are ultimately spiritual problems.

In prison ministry, we come up against what St. Paul describes in Ephesians 6:12: "For our struggle is not with flesh and blood but with the principalities, with the powers, with the world rulers of this present darkness, with the evil spirits in the heavens." Insofar as our prisons reflect the darkness of our human hearts, they are, in a sense, demonic. They are the very strongholds of the enemy of our soul against which all Christians must struggle. It is in this arena that our students, who are people of faith guided by the Holy Spirit, can bring about true reform.

This is the struggle Sobrino describes: "In the crucified people of the world, theology finds, as part of the Christian paradox, its own salvation, its proper direction and the courage to carry out its task."[25] Prison ministry should be an exercise of this kind of radical prophetic compassion.

Prison chaplains are called to struggle against a structure of oppression that robs human beings of their dignity as sons and daughters of God. This theological and political struggle is what Metz called the "mysticism of open eyes."[26] That is why theological education in a prison setting is not simply field study or immersion experiences. As Gustavo Gutiérrez says, "The poverty of the

---

24. Jon Sobrino, *Principle of Mercy: Taking the Crucified People from the Cross* (Maryknoll, NY: Orbis, 2015), 46.

25. Sobrino, *Principle of Mercy*, 46.

26. As cited in Eggemeier, "A Mysticism of Open Eyes: Compassion for a Suffering World and the *Askesis* of Contemplative Prayer," *Spiritus: A Journal of Christian Spirituality* 12, no. 1 (2012): 43.

poor is not a call to generous relief action, but a demand that we go and build a different social order."[27] The course is designed to help students ask difficult questions of themselves—to recognize the structures of racism and violence in our prison system, and to recognize, when applicable, their own complicity through class and racial privilege.

Prison ministry is, unfortunately, on the "edge" or in the margins of the greater faith community. Prison ministry is marginal because it generally functions outside the formal structures of church such as a parish. It needs to be a radical, life-altering encounter with the mystery of human suffering and the mystery of God's limitless mercy. If we are content to let our theology schools churn out suburban directors of religious education or campus ministries for the privileged who can afford to go to our schools, then we have made our choice. But it has been my experience that our students are capable of so much more and are hungry for so much more.

Conclusion: Reconciliation

> Now one of the criminals hanging there reviled Jesus, saying, "Are you not the Messiah? Save yourself and us." The other, however, rebuking him, said in reply, "Have you no fear of God, for you are subject to the same condemnation? And indeed, we have been condemned justly, for the sentence we received corresponds to our crimes, but this man has done nothing criminal." Then he said, "Jesus, remember me when you come into your kingdom." He replied to him, "Amen, I say to you, today you will be with me in Paradise."
>
> (LK 23:39–43)

---

27. Gustavo Gutiérrez, *La Fuerza Histórica de los Pobres* (Salamanca: Ediciones Sigueme, 1982), 62. Translation is mine.

I met Dennis twenty-five years after he murdered the Rainwaters. He lived in cell number 1-68 on California's death row. When I met him he was a sixty-year-old man who looked at least twenty years older than that. He was overweight, diabetic, and suffered from chronic pain in his legs and back.

A few years before we met, Dennis converted to Catholicism and was baptized on death row by my predecessor, Stephen Barber, SJ. Dennis found his way into the church pretty much on his own. In seeking God, he was seeking forgiveness and healing, and he found both, especially in the Eucharist. Every time I visited his block I brought him communion, which I gave him through a small slot at the top of the steel mesh and bar door to his cell.

Dennis shared with me early on his devotion to St. Dismas, "the good thief" who was crucified alongside Jesus. Dennis wore a small medal of Dismas around his neck. He became for me a living example of Dismas. At his trial for the murders of the Rainwaters, it was reported that he told the jury at the time of sentencing, "I have no feelings, ladies and gentlemen. I've got no heart. My heart is like a block of ice.... Death is the only appropriate sentence for me." Though he was unaware of it at the time, he was echoing the words of Dismas on the cross: "indeed, we have been condemned justly, for the sentence we received corresponds to our crimes..." (Lk 23:41).

Dennis told me that he spent the first twenty years of his time in prison mostly in solitary confinement and was constantly drunk from "pruno"—the illicit liquor brewed by inmates in their cells. He lost contact with his family and was as lost as a soul can be until the last few years of his life. A few months before he died he told me, "Father, I have lived a bad life." He said this with such sadness it brought tears to my eyes.

The Dennis I came to know was no longer the cold-blooded murderer portrayed in the news at the time of his trial. However, he never really changed his opinion that his crimes and the bad choices he made merited the death penalty. But instead of a fifteen-minute death by lethal injection or by breathing cyanide fumes inside the gas chamber, Dennis's execution lasted over thirty years.

When I began ministering to prisoners on death row in 2011, one of the biggest surprises for me was to learn that many, if not most, of the men on death row actually support the death penalty. Prisoners on death row fear aging and dying alone in a cell more than they fear the execution chamber at San Quentin.

From what he told me, it was the Catholic chaplain before Fr. Barber's time, Fr. Denis McManus, an Irish Holy Ghost Father, who began to soften Dennis's heart. Dennis admitted that at first he was verbally abusive toward the elderly priest and was not in the least interested in talking about religion. Fr. McManus, over the course of two or three years, patiently visited Dennis's cell-front every week or two, bringing with him Western novels that Dennis enjoyed. Somehow, without discussing religion, repentance, or salvation, Dennis's heart opened up to the person who showed him simple kindness and companionship. It appears God's grace did the rest because, at some point, Dennis requested information about Catholicism and over the course of the next few years found himself drawn into the life of the Church.

Dennis told me that he had confessed his worst sins to Fr. McManus and had received absolution. His poignant question to me was quite simple: "Father, is it a sin for me to pray to God to let me die?"

He had seriously considered suicide (not an uncommon fate for many men on death row) and told me how he had over time accumulated a supply of medications that, taken all at once, would have killed him. The question of suicide is tricky on death row or among prisoners serving life-without-parole sentences. While we are generally taught in theology studies that God is merciful, to tell this to an inmate contemplating suicide might be irresponsible. Fear of hell might not be so bad if it deters a man or woman from killing themselves in their prison cell. Ultimately Dennis decided on his own that his Catholic faith ruled out suicide as an option.

Dennis made a very joyful reconnection and reconciliation with his family in 2013. But even the love of his family back in Texas was eventually eclipsed by the chronic pain he felt every day and the steady, humiliating loss of control of his body due to the progression of a number of physical ailments. In October 2016 he asked me to pray with him and for him that God would take him home. I promised him I would and I did. I was again reminded of the words of Dismas: "Jesus, remember me when you come into your kingdom" (Lk 23:42). It was becoming harder and harder for Dennis to breathe. Finally, he was admitted to the hospital in December. On December 17, 2016, shortly after receiving the Sacrament of the Sick while shackled to a hospital bed, Dennis Duane Webb died. Jesus said to him, "Amen, I say to you, today you will be with me in paradise" (Lk 23:43).

Chapter Thirteen

FROM BERKELEY
TO JERUSALEM
AN EXPERIMENT IN
CONTEXTUAL EDUCATION
Gina Hens-Piazza

My iPhone indicated it was 5:09 A.M. when the muezzin's call to prayer echoed from the Ghawanima Minaret of the al-Aqsa Mosque. This day I would rise, kneel by my bed, and join with the many Muslims living in this holy city, by turning my attention and prayer to God at this early hour.[1]

What was culminating as an act of interfaith solidarity in Jerusalem for this student began in a classroom in Berkeley, California. In 1996, the Jesuit School of Theology implemented a strategic plan to become an international center for the culturally contextualized study of ministry and theology. Contextual study requires taking seriously and even featuring the dialectal dynamic between faith and culture. As faith impacts and shapes culture, so too does culture influence and qualify faith. Foregrounding culture not only privileges the local context but also gives rise to contextual theology, a local articulation and

---

1. Student who participated in the 2013 Fall semester contextual study course.

adaption of faith.[2] Educating students to do contextual theology warranted vast institutional changes. First and foremost, we needed to become a school devoted to contextual education. For the next twenty years, this vision ignited comprehensive changes in syllabi, pedagogy, course offerings, program requirements, faculty research, and even what constituted a classroom.[3] Among the many changes and new offerings that have developed during the past two decades, one recent overture has taken the form of an interdisciplinary course called Children of Sarah, Hagar, and Mary. Enlisting the disciplines of both biblical and interfaith studies, this course explores sacred texts as a means of entry into the study of interreligious issues concerning women. The focus on women serves as one avenue to understand the three great traditions of Judaism, Christianity, and Islam. It considers topics both common and distinctive that characterize these religious cultures and how they might be addressed in dialogue among women and men of these three groups. Special attention is paid to context—the sociopolitical and cultural circumstances influencing the expressions of these religions in a particular setting, a local context. Finally, the course culminates in a two-week participatory study in that context, namely, Jerusalem, a city sacred to all three religious traditions. Having studied the formal features of these three traditions, students consider how the context of Jerusalem shapes these expressions of faith and how these three religions influence the nature of that context.

---

2. There are few texts as foundational to the development of contextual theology as that of Stephen B. Bevans, *Models of Contextual Theology* (Maryknoll, NY: Orbis, 1992; rev. and exp. ed., 2002). The sustained and critical assessment of context he calls for has served as the bedrock for our own institutional shift to the culturally contextualized study for ministry and theology.

3. It takes vision, strategic planning, and administrative courage to navigate such an institutional shift. Without the leadership of Joseph Daoust, SJ, during the initial phases of this new commitment and direction for our institution, such an innovative turn for the Jesuit School of Theology in Berkeley, California, would not have been possible.

In developing such an interfaith course that features Judaism, Christianity, and Islam, a title with "Abrahamic" as the key descriptor was tempting. However, the classification "Abrahamic Religions" for Judaism, Christianity, and Islam has actually been in use for only about the past twenty years. In many ways, it has become somewhat of a cliché. Critics argue that it posits an uncritical notion of a shared or common origin that homogenizes the particulars of each of these three religions and contributes further to the problem of misunderstanding. Aaron Hughes suggests that the discourse of "Abrahamic Religions" is a reductionism flattening these differences.[4] "It presents a univocal straightjacket on what are overlapping sets of multivocal and antiphonal utterances that emerge from specific encounters."[5] Alternately, positing a title such as Children of Sarah, Hagar, and Mary attempts to allow for the fluidity and distinctiveness of each of these traditions, yet collectively invites disclosure of possible shared characteristics. The title also intentionally fixes on key women figures associated with each of these traditions. By doing so, it seeks to offer a less traditional starting point that typically features the male "founder" and his history as though it defined the entire religion. This alternative approach intends to sidestep some of the worn-out, staid presentations of Judaism, Christianity, and Islam that set forth a few key teachings or sets of practices as defining each tradition. Rather, as contextual study, Children of Sarah, Hagar, and Mary intends to make clear how religious context and particularity seriously challenge these succinct, one-dimensional summaries and affords a more engaged understanding across these traditions. Such understandings are "developed in mutually critical conversation with voices, texts, or narratives of the other religion so that students

---

4. Aaron W. Hughes, *Abrahamic Religions: On the Uses and Abuses of History* (New York: Oxford University Press, 2012), 141–42.

5. Hughes, *Abrahamic Religions*, 142.

can engage and gradually narrow the gap between their world and the world of the other religion(s)."[6]

Beyond the objectives of an interfaith course, this class also seeks to address a further agenda, that is, the larger project of religious education. Paul Knitter notes the need to move beyond mono-religious education.[7] This entails a theological education that not only builds relationships within one's own community but engages in religiously pluralistic activities in order to build relationships with other communities different from one's own. In addition, interfaith education that is contextualized as it is in this class has its own playback quality. The study of another religion, in turn, deepens students' appreciation and insights into their own tradition. Recently, one student's encounter with Judaism during the contextual experience in Jerusalem bore witness to this dynamic.

"It is not about the wall itself," she explained, "but what is behind it." We were having dinner with an Orthodox Jewish family who lived a 10-minute walk away from the Western Wall in the Old City, and I had asked them what it was like to live so close to such a holy site. The above response of the mother surprised me. For her, the wall was merely the doorway to the presence of God beyond it. Her remark helped me to make sense of what I had been seeing and experiencing so far in Israel/Palestine as a Christian. We had visited so many religious sites—the tomb of Jesus, the cave of his

---

6. In this instance, Judith A. Berling, *Understanding Other Religious Worlds: A Guide for Interreligious Education* (Maryknoll, NY: Orbis, 2004), 46, is drawing on the emphasis that Gavin Flood places on the need to wrestle with religious differences and strangeness rather than focus on similarities between traditions. See Gavin Flood, *Beyond Phenomenology: Rethinking the Study of Religion* (London: Cassell, 1999), 107–8.

7. Paul F. Knitter, "Beyond a Mono-Religious Theological Education," in *Shifting Boundaries: Contextual Approaches to the Structure of Theological Education*, ed. Barbara G. Wheeler and Edward Farley (Louisville, KY: Westminster/John Knox Press, 1991), 151.

birth, the mountain where he prayed—but oftentimes there was something disappointing about these physical spaces. When I actually got close to them, I did not "feel" their holiness. Having listened to this Orthodox Jewish woman talk about her faith, I realized that it is not just about the religious sites in themselves, but what is behind them, as it were. These places are like doorways because they point to a God who dwelt and continues to dwell in our world. They orient us toward a Presence that has touched the lives of countless believers, including myself, and in this sense they are holy.[8]

In addition to deepening and enhancing their understanding of their own tradition, interfaith education better prepares them to be effective religious agents in the arenas beyond their faith communities. Along these lines of thought, Norma Thompson notes: "Education is more than transmitting a heritage; it is learning, living and growing within a community which must relate to larger and larger communities until it encompasses the world."[9]

It Always Starts with Texts

Sacred texts—it is, after all, what every great religious tradition rests on. For Judaism, Tanak and Talmud constitute the starting point. For the Christian tradition, the roots of its faith begin with the Old and New Testaments. Similarly, the Qur'an and the Hadith serve as the stepping-off point for faith in Islam. All three religions claim the status of revelation for their sacred texts. Hence, every attempt to enter into understanding or discussion about one of these great faiths begins with the texts. Not only are they a gateway for

---

8. Student who participated in the 2017 Fall semester contextual study course.

9. Norma H. Thompson, "The Challenge of Religious Pluralism," in *Religious Pluralism and Religious Education*, ed. Norma Thompson (Birmingham, AL: Religious Education Press, 1988), 19.

understanding about a tradition, but they also host a place where interfaith dialogue may begin. Burton Visotzky, the great Jewish exegete and scholar, notes that "Interfaith dialogue takes place on all levels: local, national, and international. In each venue we start with our own traditions, our own teachings, our own texts and interpretations."[10] He suggests that "text is a way in, a place where we can meet and study, learn, and be inspired."[11] Citing a Midrash on Proverbs 31:14 by Rabbi Shimeon ben Halfota, Visotzky comments on a deepened understanding of the Hebrew word *mega-leh* and thus suggests the interfaith challenge inherent in the verse "bringing sustenance from afar." "For a Jew to learn Torah, he or she must be willing to learn it from faraway places and sources. It might require travel to Warsaw or Rome, to Egypt, or Qatar. It might require learning New Testament and Patristics, or Quran and Hadith. Sometimes travel to the other brings us home to our self."[12]

Hence, as a scripture class that is also an interfaith study, the course begins by featuring the sacred texts (Hebrew scriptures, Christian scriptures, and the Qur'an). In each of the class's nine instructional modules, texts from these traditions serve as the starting point for the topic under discussion. Modules focusing on such subjects as "Women, Anthropology, and Creation," "The Mothers," "Women Working Together," "Women, Poverty, and Violence," "Women as Religious Leaders," and so forth summon relevant and appropriate readings from each of these three sets of texts. Some texts are difficult and raise questions about the tradition in which they reside. Other texts are appealing and invite readers to entertain insights gleaned from a tradition that is unfamiliar to them. These various texts and their ancient contexts provide a starting point for students to negotiate as they read and understand from their own contemporary contexts.

---

10. Burton L. Visotzky, "It Begins with a Text," in *My Neighbor's Faith: Stories of Interreligious Encounter, Growth, and Transformation*, ed. Jennifer Howe Peace, Or N. Rose, and Gregory Mobley (Maryknoll, NY: Orbis, 2012), 40.

11. Visotzky, "It Begins with a Text," 40.

12. Visotzky, "It Begins with a Text," 41.

With the Help of Other Texts

Partnered with these sacred texts are readings by current Jewish, Christian, and Islamic scholars responding to these issues in light of the selected traditions from sacred texts. Such encounters with these ancient texts and contemporary representative scholarship offer a preliminary lens into the distinctiveness and sometimes commonality across these traditions. For the Module on "The Mothers," fine resources such as *Hagar, Sarah, and Their Children: Jewish, Christian, and Muslim Perspectives*, edited by my foremost teacher, Phyllis Trible, and her co-editor Letty Russell, have been particularly enriching for students.[13] These essays suggest how the interpretive traditions about these two biblical figures, Sarah and Hagar, have both illuminated and exacerbated the strife between religious groups. Essays in this collection by scholars from all three traditions overview the Jewish, Christian, and Islamic interpretations of these figures down through the centuries. The results disclose the troubling history of relationships among Jews, Christians, and Muslims from biblical and Qur'anic beginnings, through the history of interpretations to the events of our contemporary world. To the question of the value of studying these different religious traditions with a focus on women, in this instance on Sarah and Hagar, Trible writes: "For sure, their [Hagar and Sarah's] situations highlight issues of race, class, ethnicity, nationality, and religion that we have ignored for too long. To ask about the presence of women in the grand narrative is, by extension, to ask what the voices of all marginalized people can contribute to overcoming division and hostility."[14]

Students also grapple with the figure of Mary. Though often romanticized, in this course she is proposed, with the help of

---

13. Phyllis Trible and Letty M. Russell, eds., *Hagar, Sarah, and Their Children: Jewish, Christian, and Muslim Perspectives* (Louisville, KY: Westminster John Knox Press, 2003).

14. Trible and Russell, *Hagar, Sarah, and Their Children*, 25.

assigned readings, as a legitimate liberation figure.[15] John Kaltner's essay on Mary also assists students in discovering that there is much more attention paid to this mother of Jesus in the Qur'an than in the New Testament.[16] An essay by Jane I. Smith and Yvonne Y. Haddad, "The Virgin Mary in Islamic Tradition and Commentary," offers sound instruction on the regard that Muslim women and men have for Mary in their tradition.[17] When the module on "Women Religious Leaders" is taken up, one of the readings by Hibba Abugideiri, "Hagar: A Historical Model for Gender Jihad," offers an inspiring perspective on three modern Islamic women reformers, Hagarian style.[18] Her observation that gender jihad is, in short, a struggle for gender parity in Muslim society "in the name of divine justice" strikes notes of commonality for the study of women in Judaism and Christianity. Yet again and again, while finding points of contact between traditions, caution must be exercised. Differences also exist and must also be lifted up. In another assigned essay, "Speaking from behind the Veil," Abugideiri reflects on the misunderstanding encountered by herself and other well-educated Muslim women who choose to wear the traditional hijab.[19] She offers an important assessment of Western feminism as a problematic legacy for Muslim women. "Scholarship written in the United States about

---

15. Gina Hens-Piazza, "Woman, Symbol of the Church as Kingdom: Liberation Mariology," *Marianum* 47 (1985): 216–25.

16. John Kaltner, *Ishmael Instructs Isaac: An Introduction to the Qur'an for Bible Readers* (Collegeville, MN: Liturgical Press, 1999), 207–39.

17. Jane I. Smith and Yvonne Y. Haddad, "The Virgin Mary in Islamic Tradition and Commentary," *The Muslim World* (July/October 1989): 167–87.

18. Hibba Abugideiri, "Hagar: A Historical Model for 'Gender Jihad,'" in *Daughters of Abraham: Feminist Thought in Judaism, Christianity, and Islam*, ed. Yvonne Yazbeck Haddad and John L. Esposito (Gainesville: University Press of Florida, 2001), 81–107.

19. Hibba Abugideiri, "Speaking from behind the Veil: Does Islamic Feminism Exist?" in *Faith and Feminism: Ecumenical Essays*, ed. Phyllis Trible and B. Diane Lipsett (Louisville, KY: Westminster John Knox Press, 2014), 115–34.

women in the Middle East continues to grapple with the tricky question of 'how best to deal with the political and theoretical complexities of speaking 'about' women while still avoiding speaking 'for' other women.'"[20]

From Sacred Texts to Scholarly
Texts to Contexts—Jerusalem as Classroom

Throughout the semester-long course, students are also studying Jerusalem, where these religious traditions and the legacy of women figures from the past will be more specifically encountered. Beginning with the Canaanite Era, one each of the thirteen historical periods of Jerusalem is reviewed during the first half hour of each weekly three-hour seminar. Karen Armstrong's book *Jerusalem: One City, Three Faiths* provides one of the most comprehensive overviews of this city and serves as an introductory guide.[21] Assigned online programs that detail the current sociopolitical situation and its history supplement this textbook overview. This study of the city's history makes clear the cumulative and complex influence of Judaism, Christianity, and Islam on the culture and history of this context. At the same time, it demonstrates how this history and context continue to define and shape religious communities' self-understanding. As the semester-long study comes to a close, preparation for the fourteen-day contextual study experience in Jerusalem intensifies.

Like contextual theology, contextual education features the local setting, which brings further specificity and deeper

---

20. Abugideiri, "Speaking from behind the Veil," 133. Quoting Azam Torab, *Performing Islam: Gender and Ritual in Islam* (Boston: Brill, 2007), 246, who somewhat inaccurately quotes Henrietta L. Moore, *Feminism and Anthropology* (Minneapolis: University of Minnesota Press, 1988), 186.

21. Karen Armstrong, *Jerusalem: One City, Three Faiths* (New York: Ballantine Books, 1996).

understanding to students' grasp of these traditions.[22] But sites for contextual education are not mere data banks from which we can withdraw information to better anchor our understanding of these three faith traditions. Composed of men and women with hopes and dreams, with fulfillments and challenges, contexts are the communal places and cultural spaces in which people craft their lives. We cannot treat context as mere laboratories or sites for field study for the benefit of our knowledge. Years ago, Clifford Geertz transformed how we studied culture and its context and in the process altered the whole field of anthropology.[23] He contended that understanding comes not by studying villages, but by studying *in* the village, by participating in and engaging with a culture.[24] Hence, in this course, the formal classroom study of these three traditions now yields to contextual study that, by necessity, is participatory.

Participatory learning in a context can perform several functions. It can reinforce what one has already learned. It may qualify, amend, and even contradict textbook portraits of a religious practice or belief. More often than not, it complicates the characteristically one-dimensional learning of classroom presentations. Often, comfort zones of information that have been mastered by students in the traditional classroom are disrupted by contextual education. But despite the occasional disequilibrium, contextual experience stretches students' learning capacities and transforms informational knowledge to understanding, insight, and empathy. With adequate preparation, the richness and complexity of Jerusalem does just that!

---

22. Angie Pears summarizes contextual theology as that which not only highlights context but "which *explicitly* places the recognition of the contextual nature of theology at the forefront of the theological process." See *Doing Contextual Theology* (New York: Routledge Press, 2010), 1.

23. Clifford Geertz, *Interpretation of Cultures* (New York: Basic Books, 1973).

24. Geertz, *Interpretation of Cultures*, 22.

The Contextual Experience

During the contextual study, students reside at a religious center dedicated to interfaith relations and located in the Muslim quarter of the Old City in Jerusalem. Semester-long group work requires students' participation in one of three groups that prepared an in-depth socio-cultural orientation to Jewish, Christian, or Muslim women of Jerusalem and their traditions. During a final three-hour class, these presentations served to prepare the group for the specific local representations of one of the religious traditions in the city that they now call their classroom: Jerusalem. Representations is the operative word here, because even local manifestation of one of these religious traditions takes on a variety of forms. Each of these traditions is like a canopy under which many and varied manifestations of Judaism, Christianity, and Islam exist even in one context like Jerusalem.

Additionally, each student takes on the responsibility of functioning as a site expert. This involves a semester-long study of their assigned site and the preparation of a prospectus on the history and interfaith significance of the location, as well as its importance for women. These prepared reports are uploaded into a class document that all students can access and serve as our Contextual Study Guide when we are in Jerusalem and beyond. Such sites include Huldah's Tomb, excavations at Migdol, Rachel's tomb, Women of the Wall, and so on. On location in Jerusalem, the student site expert presents further orientation, history, importance, and relevant details of an assigned site, paying attention to the interreligious components. The history suggesting that a site has significance for several religious traditions is especially key. For example, one student's presentation on Huldah's tomb reveals that this site has actually been associated with three different women down through the ages: Huldah, the Old Testament woman prophet; Pelagia, a devout Christian woman; and Rubia, a remarkable Islamic mystic. Here an interfaith history continues to be built in the view of students. Gradually, this interfaith history discloses just how intertwined these various faiths are in their development over the centuries and across this culture.

For example, one student expert presenting on the site of Mary's tomb not only pointed out the elements of different Christian groups whose influence is embedded in the artwork there; she also noted the *mihrab* (an eastern-facing niche in the wall) that is visible in the cave stemming from the period when Arab Muslims controlled this part of Jerusalem and represented their devotion to Mary by crafting a prayer space there.

Students were asked to attend to the dialectic dynamic of context on interfaith relations and interfaith relations on context. Context here, broadly defined, was to include cultural, social, and political circumstances. One student's reflection notes well the utter ensnarement of these religious sites commemorating ancient matriarchs and their significance with the sociopolitical strife of the contemporary era:

> As I stood outside the site revered as the burial place of the biblical matriarch, Rachel, a young Israeli soldier fired off tear gas canisters through an opening in the West Bank separation barrier, targeting young Palestinian protesters on the other side of the immense and imposing wall. The imperviousness of the wall facilitated a sense of safety despite the tension and confusion bubbling up nearby. The site commemorates events narrated in the book of Genesis, noting that Rachel "died; and she was buried on the road to Ephrath (now Bethlehem)" but not before giving birth to a son. "With her last breath... she named him Ben-oni," a Hebrew name meaning "son of my sorrow." After such an encounter, I was struck by the tragic irony of the situation. The site regarded as Rachel's tomb and the place where she gave birth to the son of her sorrow is a site that continues to be marred by the sorrow of conflict, violence, separation, and bitter land disputes. Rachel's story, however, does not call us simply to revere

her burial place as a symbol of the death and sorrow that took place there, but rather as a reminder of the possibility for new life to emerge from the death and sorrow that took place there. Our remembrance of the creative and life-giving forces of a figure like Rachel leads us to seek new life amidst the death and sorrow that continues to plague such a holy land. As a student of theology, this encounter has not only illuminated the dynamism of the biblical text itself, but brings that text crashing into a turbulent reality in need of wisdom, interfaith healing, and political peacemaking.[25]

Beyond the importance of the complex sociopolitical setting that informs our understanding of interfaith relations, Eboo Patel identifies the capacity for relationship as one of the essential skills for sound interfaith understanding.[26] Thus students were urged to enter into conversations and initiate relationships during the contextual study. Here the learnings thicken and multiply. One student wrote of her experience as follows:

> When I first met Hallah, she and her daughter joined their Jewish friend in sharing their experiences of the women's interfaith group, Trust-Emun. Hallah shared a moving story about her husband who had offered shelter to an enemy soldier in battle. She passed along what he had told her: "He was just as afraid as I was, so I had to help him." Her husband had since died, and as she told her story, her enduring love for him became plainly clear. The love in her drew me in, and I found a quiet moment after our formal discussion to tell her so.

---

25. Student who participated in the 2015 Fall semester contextual study course.
26. Eboo Patel, *Interfaith Leadership: A Primer* (Boston: Beacon Press, 2016), 142–45.

"I see more love in you than I have myself," she replied. It was a disarmingly sacred moment for me, to have the love I carry seen by a stranger. Hallah and her daughter invited me into their home following the discussion. Ascending to their home in the Old City in Jerusalem still feels like a dream. The hospitality they showed me stays with me even now, as I remember them making tea and showing me their family treasures. Hallah even removed her headscarf. Though we had just met, it felt like we were family. The day before we left Jerusalem, Hallah and her daughter invited me back with two other women from our group. That evening, Hallah sang to us verses from the Qur'an—an art she had begun to study recently—as her voice mingled with the shouts and songs of those celebrating Muhammad's birthday at Al Aqsa mosque just next door.

Hallah showed me that interreligious dialogue isn't, at its core, theological discussion or agreeing to disagree on doctrines. Its work is in revealing that, in this messy world, we are one human family. It is recognizing love in one another and celebrating that; it is getting close enough and being courageous enough to see that we share the same fear and letting that change us; it is giving and receiving the hospitality that is spoken of so often in our biblical tradition. Hallah revealed to me the face of God, a God who welcomes me into her home, introduces me to her beloved family, shows me her treasures, tells me her stories, and sings to me the most sacred words she knows. Hallah taught me that to dialogue, the first step is one of vulnerability and of opening oneself. I keep her and her teaching close as I go about my life and my ministry.[27]

---

27. Student who participated in the 2013 Fall semester contextual study course.

Getting to know a family while experiencing Shabbat in their home transformed another student's knowledge of this weekly Jewish observance into a cherished understanding of this family and their deep faith.

> Our Shabbat experience with an Orthodox Jewish family was a moving experience. I had read about this Jewish holy practice but had never taken part in it. Our host and his wife, let me call them Yacob and Rahab, are blessed with five children. Rahab offered each of us a warm greeting as we entered their simple home on the hillside in the city of David. Rahab had already lit the candles. She told me the lighting of candles by the women of the house is a custom during Shabbat that is supposed to create peace. As she spoke I reflected upon the role of women as conduits of peace. After we washed our hands, silence was observed as the parents blessed each of their children. This was a powerful symbol for me of how we are all blessed in different ways and we need to celebrate those differences. Afterward, the meal was punctuated by prayers, moments of silence, sharing of experiences and laughter. I felt connected with everyone at the table. Eating a meal brought us together with this Jewish family in a profound way. I thought that it is not surprising that both Christianity and Judaism have table fellowship at the center of their liturgical observances.[28]

Even experiencing a distinguished Islamic professor's treatment of an unidentified bystander who wanted to offer his own thoughts

---

28. Student who participated in the 2015 Fall semester contextual study course. These remarks are drawn from an article he since published reflecting on this educational experience. See Oscar Momanyi, SJ, "The Children of Sarah, Hagar and Mary: A Feminist Perspective on Judaism, Islam and Christianity," *The Way* (April 2017): 56, 73–87, https://www.theway.org.uk/back/562Momanyi.pdf.

about the Dome of the Rock and Al Aqsa mosque during the professor's comments became a source of instruction about one of the principles of Islam.

Before visiting the Noble Sanctuary, our group was informed that we would be greeted and accompanied around the holy site by Professor Mustafa Abu Sway. He was a prominent philosopher and Islamic scholar in Jerusalem, a man working tirelessly for justice on behalf of Palestinians in the region. So naturally, when we arrived, I assumed the man who greeted us at the entrance to the holy grounds was Professor Abu Sway. He spoke at a very rapid pace, with a thick accent so I was having a hard time following him. To my surprise, he was constantly smoking, appeared unkempt, homely... and, if I am honest, I was totally judging him. This was the professor? I was trying extremely hard to not feel utterly confused inside. After about ten minutes of walking the grounds, another man named Mustafa Abu Sway introduced himself... the first man was not him. My confusion lifted and I felt strangely relieved.

However, even though Professor Abu Sway had arrived, the other man proceeded to join us for our tour. As I observed Professor Abu Sway interact with him, I was absolutely stunned by the genuine kindness the professor extended to this man. I do not exaggerate: he acted as his equal, which was a far cry from my initial judgments. Professor Abu Sway allowed this man to share airtime in explaining different events that had recently occurred— like the damage done to Al Aqsa mosque by Israeli soldiers only a few months before, and their experience of Jewish settlers. Seeing this distinguished professor engage so kindly and with such humility to a man that I perceived as "below" him was a true window for me into lived Islamic faith. My way of "measuring" the world was called into question by the authenticity of this man.

After the tour of the sites, Professor Abu Sway came back to our residence in the Muslim quarter, further educating us about what has transpired for Palestinians in the region and the horrible human rights violations that had been taking place. As he spoke, the images of the way he treated that man back at the Noble Sanctuary ran through my mind. The complete lack of judgment. The lack of intellectual superiority. The pure acceptance. And it changed the way I received his stories about the plight of Palestinians. It allowed me to hear and see with more clarity the real atrocities that were and continue to take place.[29]

Learning about other faiths begins with encounters and building relationships. Such experiences dismantle stereotypes and prejudices that one might not own or even be aware of harboring. However, contextual learning does more when it comes to interfaith education. Such encounters on location cultivate narratives of social cohesion among people with different beliefs. These become networks through which individuals can articulate their own religious identity and still find common ground for building community with people who believe differently than they. One student's brief encounter bears a beginning witness to this unifying narrative:

While visiting a shop in the Old City of Jerusalem, I began chatting with Assusu, a storekeeper. I shared that I had just come from praying at the Wailing Wall and he asked if I was Jewish. I asked if he was religious and he responded that he was a human. He added he was a Muslim. As I asked about the menorahs he sold in his shop, he explained that his store was for everyone. As we continued to talk, Assusu demonstrated a remarkable openness. He never asked me to buy anything and expressed gratitude for

---

29. Student who participated in the 2015 Fall semester contextual study course.

our open conversation. His openness to my faith, and my reason for being in Jerusalem established an unexpected interconnectedness. Though we have different beliefs, our respect for each other and the time spent in conversation suggest a kind of unity that eclipsed our differences. I continue to think about that encounter and feel heartened by what I learned.[30]

Conclusion

Contextual studies for a scripturally based interfaith course have had significant educational yields. Students learn more about their own tradition by studying other religions. Unconscious stereotypes and prejudices begin to be dismantled. Places for bridge building and interdependence across traditions begin to surface. The narratives of one's individual tradition find points of contact with other traditions and histories. New narratives of social cohesion begin to develop. Students become more aware and critical of the forces of culture and context that influence belief. At the same time, they also begin to see common projects that emerge with other traditions that can improve and create a more just culture.

However, this contextually based study also illuminates features that exacerbate conflicts and lead to misunderstandings between faiths. A study of interfaith theology in contexts like Jerusalem sometimes makes such hostilities palpable. One final encounter in context during our immersion sought to wrestle with these divisions and offer one way forward. On the final day of our time in Jerusalem, we visited Neve Shalom Wahat a Salam, a cooperative community of Palestinian Muslims, Christians, and Israeli Jews living on the outskirts of Jerusalem. It has been in existence for over forty years and currently houses seventy families. Their goal

---

30. Student who participated in the 2017 Fall semester contextual study course.

is simple—to live together and respect each other's religious differences. Children go to a bilingual school (Hebrew and Arabic) on the grounds, and a popular spirituality center hosts groups from the surrounding region. Here people of three different faiths, national backgrounds, and histories all admit to being concerned about ultimate matters, putting those concerns into action, and adopting a lifestyle that builds community with those who are different from themselves. As one student observed, "The decision to become part of this community is such an utterly intentional acceptance on the part of both Israelis and Palestinians, and on the part of Jews, Christians, and Muslims of each other as one's neighbor...ensuring that children will grow up knowing 'the other' as not really 'the other' but as true sisters and brothers."[31]

As much as seeing is believing, learning in context fosters something more. Contextual education nudges knowledge to permeate the personal and intersubjective spaces of shared understanding. We begin to know locally and in more complex terms what we previously knew only informationally. As one student so aptly summarized:

> Learning and studying contextually was essential; being with people, living in their setting, participating with them in conversations and in their religious practices drew out something deeper in me about their faith and about my own. As I participated in this context, it began to work on me. I learned in ways that I had not expected and gained insights that moved beyond what I thought I knew. This course has changed the way I think about education.[32]

---

31. Student who participated in the 2017 Fall semester contextual study course.
32. Student who participated in the 2017 Fall semester contextual study course.

Chapter Fourteen

POPE FRANCIS
AS A CONTEXTUAL
THEOLOGIAN

Kevin O'Brien, SJ

For a few moments, the world fell silent.

Jorge Mario Bergoglio stepped out onto the balcony overlooking St. Peter's Square so that the world could meet the newly elected pope who took the name Francis. His white cassock plainly visible amid the darkness of the Roman night, Francis offered a brief greeting and then asked for the people's blessing and bowed slightly. The silence that covered the square where thousands of people had gathered washed over the world as millions more watched on television and online. In the silence, the pope listened and received all the needs and hopes, the joys and anguish of those he was called to serve. Before teaching and preaching as pope, he listened.

If there is one posture that describes contextual theology, it is listening. According to Steve Bevans, this listening includes listening both to the past and the present:

> We can say, then, that doing theology contextually means doing theology in a way that takes into account two things: First, it takes into account the faith experience of the past that is recorded in scriptures and kept alive, preserved, defended—and perhaps even neglected or suppressed—in tradition.... Second, contextual theology

takes into account the experience of the present, the context.[1]

For Bevans, to speak of theology that is contextual is redundant. Theologians, he observes, have always taken contexts into consideration, but they have not always been intentional about it. He writes:

> In contextual theology, experience plays a key role. Contextual theology recognizes that the scriptures, though certainly normative for Christian theologizing, are the record of God's revelation as experienced in the history of Israel, in the life and ministry of Jesus of Nazareth, and in the earliest years of the Christian church. In the same way, Christians committed to contextual theologizing realize that the received doctrinal tradition comes as the result of Christians through the ages in various contexts who have reflected on their experience in light of the scriptures and of Christian tradition. Contextual theology involves what the authors of scripture and Christians of the past did: reflecting on their experience in the light of their faith, in dialogue with inherited wisdom.[2]

Lacking consciousness of context risks universalizing theology so that it never touches the human. Unmoored from history, theology fails to address human needs and longings. Lacking intelligibility, it loses meaning, and thus it is not helpful for those the Church seeks to serve.

---

1. Stephen B. Bevans, SVD, *Models of Contextual Theology* (Maryknoll, NY: Orbis, 2002), 5.

2. Stephen Bevans, SVD, "Contextual Theology as Practical Theology," in *Opening the Field of Practical Theology: An Introduction*, ed. Kathleen A. Cahalan and Gordon S. Mikoski (Lanham, MD: Rowman and Littlefield, 2014), 49–50.

This kind of universalized theology is far from the theology that Pope Francis has practiced since that night he stepped onto the balcony and asked the people's blessing. He listened, and continued to listen. He has listened to scripture and the Church's tradition, privileged loci of God's revelation. He has listened to the experience of ordinary people, especially the most vulnerable and poor, who reveal something distinctive about who God is and what God wants for us and our world. He has listened to the cry of nature. Because God is always trying to get our attention in the experience of the past and the present, we listen, learn, and only then—as Francis shows—do we teach, preach, and counsel.

Throughout his papacy, Francis has contended with the not-so-subtle critique that he is a pastor, not a theologian, especially when compared to his immediate predecessors.[3] This charge provides cover to minimize, even dismiss, what he teaches and how he is moving the Church forward to meet the needs of the current era. Such critics miss the point. If all theology is contextual, it is necessarily pastoral, because the reason theologians and ministers attend to cultural contexts in the first place is to put their teaching and learned ministry in service of God's people, especially those on the margins of church and society. Marking the 100th anniversary of the Faculty of Theology of the Catholic University of Argentina (UCA), Pope Francis put it succinctly: "Understanding theology is understanding God, who is Love."[4]

---

3. Vatican correspondent John Allen makes the astute observation that Francis tends to refer to theologians in the third person. John L. Allen, "Pope Urges Theologians to Be 'Faithful, Anchored' to Vatican II," *Crux*, December 29, 2017, https://cruxnow.com/vatican/2017/12/29/pope-urges-theologians-faithful-anchored-vatican-ii/.

4. Francis, Letter to the Grand Chancellor of the Pontificia Universidad Católica Argentina, for the 100th anniversary of the founding of the Faculty of Theology (March 3, 2015), https://w2.vatican.va/content/francesco/en/letters/2015/documents/papa-francesco_20150303_lettera-universita-cattolica-argentina.html.

For Francis, the work of theologians is a ministry.[5] Contextual theologians, like Pope Francis, are grounded in the real world, close to people, and address their joys and concerns. In his letter to the UCA faculty in his native Argentina, Francis noted that theologians today must realize the renewal of the Second Vatican Council, "which was an updating, a re-reading of the Gospel from the perspective of contemporary culture."[6] This means "living on a frontier, one in which the Gospel meets the needs of the people to whom it should be proclaimed in an understandable and meaningful way." Francis cautioned that "We must guard against a theology that is exhausted in academic dispute or one that looks at humanity from a glass castle. You learn so as to live: theology and holiness are inseparable."[7] For Francis, learning theology goes hand in hand with living theology. He continued:

> Let the theology that you elaborate therefore be rooted and based on Revelation, on Tradition, but also correspond with the cultural and social processes.... Do not settle for a desktop theology. Your place for reflection is the frontier. Do not fall into the temptation to embellish, to add fragrance, to adjust them to some degree and domesticate them. Even good theologians, like good shepherds, have the odour of the people and of the street and, by their reflection, pour oil and wine onto the wounds of mankind.[8]

---

5. Francis, Audience with Members of the Italian Theological Association (December 29, 2017), http://press.vatican.va/content/salastampa/en/bollettino/pubblico/2017/12/29/171229c.html#.

6. Francis, Letter to Pontificia Universidad Católica Argentina. To a group of Italian theologians, he similarly maintained that theologians today must "receive" the council with a "creative fidelity" and anchor their work in the council (Francis, Audience with Italian Theological Association).

7. Francis, Letter to Pontificia Universidad Católica Argentina.

8. Francis, Letter to Pontificia Universidad Católica Argentina.

In contrast to these "shepherd theologians," Francis posed the following images to the UCA faculty in his plainspoken and evocative style:

> Who then is the student of theology that the UCA is called to form? Certainly not a "museum" theologian who gathers data and information on Revelation without, however, really knowing what to do with it. Nor a passive onlooker on history. The theologian formed at the UCA should be a person capable of building humanity around him, passing on the divine Christian truth in a truly human dimension, and not a talentless intellectual, an ethicist lacking in goodwill or a bureaucrat of the sacred.[9]

Pope Francis has something to teach us about doing theology and living theology today. We thus do well to explore Pope Francis as a contextual theologian. In this chapter I will first describe Francis's theological method as reflected in the seminal writings of his papacy. I will then articulate three practices—mercy, accompaniment, and discernment—that flow from his method of contextual theology and his understanding of theology as ministry. Finally, I will suggest the significance of Francis's approach to theology for those teaching, learning, and living theology today.

Francis's Theological Method

The way we do theology determines in part the conclusions we reach. Contextual theologians study, write, and teach in dialog with

---

9. Francis, Letter to Pontificia Universidad Católica Argentina. In his apostolic exhortation *Evangelii Gaudium* (2013), the pope also urges evangelizers of all kinds to "take on the 'smell of the sheep'" (24), http://w2.vatican.va/content/francesco/en/apost_exhortations/documents/papa-francesco_esortazione-ap_20131124_evangelii-gaudium.html.

particular communities, however they are defined. For example, theologians might consider the city or nation in which they teach, or a particular economic class, or a racial or ethnic group.[10] Relying on the expertise found in other disciplines such as sociology, anthropology, economics, history, and political science, theologians try to better understand the context with which they are engaged. They also are wise to immerse themselves in the liturgical life and the literary and artistic expression of the community. Finally, they might reflect on their own personal interactions with the community. They listen intently to a variety of voices in the community so that, by understanding better the community's needs and hopes, their work is helpful. In these ways, contextual theologians begin their inquiry not with first principles or timeless ideals, but with experience and history. The community then receives what the theologian says or writes. This reception gives life to the theologian's work in ways both predictable and unexpected to the theologian. Their response can help the theologian further refine his or her work, which can then be offered to the community again in a dialectical process.[11]

In his seminal writings thus far, Francis grounds his theological reflection in certain contexts.[12] In chapter 2 of his apostolic

---

10. In *Laudato si'* (2015), Francis raises a novel context: future generations of people who will inhabit the earth. He does so by extending the notion of the common good to future generations and proposes "intergenerational solidarity" as a key component of Catholic social thought (159), http://w2.vatican.va/content/francesco/en/encyclicals/documents/papa-francesco_20150524_enciclica-laudato-si.html.

11. The process I have described here is similar to the "*communio* model of reception" that Richard Gaillardetz describes in his explanation of how doctrine is fashioned between bishops and the Christian faithful. Richard R. Gaillardetz, *By What Authority?* (Collegeville, MN: Liturgical Press, 2003), 110–17.

12. Here I refer to Francis's three major writings thus far as pope: two apostolic exhortations and one encyclical. Just over three months after his election in 2013, Francis published his first encyclical, *Lumen Fidei* (The Light of Faith). In the encyclical's opening, Francis explains that Benedict XVI had mostly completed a first draft of the encyclical when he retired: "I have taken up his fine work and added a few contributions of my own"

exhortation *Evangelii Gaudium* (The Joy of the Gospel), he lists in great detail the impediments to effective evangelization both internal and external to the Church. In chapter 4, he outlines the social, cultural, and economic dimensions that touch on the Church's evangelical mission. In his encyclical *Laudato si'*, "Praise Be to You": On Care for Our Common Home, Francis observes at the outset that "Theological and philosophical reflections on the situation of humanity and the world can sound tiresome and abstract unless they are grounded in a fresh analysis of our present situation" (LS 17). With this cue, he then devotes chapter 1 to an exhaustive analysis of the environmental crises facing the earth. In chapter 3, he identifies human causes for the crises, and in chapter 5, he assesses specific policies and proposals to address the crises. Finally, in chapter 2 of the apostolic exhortation *Amoris Laetitia* (The Joy of Love), Francis describes the various realities and challenges of family life.[13] In subsequent chapters, he suggests concretely how the Church must respond pastorally and meaningfully to these challenges. The concreteness of Francis's approach is apparent across his writings, and somewhat novel in papal magisterium. To name just a few examples, Francis walks pastors through his step-by-step process in preparing a homily that speaks to people's needs and hopes (EG 135–59), raises cautions about city parking (LS 153) and air conditioning (LS 55), and offers homespun advice to married couples, such as sharing a morning kiss and evening blessing (AL 226) and saying "please," "thank you," and "sorry" (AL 133).

While such specificity is unique, Francis's consideration of human condition and social context is not novel. Vatican II's

---

(7). Given that Benedict is the principal author of the first encyclical, I have focused my attention on major writings that are attributed only to Francis, http://w2.vatican.va/content/francesco/en/encyclicals/documents/papa-francesco_20130629_enciclica-lumen-fidei.html.

13. Francis, *Amoris Laetitia* (AL) (On Love in the Family) (2016), https://w2.vatican.va/content/dam/francesco/pdf/apost_exhortations/documents/papa-francesco_esortazione-ap_20160319_amoris-laetitia_en.pdf.

Gaudium et Spes (Pastoral Constitution on the Church in the Modern World) begins with the then-remarkable statement: "The joys and the hopes, the griefs and the anxieties of the [people] of this age, especially those who are poor or in any way afflicted, these are the joys and hopes, the griefs and anxieties of the followers of Christ."[14] *Gaudium et Spes* then surveys a host of trends and challenges faced by people in the modern world. The council names at length cultural developments and political and economic realities that demand the Church's attention. To varying degrees, the conciliar and postconciliar popes weaved context into their papal teaching. They have thus been faithful to the mandate of *Gaudium et Spes*:

> In every age, the church carries the responsibility of reading the signs of the times and of interpreting them in the light of the Gospel, if it is to carry out its task. In language intelligible to every generation, it should be able to answer the ever recurring questions which people ask about the meaning of this present life and of the life to come, and how one is related to the other. We must be aware of and understand the aspirations, the yearnings, and the often dramatic features of the world in which we live. (GS 4)[15]

Francis affirms this tradition and extends it.

Francis's insistence that we begin inquiry from experience and context is based on the theological conviction that God is present

---

14. Second Vatican Council, *Gaudium et Spes* (GS) (1965), 1, http://www.vatican.va/archive/hist_councils/ii_vatican_council/documents/vat-ii_cons_19651207_gaudium-et-spes_en.html.

15. Similarly, in *Evangelii Gaudium* (EG), Francis, relying on the words of Paul VI, writes: "It is not the task of the pope to offer a detailed and complete analysis of contemporary reality, but I do exhort all the communities to an 'ever watchful scrutiny of the signs of the times'" (51).

and laboring in and through all of creation. Francis makes this point most eloquently in *Laudato si'*, quoting Ecumenical Patriarch Bartholomew, a kindred spirit who shares Francis's environmental concerns: "'[T]he divine and the human meet in the slightest detail in the seamless garment of God's creation, in the last speck of dust of our planet'" (LS 9). Drawing on the example of his namesake, St. Francis of Assisi, the pope describes nature as a "magnificent book in which God speaks to us and grants us a glimpse of his infinite beauty and goodness" (LS 12).[16] The human person, who is created in the image and likeness of God, has a privileged place in creation (LS 65).[17] That God chose to be human in the person of Jesus Christ deepens the bond between the divine and the human and reaffirms the dignity of each person, who is the "prolongation of the incarnation" (EG 179). Families, too, are a living reflection of the communion of love that describes the triune God (AL 11): "The Lord's presence dwells in real and concrete families, with all their daily troubles, and struggles, joys, and hopes" (AL 315). Among humanity, Francis insists that the poor and marginalized particularly have something to teach us about God and authentic human living: "We are called to find Christ in them, to lend our voice to their causes, but also to be their friends, to listen to them, to speak for them and to embrace the mysterious wisdom which God wishes to share with us through them" (EG 198).

Humanity's unique place in creation does not diminish the importance of other created things in God's revelation. By becoming a human being, Jesus Christ "has taken unto himself this material world and now, risen, is intimately present to each being, surrounding it with his affection and penetrating it with his light" (LS 221). Because all of creation participates in the ongoing revelation of God, Francis calls us to be attentive in order to "discover in each

---

16. See also LS 221: "[E]ach creature reflects something of God and has a message to convey to us."

17. See also EG 274: "God created that person in his image, and he or she reflects something of God's glory."

thing a teaching which God wishes to hand on to us" (LS 85).[18] To restrict theological inquiry to traditional sources of revelation— tradition and scripture—is to impoverish it. By also considering both the awesome and painful realities of human living and the natural world, theologians deepen their studies and fortify their voices in saying something meaningful and helpful.

If theologians and ministers take seriously revelation that awaits in the created order, then they must bring the traditional sources of revelation into dialog with culture. According to the Second Vatican Council, "There are many links between the message of salvation and culture. In his self-revelation to his people, fully manifesting himself in his incarnate Son, God spoke in the context of the culture proper to each age" (GS 58). Because the human person cannot be properly considered apart from his or her culture and the web of relationships that compose it, Francis concludes: "Grace supposes culture, and God's gift becomes flesh in the culture of those who receive it" (EG 115).

As theologians consider cultural context, they do not simply describe how grace influences culture, but also how the culture enriches the way the Gospel is expressed, understood, and lived. This process of inculturation, Francis explains, reveals the depth, diversity, and beauty of the Church's tradition, which no one culture or person could do on his or her own (EG 116–17). He writes: "Each portion of the people of God, by translating the gift of God into its own life and in accordance with its own genius, bears witness to the faith it has received and enriches it with new and eloquent expressions" (EG 122). Given this conviction, Francis freely references, in a way not seen before in papal documents, statements from national and regional bishops' conferences, as well as those from previous popes. Regions and countries, he explains, "can seek solutions better suited to its culture and sensitive to its traditions and local needs" (AL 3).

---

18. Quoting John Paul II, Francis writes: "We can say that 'alongside revelation properly so-called, contained in sacred Scripture, there is a divine manifestation in the blaze of the sun and the fall of night'" (LS 85).

Thus, theologians properly concern themselves with culture, as they would any locus of the divine. In so doing, they must balance faithfulness to the tradition with a certain intellectual boldness. In his Apostolic Constitution, *Veritatis Gaudium* (The Joy of Truth), Francis writes:

> Theology and Christian culture have lived up to their mission whenever they were ready to take risks and remain faithful on the borderline. "The questions of our people, their suffering, their battles, their dreams, their trials, their worries possess an interpretational value that we cannot ignore if we want to take the principle of the Incarnation seriously. Their wondering helps us to wonder ourselves, their questions question us. All this helps us to delve into the mystery of the Word of God, the Word that requires and asks that we dialogue, that we enter into communion."[19]

Considered as a whole, Francis's major writings exhibit a generally hopeful and optimistic view of humanity and human culture. Yet he also knows the reality of sin. Speaking to the International Theological Commission in 2013, Francis observed that the Church's dialogue with culture must be "at once critical and benevolent."[20] Francis does not hesitate to confront the cultural dispositions and

---

19. Francis, *Veritatis Gaudium* (2017), 5, https://w2.vatican.va/content/francesco/en/apost_constitutions/documents/papa-francesco_costituzione-ap_2017 1208_veritatis-gaudium.html. Here he is quoting himself from a video address, *Video Message to Participants in an International Theological Congress Held at the Pontifical Catholic University of Argentina* (September 1–3, 2015), https://w2.vatican.va/content/francesco/en/messages/pont-messages/2015/documents/papa-francesco_20150903_videomessaggio-teologia-buenos-aires.html.

20. Francis, Address to Members of the International Theological Commission (December 6, 2013), https://w2.vatican.va/content/francesco/en/speeches/2013/december/documents/papa-francesco_20131206_commissione-teologica.html.

trends that dehumanize, diminish, and desecrate human beings and the natural world, naming, for example, individualism, unbridled freedom, materialism, consumerism, relativism, excessive anthropocentrism, and clericalism.[21] Francis thus teaches contextual theologians to be nimble in their work. At times they are descriptive and expository about culture, laying the foundation for a richer dialogue between faith and culture. They are also free to defend and advocate as well as criticize culture. In these postures, theologians offer a vital service to the Church by fostering dialog with cultures. Francis urges theologians "to carry out this service as part of the Church's saving mission. In doing so, however, they must always remember that the Church and theology exist to evangelize, and not be content with a desk-bound theology" (EG 133).

The Practices of Mercy, Accompaniment, and Discernment

Theologians and pastors who take culture seriously must be willing to get close to the communities they encounter. Instead of looking for "those personal and communal niches which shelter us from the maelstrom of human misfortune," Francis urges ministers in the Church to "enter into the reality of other people's lives and know the power of tenderness. Whenever we do so, our lives become wonderfully complicated and we experience intensely what it is to be a people, to be part of a people" (EG 270). It is tempting to run from the complex reality of people's lives, retreating to the comfort of predictable work and the realm of ideas untouched by the messiness of humanity. Francis urges us to resist "renouncing the realism of the social aspect of the Gospel" and reducing Jesus to "a purely spiritual Christ, without flesh and without the cross" (EG

---

21. See, for example, EG 53, 59, 64, 67, 89, 102; LS 66, 109, 116, 122; AL 33, 34, 39, 124, 127.

88). To the contrary, theologians, like other ministers in the Church, must "run the risk of a face-to-face encounter with others, with their physical presence which challenges us, with their pain and their pleas, with their joy that infects us in our close and continuous interaction" (EG 88). Francis puts it plainly: "I prefer a Church which is bruised, hurting and dirty because it has been out on the streets, rather than a Church which is unhealthy from being confined and from clinging to its own security" (EG 49). Leaving their desks and walking out onto the streets, theologians benefit from cultivating three practices: mercy, accompaniment, and discernment.

The point of getting close to people is to help them, which for Francis means sharing with them God's abundant, merciful love (EG 24, 39). In their indispensable role of helping the Church do its thinking, theologians are vital partners in Francis's "revolution of tenderness" (EG 88),[22] as long as they do not just think about problems and ruminate on ideas at a safe remove from people. To the contrary, for Francis, the Church is like a field hospital after battle, close enough to heal people's wounds and warm their hearts.[23] In his letter to the theology faculty in Argentina, Francis applies this image to their work as theologians and scholars:

Theology is an expression of a Church which is a "field hospital," which lives her mission of salvation and healing in the world. Mercy is not just a pastoral attitude but it is the very substance of the Gospel of Jesus. I encourage you to study how the various disciplines—dogma, morality, spirituality, law, and so on—may reflect the centrality of mercy. Without mercy our theology, our law, our pastoral

---

22. See also Francis, *The Name of God Is Mercy* (New York: Random House, 2016). This book-length interview with Italian journalist Andrea Tornielli was published during the Holy Year of Mercy, declared by Francis for December 8, 2015, to November 20, 2016.

23. Francis, *Name of God Is Mercy*, 52–53; Francis, *A Big Heart Open to God*, interview with Antonio Spadaro (New York: HarperOne, 2013), 30–31.

care run the risk of collapsing into bureaucratic narrow-mindedness or ideology, which by their nature seeks to domesticate the mystery.[24]

Relying on a traditional image of the Church steeped in Vatican II, Francis also describes the Church as more than a hierarchical institution: "[S]he is first and foremost a people advancing on its pilgrim way toward God. She is certainly a mystery rooted in the Trinity, yet she exists concretely in history as a people of pilgrims and evangelizers, transcending any institutional expression, however necessary" (EG 111). As part of the people of God, the theologian walks with others, not as an observer, but as a fellow pilgrim. As such, those serving in the Church must learn the art of accompaniment. To accompany another is to reverence the other, to walk closely, patiently, and faithfully with them, to listen attentively to them, and to encourage them along the way (EG 169, 171). One who accompanies another with "an openness of heart" (EG 171) realizes that "each person's situation before God and their life in grace are mysteries which no one can fully know from without" (EG 172). In this way, humility is intrinsic to accompaniment.

Doing theology within the beauty and brokenness of human lives is not easy. Given the complex challenges, theologians who practice culturally contextualized theology must cultivate the art of discernment as well. As a Jesuit, Pope Francis is well versed in discernment, which is central to the *Spiritual Exercises* of St. Ignatius. In this tradition, discernment means being attentive to our experience and our interior reactions to that experience. We acknowledge gratefully how God labors in creation at every moment, but also recognize how sin distorts that divine presence. In a prayerful spirit, we reflect on our experiences and sift through our interior reactions, assessing which come from God and which do

---

24. Francis, Letter to Pontificia Universidad Católica Argentina.

not—or, put another way, which lead us to greater faith, hope, and love and which do not. We then make concrete decisions in the hope of acting consistently with what God desires for us.[25] Francis encourages those who work in the Church to collaborate with others as they regularly engage in "evangelical discernment," which helps us labor wisely, boldly, and creatively (EG 33, 50).

Theologians wisely rely on discernment to navigate the many "gray areas" and ambiguities of human living and to understand their own reactions when they engage cultures, communities, and persons. When removed from this sometimes messy reality, it is easy to become, as Francis notes, "like spiritual masters and pastoral experts who give instructions from on high" (EG 96) and who, "thinking that everything is black and white... close off the way of grace and of growth" (AL 305). From this personal distance and antiseptic clarity, we fail to appreciate the totality of a situation and how various factors mitigate responsibility for one's actions (EG 44; AL 301–2). In contrast, those entrusted with leadership in the Church are called to practice a "spiritual discernment that responds to a need that arises by looking at things, at people, and from reading the signs of the times."[26] While not hesitating to be prophetic and to present certain ideals, contextual theologians and pastors are also realistic and compassionate as they try to serve people (AL 307–8).

In his exhortation *Amoris Laetitia*, which followed a two-year synod on family life, Francis counseled on how to strike that difficult balance. Acknowledging the pain and difficulties faced by many families, he writes: "[W]hile clearly stating the Church's teaching, pastors are to avoid judgments that do not take into account the complexity of various situations, and they are to be attentive, by necessity, to how people experience and endure distress because of their situation" (AL 79). In difficult situations, careful

---

25. Francis alludes to this process of discernment in EG 51.
26. Francis, *Big Heart Open to God*, 14.

discernment must be exercised (AL 79, 298). Such discernment requires dialog with those who are struggling or living objectively in ways that conflict with Church teaching (AL 293).[27] The point of such dialog is to understand people's goodness and limitations, to appreciate particular challenges of their situation, and to discern a path forward as they grow in holiness (AL 294–95). For Francis, such accompaniment and discernment are how the Church extends mercy to people in tough situations (AL 296).

In chapter 8 of *Amoris Laetitia*, which is appropriately titled "Accompanying, Discerning, and Integrating Weakness," Francis addresses at length the contentious issue of how to care for divorced Catholics who are civilly remarried. In preparation for the synod, he asked bishops to survey families so that they could share their experiences.[28] Having listened in this way, he was able to articulate various reasons why couples find themselves in difficult situations. Francis admits that no easy answers exist (AL 298), and he refuses to provide a general rule that could apply to all such cases (AL 300). Instead, not surprisingly, he urges a "process of accompaniment and discernment," weighing a host of factors in the former and current marriages (AL 298, 300).[29] Insisting on the need to consider such concrete factors, Francis observes that "individual conscience needs to be better incorporated into the Church's praxis in certain situations which do not objectively embody our understanding of marriage" (AL 303).

---

27. Francis names in particular those in civil unions, those who are cohabitating without marriage, and divorced and civilly remarried Catholics (AL 293, 294, 297–98).

28. See Jim McDermott's excellent series of four articles on the surveys, "The Surveys for the Synod on the Family," *America*, February 26, 2015 ("Initial Observations"), March 2 ("Taylor Swift Saves My Family"), March 3 ("How Did We Get Here?"), and March 3 ("What's Everyone Else Up To?"), https://www.americamagazine.org/voices/jim-mcdermott?page=20.

29. Francis notes that the following must be present in the discernment: humility, discretion, respect for the Church and its teaching, a sincere desire to know God's will and to follow it (AL 300).

Accompaniment and discernment presume that people have something meaningful to say about the faith of the Church and how to live it. Professional theologians or bishops do not have a monopoly on teaching:

> God furnishes the totality of the faithful with an instinct of faith—*sensus fidei*—which helps them to discern what is truly of God. The presence of the Spirit gives Christians a certain connaturality with divine realities, and a wisdom which enables them to grasp those realities intuitively, even when they lack the wherewithal to give them precise expression. (EG 119)[30]

Francis encourages theologians to listen to the "reality of faith" revealed in people not expert in theology: "It is in this living faith of the holy faithful people of God that every theologian must feel immersed and by which he [or she] must also know how to be sustained, carried and embraced."[31] Given this spiritual intuition in each person, the pope encourages pastors to help people follow their conscience in discerning the complexities of life: "We have been called to form consciences, not to replace them" (AL 37).

Accompanying people with mercy necessitates meeting them where they are. While affirming certain ideals, theologians and ministers must also accommodate the person's actual situation, being realistic about what a person is able to do or achieve as

---

30. Elsewhere, Francis described this *sensus fidei* in the following way: "Through the gift of the Holy Spirit, the members of the Church possess the '*sense of the faith.*' It is a kind of 'spiritual instinct' which allows them to *sentire cum Ecclesia* [think with the Church] and to discern what conforms to the Apostolic faith and to the spirit of the Gospel. Of course, it is clear that the *sensus fidelium* [sense of the faithful] must not be confused with the sociological reality of majority opinion. It is something else" (Francis, Address to International Theological Commission).

31. Francis, Audience with Italian Theological Association.

they grow in holiness on their journey of faith (EG 44).[32] In other words, attraction works better than compulsion. Francis urges servants in the Church to avoid rigidity and defensiveness: "Frequently, we act as arbiters of grace rather than its facilitators. But the Church is not a tollhouse; it is the house of the Father, where there is a place for everyone, with all their problems" (EG 47).[33] Francis hopes that those who serve in the Church cultivate a "missionary heart," one humble enough to realize that "it has to grow in its own understanding of the Gospel and in discerning the paths of the Spirit, and so it always does what good it can, even if in the process, its shoes get soiled by the mud of the street" (EG 45).

Through their expertise and their attentiveness to the breadth of revelation, theologians offer indispensable help in forming consciences and empowering the proper exercise of conscience. They also help ministers and lay persons grow in understanding and expressing scripture and tradition in ways that are meaningful for today (EG 40). Recognizing that the Church grows in holiness and matures in understanding of the divine mystery, Francis calls on theologians and other academics to study and debate a variety of issues pertinent to people's lives (EG 40). In an address to the Italian Theological Association in 2017, Francis encouraged their work of "free and responsible reflection" and named some "unprecedented challenges" faced by the Church today: "the ecological crisis; the development of neurosciences and techniques that may modify man; growing social inequalities or

---

32. See also AL 303: An informed conscience, aided by discernment, can acknowledge "with sincerity and honesty what for now is the most generous response which can be given to God, and come to see with a certain moral security that is what God himself is asking amid the concrete complexity of one's limits, while yet not fully the objective ideal."

33. See also AL 134: "Marital love is not defended primarily by presenting indissolubility as a duty, or by repeating doctrine, but by helping it to grow ever stronger under the impulse of grace."

the migrations of entire peoples; both theoretical and practical relativism."[34] Because those issues are complicated, debate and inquiry about them will also be so. Just as Francis empowers lay persons to "own" their faith as mature adults, he also leaves room for theologians and pastors to wrestle sincerely and courageously with the ambiguities of Christian life. Francis offers this assurance: "For those who long for a monolithic body of doctrine guarded by all and leaving no room for nuance, this might appear as undesirable and leading to confusion. But in fact such variety serves to bring out and develop different facets of the inexhaustible riches of the Gospel" (EG 40).

Lessons for Theologians Today

Engaging particular contexts prevents theologians from becoming, to use Francis's images, "museum" or "desktop" theologians, writing from "glass castles" or becoming "bureaucrats of the sacred," domesticating the inexhaustible mystery of God. Attentive to the geographic, economic, cultural, and ideological frontiers of church and society, theologians who immerse themselves in the lives of people have the "smell of the sheep" on them because they write and research not from a distance but in proximity to them. Surrounded by humanity, in all of their beauty and brokenness, they know the community enough to offer God's mercy in some concrete way. They are also close enough to be changed professionally and personally.

In his commencement address at the Jesuit School of Theology in Berkeley in May 2017, Bishop Robert McElroy of San Diego challenged the faculty and graduating students to join Pope Francis's theological project: for pastoral theology to claim its rightful place as a central element of Catholic doctrine and practice. Pastoral theology, McElroy argued, was traditionally considered "a derivative

---

34. Francis, Audience with Italian Theological Association.

branch of theology, confined to the application of the fruits of the
other branches of theology to the practice of the salvation of souls."
Instead, McElroy argued that Francis's pastoral outlook

> demands that all of the other branches of theology attend
> to the concrete reality of human life and human suffering
> in a much more substantial way in forming doctrine.
>
> It states that the lived experience of human sinfulness
> and human conversion are vital to understanding the cen-
> tral attribute of God in relation to us, which is mercy.
>
> It demands that moral theology process from the ac-
> tual pastoral action of Jesus Christ, which does not first
> demand a change in life, but begins with an embrace of di-
> vine love, proceeds to the action of healing and only then
> requires a conversion of action in responsible conscience.
>
> The pastoral theology of Pope Francis requires that the
> liturgical and sacramental life of the Church be formed
> in compassionate embrace with the often overwhelming
> life challenges which prevent men and women at periods
> of their life from conforming adequately with important
> Gospel challenges.
>
> And the pastoral theology of Pope Francis rejects a
> notion of law which can be blind to the uniqueness of
> concrete human situations, human suffering, and human
> limitation.

McElroy thus sees a more vital interplay between pastoral theology and other disciplines in the Catholic theological tradition. If
Francis's vision is realized, pastoral realities and the lived experience of people in their noble striving would be primary sources of
theological reflection for understanding Christian life. Accompaniment and mercy would become fundamental to every form of
theological inquiry.

McElroy closed his address by offering a challenge to the Jesuit School of Theology and, by extension, other theology centers

interested in contextual theology: "It will be one of the greatest theological projects of our age to understand how this new theological tradition should be formed, how it can be integrated into the wider doctrinal life of the Church, and how it can bring unity, energy, and insight into the intersection of Catholic faith and the modern world."[35] The question for theology professors and students is how to summon the courage, creativity, boldness, and insight to meet this challenge.

Bringing mercy, accompaniment, and discernment into the heart of theological inquiry and the life of a school is transformative. Approaching theology in a culturally contextualized way means adjusting syllabi and curriculum to consider specific contexts. It means collaborating with professionals from other academic disciplines and building connections within theological areas, breaking down the proverbial silos in the academy. It means leaving the "ivory tower" and getting close to the people we are called on to serve so that we can better understand their lives. It means identifying peripheries and margins in church and society that are often overlooked and making them the center of theological reflection. It also means embracing theology not simply as a profession but as a vocation, for if, as Francis says, theology and holiness are inseparable, then it is not just for the persons "helped" to grow in holiness but for the theologian, too, to learn something new about God and humanity and our mission in the world.

Bringing pastoral theology to the heart of theological inquiry means asking some challenging questions: What does mercy demand in this case? Whom are we called to accompany? To what frontier must I go? What do people need and what can we learn from them? How do we best discern the complexities of a context, faithful both to the tradition and to the persons whom we accompany? How willing am I to grow in faith, hope, and love in this

---

35. Robert McElroy, "The Pastoral Theology of Pope Francis" (unpublished commencement address, Jesuit School of Theology, Berkeley, May 2017).

encounter? While Francis respects theologians too much to give easy answers, he does offer us an example of a way forward. Like he did on the night of his election, we, too, can bow before the mystery of God and the people we wish to serve. We, too, can listen, confident that if we are attentive, discerning, and close enough, we can pour words, like oil, on the wounds of the world, and find blessings returned to us in unimaginable ways.

AFTERWORD

For the last year or so, it has been my pleasure—and honor—to work with Eddie Fernández and Deborah Ross in preparing the essays in this book for publication. It has been a pleasure on the one hand because it has been great to work with my old friend Eddie and my new friend Deborah. On the other hand, I have really enjoyed reading, commenting on, and engaging with the work of the various authors who have contributed to this collection of essays. I have learned a lot, not only about new and creative uses of contextual theology as such, but about the role of contextual theology in education. Whether it has been learning about how classical Christological formulas are actually exercises in doing contextual theology and can be models of doing Christology today, or learning how doing interreligious dialogue can be understood as doing contextual theology, I have been personally enriched. I have been inspired by how a contextual approach to theological education can be deepened by reflection during study trips to the Middle East, by reflection on the experience of the poor in Africa, and by reflection on prisoners' experiences in San Quentin. These and the other essays in this book have been exciting to read.

But working on this book with Eddie and Deborah, and with the JST Faculty, has also been an honor. That my book *Models of Contextual Theology* has been so important in inspiring and shaping JST's curriculum and its approach to theology has been truly humbling, and I am deeply grateful for my JST colleagues' trust and enthusiasm in and for my work. It is every author's dream that what she or he writes will be actually read by other people and could actually make a difference in their lives. This dream has been realized in these pages in more ways than I could have ever hoped for. A long time ago, I remember reading Bernard Lonergan's remark that often the interpreter of a work understands an author's development more than the author him/herself.[1] I think this is really true in the case of this book. Just to give one example, I never realized how powerful my "translation model" could be in certain circumstances. I always conceived of it as one of the weaker models of contextualization. But in the context of the San Quentin prison it takes on a meaning beyond anything I ever intended for it.

My hope for this book is that other theological educators might be inspired and learn from the women and men who have shared their experiences in these pages. In this way, perhaps, they might begin—however modestly—to shape their own curricula by paying attention to context and contextual method. In doing this, they will not only be imitating the JST faculty and the JST curriculum. They will no doubt discover for themselves the importance of doing theology that honors the experience of their students and challenges them to think for themselves. They will also be answering the call from Pope Francis not to settle for a "desktop theology," but to do theology "for the frontier." Like good pastors, Francis says in an allusion to a now famous line, theologians need to "have the odour of the people and of the street."[2]

The contributors to this volume, *Doing Theology as If People Mattered*, have the odor of Jerusalem, of Asia, of prisons, of Africa, of a poor parish, of engagement with other Christians, and of people of other faiths. To my mind, this is the odor of real theology—an engaged, faith-filled, passionate, contextual, culturally

---

1. Bernard Lonergan, foreword to *The Achievement of Bernard Lonergan*, by David Tracy (New York: Herder and Herder, 1970), xii.

2. See Kevin O'Brien's essay on "Pope Francis as a Contextual Theologian," (chap. 14 in this volume).

sensitive theology that has the "smell of the sheep."[3] It is in learning to do this kind of theology that is perhaps the only way to form ministers for our globalized, multicultural, and fragmented world of today.

Steve Bevans, SVD
August 2, 2018

---

3. Francis, *Evangelii Gaudium* (2013), 24, http://w2.vatican.va/content/francesco/en/apost_exhortations/documents/papa-francesco_esortazione-ap_20131124_evangelii-gaudium.html.

NOTES ON CONTRIBUTORS

KATHRYN R. BARUSH is Assistant Professor of Art History and Religion. She earned her DPhil from the University of Oxford in 2012 and is the author of the monograph *Art and the Sacred Journey in Britain, 1790–1850*. Prior to coming to JST, she held positions at the National Gallery of Art in Washington, DC, and at the Yale University Center for British Art.

ALISON M. BENDERS serves as Associate Dean and Senior Lecturer. Her degrees include a BA in Philosophy from Yale University, a JD from the University of Virginia, and a PhD in Systematic Theology from Boston College. In addition to administrative responsibilities, she teaches and researches on the issue of race and privilege as an intersectional exploration of human beings enmeshed in society, culture, and church. Her book *Just Prayer: A Book of Hours for Peacemakers and Justice Seekers*, earned the Catholic Book Award in Spirituality in 2016.

STEPHEN B. BEVANS, SVD, is a priest in the missionary congregation of the Society of the Divine Word and Louis J. Luzbetak, SVD, Professor of Mission and Culture, Emeritus at Catholic Theological Union, Chicago. He has written or edited eighteen books, among them *Models of Contextual Theology* and, most recently, *Essays in Contextual Theology*. He is a member of the World Council of Churches' Commission on World Mission and Evangelism.

THOMAS CATTOI is Associate Professor of Christology and Cultures and teaches early Christian theology and interreligious dialogue. In addition to serving as the co-editor of the journal

Buddhist-Christian Studies, he has authored six volumes, among them *Divine Contingency: Theologies of Divine Embodiment in Maximos the Confessor and Tsong kha pa*, and *Theodore the Studite: Writings on Iconoclasm*.

EDUARDO C. FERNÁNDEZ, SJ, is Professor of Pastoral Theology and Ministry, having earned an STD in missiology at the Pontifical Gregorian University in Rome. He publishes, gives workshops and retreats, and assists at local parishes. He has penned several books, including *La Cosecha: Harvesting Contemporary United States Hispanic Theology (1972–1998)* and *Mexican American Catholics*, and co-authored, with James Empereur, *La Vida Sacra: Contemporary Hispanic Sacramental Theology*.

CHRISTOPHER M. HADLEY, SJ, is Assistant Professor of Systematic Theology. He teaches in the areas of Trinity, fundamental theology, and theological aesthetics in the context of race. His recent scholarship has covered topics in political theology, method, New Testament theology, the thought of Bernard Lonergan, and Gregory of Nyssa. His current project is a book on Balthasar's trinitarian theology.

GINA HENS-PIAZZA, Professor of Biblical Studies, holds the Joseph S. Alemany Endowed Chair. She is the author of six books, including the *Wisdom Commentary on Lamentations* and the forthcoming *The Supporting Cast of the Bible*, as well as numerous articles. She frequently lectures nationally and internationally on biblical topics and social justice, particularly in regard to women.

PAUL A. JANOWIAK, SJ, is Associate Professor of Liturgical and Sacramental Theology and the Theology of Preaching. His interests include liturgical spirituality, preaching, and contemporary sacramental practice. His books include *The Holy Preaching: The Sacramentality of the Word in the Liturgical Assembly* and *Standing Together in the Community of God: Liturgical Spirituality and the Presence of Christ*.

KEVIN O'BRIEN, SJ, is the President of Santa Clara University and former Dean and University Professor of the Jesuit School of Theology. He is the author of the award-winning book *The Ignatian Adventure: Experiencing the Spiritual Exercises of Saint Ignatius in Daily Life*, published in Spanish and English.

WILLIAM O'NEILL, SJ, currently holds the Lo Schiavo Chair in Catholic Social Thought at the University of San Francisco. His writings address questions of human rights, social reconciliation, restorative justice, refugee and immigration policy, race and mass incarceration, and the Church and public reason. He serves as Catholic Chaplain at the Federal Correctional Institution for women in Dublin, California.

HUNG TRUNG PHAM, SJ, is Assistant Professor of Ignatian Spirituality. Besides publishing, he gives workshops and retreats domestically and internationally. His teaching and research interests are in the area of Ignatian Spirituality and Immigrant Spirituality.

JULIA D.E. PRINZ, VDMF, lecturer in Christian Spirituality, teaches and writes in the area of biblical hermeneutics, political theology, aesthetics, and healing. She authored *Endangering Hunger for God* and, since 1995, has been working with recent immigrant populations in the San Francisco Bay Area. She has been the director of Women of Wisdom and Action in Asia since 2012.

JEAN-FRANÇOIS RACINE is Associate Professor of New Testament. His current research interests include literary study of Luke-Acts, as well as dreams and visions in early Christian literature. He has authored *The Text of Matthew in the Writings of Basil of Caesarea* and, with Richard J. Bautch, edited *Beauty and the Bible: Toward a Hermeneutics of Biblical Aesthetics*.

DEBORAH ROSS is Lecturer and Director of Ministerial Formation. Her research interests include practical theology, sacramental and liturgical theology, and theological anthropology. She is co-author of *Talking About God in Practice: Theological Action Research and Practical Theology* and wrote the introduction to the revised edition of *Image and Pilgrimage in Christian Culture* by Victor and Edith Turner.

SANDRA M. SCHNEIDERS, IHM, is Professor Emerita of New Testament Studies and Christian Spirituality. She has also been a professor of spirituality at the Graduate Theological Union in Berkeley, California, for forty years. She is author of the trilogy *Religious Life in a New Millennium*, three volumes on biblical interpretation: *The Revelatory Text; Written That You May Believe; and Jesus Risen in Our Midst*, as well as several other books and over one hundred articles in professional journals and chapters in books. She currently teaches occasional courses and gives lectures on scripture, spirituality, and religious life, as well as directing retreats, consulting, and participating in scholarly conferences.

ROBERT SCHREITER, CPPS, is Professor of Systematic Theology and holds the Vatican Council II Chair in Theology at Catholic Theological Union in Chicago. He is past president of the American Society of Missiology and the Catholic Theological Society of America. His research interests include theology and culture, the mission of the Church, developments in World Christianity, and the theology and ministry of reconciliation. Among his books are *Constructing Local Theologies* and *The New Catholicity: Theology between the Global and the Local*.

ANH Q. TRAN, SJ, is Associate Professor of Historical and Systematic Theology and holds a PhD from Georgetown University. His teaching and research interests involve ecclesiology, missiology, intercultural and interreligious dialogue, comparative religion/theology, Asian theology, and Christian mission in Asia. He is the author of *Gods, Heroes, and Ancestors* and a co-editor and contributor to *World Christianity: Perspectives and Insights*.

GEORGE T. WILLIAMS, SJ, is the Catholic Chaplain at San Quentin State Prison, serving 4,000 prisoners, 750 of whom are on California's Death Row. Fr. Williams holds a doctorate in Criminology from Northeastern University, has worked in prison ministry for twenty-five years, and teaches a course in this area for JST.

INDEX

Subjects

Names